The
South
Atlantic
Quarterly
Spring 2006
Volume 105
Number 2

Visit Duke University Press Journals at www.dukepress.edu/journals.

Subscriptions. Direct all orders to Duke University Press, Journals Fulfillment, 905 W. Main St., Suite 18B, Durham, NC 27701. Annual subscription rates: print-plus-electronic institutions, $155; print-only or e-only institutions, $140; individuals, $35; students, $21. For information on subscriptions to the e-Duke Scholarly Collection through HighWire Press, see www.dukepress.edu/edukecollection. Print subscriptions: add $12 postage and 7% GST for Canada; add $16 postage outside the U.S. and Canada. Back volumes (institutions): $140. Single issues: institutions, $35; individuals, $14. For more information, contact Duke University Press Journals at 888-651-0122 (toll-free in the U.S. and Canada) or 919-688-5134; subscriptions@dukepress.edu.

Permissions. Photocopies for course or research use that are supplied to the end user at no cost may be made without explicit permission or fee. Photocopies that are provided to the end user for a fee may not be made without payment of permission fees to Duke University Press. Address requests for permission to republish copyrighted material to Permissions Coordinator, permissions@dukepress.edu.

Advertisements. Direct inquiries about advertising to Journals Advertising Coordinator, journals_advertising@dukepress.edu.

Distribution. The journal is distributed by Ubiquity Distributors, 607 DeGraw St., Brooklyn, NY 11217; phone: 718-875-5491; fax: 718-875-8047.

The *South Atlantic Quarterly* is indexed in *Academic Abstracts FullTEXT Elite, Academic Abstracts FullTEXT Ultra, Academic Research Library, Academic Search Elite, Academic Search Premier, America: History and Life, American Humanities Index, Art Index Retrospective, 1929–1984, Arts and Humanities Citation Index, Corporate ResourceNet, Current Contents/Arts and Humanities, Discovery, Expanded Academic ASAP, Historical Abstracts, Humanities Abstracts, Humanities and Social Sciences Index Retrospective, 1907–1984, Humanities Full Text, Humanities Index, Humanities Index Retrospective, 1907–1984, Humanities International Index, MasterFILE Elite, MasterFILE Premier, MasterFILE Select, MLA Bibliography, News and Magazines, OmniFile Full Text V, OmniFile Full Text, Mega Edition, Research Library, Social Sciences Index Retrospective, 1907–1984,* and *Student Resource Center College with Expanded Academic ASAP.*

The *South Atlantic Quarterly* is published, at $155 for (print-plus-electronic) institutions and $35 for individuals, by Duke University Press, 905 W. Main St., Suite 18B, Durham, NC 27701. Periodicals postage paid at Durham, NC, and additional mailing offices. Postmaster: Send address changes to *South Atlantic Quarterly*, Box 90660, Duke University Press, Durham, NC 27708-0660.

ISSN 0038-2876

The Pleasure Principle:
Sport for the Sake of Pleasure

SPECIAL ISSUE EDITOR: DAVID L. ANDREWS

The
South
Atlantic
Quarterly
Spring 2006
Volume 105
Number 2

David L. Andrews

Introduction: Playing with the Pleasure Principle

> I want to start with the fact that people spend time with popular culture and that it matters to them, that it is often an important site of people's passion.
> —L. Grossberg, *We Gotta Get Out of This Place: Popular Conservatism and Postmodern Culture*

At this introductory juncture of an issue focused on the emotive purchase and resonance of sport, the reader is probably expecting me to provide a pithy personal observation as a means of bringing the topic into focus. While I have tried to avoid such hackneyed conventions, sometimes our own experiences cannot be avoided. During a baptism recently held in one of Baltimore's numerous Catholic churches, I was forced, during what seemed to be an important point during the mass, to do my fatherly duty and take my four-year-old son to the bathroom after one of his interminable "Daddy, I need to make a wee" implorings. Not being familiar with the layout of this, or indeed any other, house of worship, we soon stumbled across a group of slightly wizened elderly male parishioners squeezed into a cramped vestibule. This genial, homily-avoiding assemblage acknowledged our existence with knowing smiles, but otherwise

The *South Atlantic Quarterly* 105:2, Spring 2006.
Copyright © 2006 by Duke University Press.

did not deviate from their mutual preoccupation: they were discussing, with an unnerving degree of intensity, the merits of the Baltimore Orioles pitching rotation. Other than the fact that I had not as yet found our desired destination, I was not immediately struck by my encounter with this unself-conscious Orioles cabal. Only having returned to our pew, to be confronted by my genuflecting family (immediate and partially extended), did I begin to reflect upon the scene just encountered. I wondered whether these venerable souls would have been so animated if they were debating the virtues of their priestly retinue, or even that of the apostolicity, during the bottom of the ninth in a Camden Yards broom cupboard. I concluded that they would not. This is not to assert that these men were somehow irreligious or lacking spirituality. Rather, my overriding sense from this briefest of encounters was that sport, and in particular men's observable passion for the Baltimore Orioles, constituted an important vehicle through which they brought pleasure, substance, and meaning into their everyday lives (even if it meant impinging, at least this once, on their formal religious observances).

The point of reciting this encounter with the Baltimore Four is not to draw attention to the uniqueness of this happening: quite the opposite, in fact. The aim, rather, is to illustrate that such emotional investments in, and attachments to, sport are so commonplace that we barely register them as being anything other than reassuringly familiar and unexceptional aspects of everyday life. Despite the considerable affective purchase of other popular cultural forms (I am led to believe that people have been known to display an intense passion for, among other things, cooking, music, home decoration, and even gardening), arguably none of them display the intensity and extensity of passions generated by engaging with the culturally regulated, socially sanctioned, and increasingly economically (re)organized expressions of physicality that constitute the diverse landscape of contemporary sport culture. Sport's tacit visceral physicality, dramatic uncertainty, and subjective interpellation make it a compelling and seductive aspect of popular existence for both spectators and participants alike. Indeed, it could be argued that it is these affective capacities which make "popular [*sporting*] culture popular."[1] This becomes ever more apparent when considering the relationship between sport and another primary source of people's emotional attachments: the nation. Of course, Eric Hobsbawm most succinctly captured this mutually affecting (in terms of the capacity to stir the emotions) relationship:

What has made sport so uniquely effective a medium for inculcating national feelings, at all events for males, is the ease with which even the least political or public individuals can identify with the nation as symbolized by young persons excelling at what practically every man wants, or at one time in life has wanted, to be good at. The imagined community of millions seems more real as a team of eleven named people. The individual, even the one who only cheers, becomes a symbol of his nation himself.[2]

As Hobsbawm insinuated, sport practices and bodies are always potentially politicized, inasmuch as their faculty for emotive engagement is liable to be mobilized by those encouraging positive popular investment in specific national political agendas. This was most famously illustrated in the Third Reich's co-optation of the 1936 Berlin Olympic Games. It is also evident in more benign political regimes, as when British prime minister Harold Wilson sought to articulate England's 1966 FIFA World Cup victory to his modernist "white heat of technology" mantra in an attempt to bolster support for the Labour government. More recently, the very public death of the ex-NFL player Pat Tillman while serving as an Army Ranger in Afghanistan further exemplified the manner in which sport helps to structure and direct people's investment in the political. Far from being based in the reality of events as they tragically unfolded, George W. Bush and his supporters gleefully appropriated this tragic occurrence, and cynically re-presented it, for their own political purposes. Through various eulogistic statements and ceremonies (not least being his funeral, televised live to the nation), Tillman was positioned as the ultimate American hero: the fallen soldier-athlete whose ultimate sacrifice came when, to use a Bush idiom, heroically *defending freedom* from the threatening infidel; in actuality, Tillman was killed by fellow Army Rangers in a tragic accident described in an official report as an act of "gross negligence."[3] The objective of such discursive repackaging would seem to have been plain. Tillman was, after all, "the Army's most famous volunteer in the war on terrorism, a charismatic former pro football star whose reticence, courage and handsome beret-draped face captured for many Americans the best aspects of the country's post-Sept. 11 character."[4] Hence, the fictionalized heroism of his demise was used as a means to generate the emotive capital (the very climate of positive public sentiment and support) necessary to validate the administration's war-mongering policies in Afghanistan, in Iraq, and seemingly beyond. Thus, sport was used as an affective constituent of the "new conservatism" that "depoliticizes politics" as it repoliticizes everyday life."[5]

Whether resonating at the level of national, local, or individual constituencies, it is evident that sport constitutes an important component of the "mattering maps" of our everyday lives, through which we inculcate feelings of belonging and pleasure into our all-too-brief existences.[6] In terms of the latter, while the ascendant sport(s) may change from one sociohistoric context to another, associated expressions of positive public sentiment would appear remarkably similar (in both form and intensity) across time and space. As an illustration of the longevity of sport's vernacular affective resonance, Juvenal's (55–130 A.D.) familiar castigation of the political apathy displayed by the Roman citizenry pointed to that which truly ignited popular emotions: "Now that no one buys our votes, the public has long since cast off its cares; the people that once bestowed commands, consulships, legions and all else, now meddles no more and longs eagerly for just two things—bread and circuses." The "circuses" to which Juvenal referred were, of course, the savage gladiatorial contests staged in the Roman Empire's vast amphitheaters. Choreographed by the social and political elite to entertain mass ranks of spectators, these visceral physically based spectacles engaged—and thereby covertly governed—the Roman public's emotional investments. Shifting millennia, while the emergence of modern spectator sport in the late nineteenth and early twentieth centuries incorporated considerably less bloodthirsty forms of competitive physicality than their ancient antecedents, they did nonetheless perform similar social, political, and cultural functions. Within the modern industrial era, and specifically its newly defined realm of leisure time, institutionalized sport became an important site of "surveillance, spectacle, and profit."[7] The patrician-industrialist power bloc ensured that sport helped constrain working bodies to the demands and discipline of the industrial order (by codifying and regulating sport practice), while simultaneously managing and compounding their sporting passions (by commandeering the organization and delivery of popular sport contests).

In his seminal exposition of working-class culture in postwar Britain, *The Uses of Literacy*, Richard Hoggart drew attention to the broad-ranging popular appeal of sport, and thereby initiated a consistent strand within cultural studies research.[8] Hoggart's particular rendition of literary humanism posited sport as a popular practice seamlessly sutured into the structural rhythms and affective sensibilities of working-class existence:

At work, sport vies with sex as the staple conversation. The popular Sunday newspapers are read as much for their full sports reports as for their accounts of the week's crimes. Sports conversations start from personalities, often spoken of by their Christian as well as by their surnames, as "Jim Motson," "Arthur Jones," and "Will Thompson": technical details of play are discussed, often to the accompaniment of extraordinary feats of memory as to the history of matches many seasons back. The men talk about individuals whom they know, at least as figures on the field, in situations eliciting qualities they can respect and admire.[9]

In a less accommodating vein, but equally illustrative of the popular passions generated by contemporary sport culture, Jean Baudrillard vilified the French public for being transfixed by the televised drama of a qualifying game for the 1978 FIFA World Cup Finals, while ignoring the politically charged issue pertaining to the extradition of the German lawyer Klaus Croissant on the same evening. As he lamented, "A few hundred people demonstrated in front of the Santé prison, there was some furious nocturnal activity on the part of a few lawyers, while twenty million people spent the evening in front of their TV screens" seduced by the affective of a "dramatic [*sporting*] sequence."[10] Extrapolating Baudrillard's observation to a global frame of analysis, within his 1994 documentary film, *The Final Kick*, Andreas Rogenhagen documented the simultaneous response, within forty different national cultural settings, to the unfolding drama of the 1994 FIFA World Cup Final between Brazil and Italy. This multicultural, if nonscientific, cinematic sampling of the game's more than 2 billion worldwide viewers pivoted on the climactic moment when Roberto Baggio's penalty shootout miss handed the trophy to Brazil. *The Final Kick* graphically depicted the boundary-crossing interest in this globalized sporting spectacle, while also illustrating the inflected subtleties (or, in places, not-so-subtleties) of the localized emotive investments and responses to Baggio's, and thus Italy's, dramatic denouement. To put it simply, the emotive responses in Brazil and Italy, while of arguably equal intensity and duration, were substantively different in form, one fan's delight being another's despair.

Perhaps the most prescient insights into the range of sporting emotions (from the euphoric to the disconsolate, with every emotive gradation in between, lest it not be forgotten that investing the self in sport can be a mundane, tedious, and/or frustrating experience) can be found within the work of the English novelist Nick Hornby. Despite the relentless appropriation of his work by Hollywood's trivializing production aesthetic,[11] Hornby continues to produce prescient expositions of the emotional travails and intensities characteristic of the contemporary, bourgeois, white male experience. Involved in a seeming never-ending search for a balance between the pursuit of pleasure(s) and the various responsibilities (primarily economic, social, and psychic) associated with Western urbane adulthood, the Hornbyesque protagonist—like Hornby himself, perhaps—is most likely to find emotional fulfillment in, and through, obsessive and irrational relationships with (English) football and/or popular music. Hornby's football-related emotional resume provides the focus of his highly influential autobiographical work *Fever Pitch: A Fan's Life*. In one of the book's most memorable passages, he describes the moment of transcendent euphoria precipitated by his beloved Arsenal's last-gasp, improbable, and thereby instantaneously legendary Championship triumph over Liverpool in 1989:

> There is, then, literally nothing to describe it. I have exhausted all the available options. I can recall nothing else that I have coveted for two decades (what else *is* there that can reasonably be coveted for that long?), nor can I recall anything else that I have desired as both man and boy. So please, be tolerant of those who describe a sporting moment as their best ever. We do not lack imagination, nor have we had sad and barren lives; it is just that real life is paler, duller, and contains less potential for unexpected delirium.[12]

Hornby also acquaints the reader with some of the less exultant experiences of football fandom:

> Football teams are extraordinarily inventive in the ways they find to cause their supporters sorrow. They lead at Wembley and then throw it away; they go to the top of the First Division and then stop dead; they draw the difficult away game and lose the home replay; they beat Liverpool one week and lose to Scunthorpe the next; they seduce you, half-way through the season into believing that they are promotion candidates and then go the other way. . . . always when you think you have anticipated the worst that can happen, they come up with something new.[13]

As Hornby intimated, the potential for the intoxicating experience of sporting triumphs is compounded by the very real possibility (in some cases, inalienable likelihood) of impending defeat, and the abject despair that routinely accompanies it. Many (and we know who we are) live in a perpetual state of tension between sport-related feelings of angst and anticipation — a condition sustained by the minutest victories, or the mere possibility thereof. Somewhat perversely, therefore, emotional investments in sport do not necessarily require immediate, if indeed any, dividends. Few *other* business can rely on such dutiful forms of consumer behavior. That is, perhaps, another issue.

In conclusion, this is by no means *South Atlantic Quarterly*'s first engagement with sport (nor, hopefully, will it be its last). In addition to Paul Smith's illuminating study of English football culture,[14] as recently as 1996 the journal dissected the "*media* of sports, both in the contemporary sense — as in print and broadcast journalism — and in the environmental and aesthetic contexts traditionally implied by the term."[15] However, in introducing this "Real Sports" issue, James T. Fisher expressed a common sentiment toward the awareness and, indeed, the very idea, that sport could be examined from a critical scholarly perspective. As he appreciatively intoned, "The worlds of sports have remained generally immune from such concerns," as "the prospect of a 'sport studies' is not pleasant to behold."[16] In one fell swoop, and clearly unknowingly, Fisher dismissed the voluminous body of literature focused on the serious analysis of sport culture generated over the last four decades or so.[17] Rather than ignoring sport studies, the present issue seeks to make a contribution to this thriving field of intellectual inquiry. However, it is a consciously unconventional project in that it explicitly sought out researchers largely unaware of, and so generally unencumbered by, the established trajectories and internal debates within sport studies scholarship; the idea was to initiate a dialogue with the field of sport studies, while simultaneously introducing it to the broader academic community. Hence, this special issue provides an opportunity for non–sport specialist scholars to utilize fully their not inconsiderable interpretive and analytical powers in examining the derivation and implications of their own sporting passions and preoccupations. The contributions collected herein thus empirically interrogate that which arguably constitutes sport's most unique characteristic as a form of contemporary popular culture: the irrational and obsessive passions it frequently engenders even in the most (seemingly) rational of people. For, if nothing else, sport *matters* to people, even to academics, as a source of pleasure, excitement, and identification that "gives 'color,' 'tone' or 'texture' to the lived."[18]

Notes

1   L. Grossberg, *We Gotta Get Out of This Place: Popular Conservatism and Postmodern Culture* (London: Routledge, 1992), 75.

2   E. J. Hobsbawm, *Nations and Nationalism since 1870: Programme, Myth, Reality* (Cambridge: Cambridge University Press, 1990), 143.

3   Although carried out prior to Tillman's nationally televised funeral, the official army report into his death was withheld from his family until some weeks later. See J. White, "Army Withheld Details about Tillman's Death: Investigator Quickly Learned 'Friendly Fire' Killed Athlete," *Washington Post*, May 4, 2005.

4   S. Coll, "Army Spun Tale around Ill-Fated Mission," *Washington Post*, December 6, 2004.

5   Grossberg, *We Gotta Get Out of This Place*, 281.

6   Ibid., 75.

7   T. Miller and A. McHoul, *Popular Culture and Everyday Life* (London: Sage, 1998), 61.

8   See D. L. Andrews and J. W. Loy, "British Cultural Studies and Sport: Past Encounters and Future Possibilities," *Quest* 45.2 (1993): 225–76.

9   R. Hoggart, *The Uses of Literacy* (London: Chatto and Windus, 1957), 91.

10 J. Baudrillard, "The Implosion of Meaning in the Media and the Implosion of the Social in the Masses," in *The Myths of Information: Technology and Postindustrial Society*, ed. K. Woodward, 137–48 (Madison, WI: Coda Press, 1980), 143.

11 Ably illustrated in the U.S. filmic versions of *High Fidelity* (2000), *About a Boy* (2002), and, particularly, *Fever Pitch* (2005).

12 N. Hornby, *Fever Pitch: A Fan's Life* (London: Victor Gollancz, 1992), 231.

13 Ibid., 127.

14 P. Smith, "Playing for England," *South Atlantic Quarterly* 90.4 (1991): 737–52.

15 J. T. Fisher, Editor's note, *South Atlantic Quarterly* 95.2 (1996): 280.

16 Ibid.

17 Apparently a novel domain to researchers outside the field, there is in fact a highly productive, and truly global, sociology of sport community, evidence of which can be discerned from the existence of at least four refereed journals (*International Review for the Sociology of Sport, Journal for Sport and Social Issues, Sociology of Sport Journal, Sport in Society* [formerly *Culture, Sport, Society*]); a proliferating body of single-authored texts and edited anthologies, many of which appear in sport-oriented book series developed by major scholarly publishers (including Berg's two series, Global Sport Cultures and Sport, Commerce, and Culture; Routledge's Sport in the Global Society series; the University of Illinois Press Sport in Society series; the University of Minnesota's Sport and Culture series; State University of New York Press's Sport and Social Relations series; and Syracuse University Press's Sports and Entertainment series); two international organizations (the North American Society for the Sociology of Sport [www.nasss.org] and the International Sociology of Sport Association [u2.u-strasbg.fr/issa/]) and their associated annual conferences; and a focused research database (www.sportdiscus.com/).

18 Grossberg, *We Gotta Get Out of This Place*, 81.

George Ritzer

Rooting for the "Devil":
Baseball, the Yankees, Shane Spencer
(Who?), and Social Theory

Born in New York City, specifically Manhattan, I was destined to be a fan of New York teams, especially the baseball teams of the 1940s and 1950s—the Yankees, Giants, and Dodgers (the latter two have long since departed for the West Coast). To narrow that field further, the Dodgers were out—Brooklyn was basically another "country," a place Manhattanites passed over on the "El" en route to a day at Coney Island. The Giants were likely, since their home stadium, the Polo Grounds, was just a few miles away from my apartment in Manhattan, so my father was an avid Giants fan, and later my younger brother was too. I still retain a powerful memory of watching on television Bobby Thompson's famous 1951 home run, the one that won the pennant (and announcer Russ Hodges's almost equally famous, near hysterical, rant: "The Giants win the pennant, the Giants win the pennant . . ."). I also have a vivid recollection of being at a Giants game at the Polo Grounds with my father in 1950 and seeing a young kid—the future Hall-of-Famer Willie Mays, on leave from the army, I think—work out before the game started and how it was clear to us all that he was going to be a superstar. But still somehow

The *South Atlantic Quarterly* 105:2, Spring 2006.
Copyright © 2006 by Duke University Press.

I became a Yankees fan and remain one to this day, despite my best efforts to rid myself of the "affliction." I call it an affliction because the Yankees are considered by most observers of baseball and professional sports in general to be the devil incarnate. Furthermore, many of my favorite theoretical perspectives, to say nothing of my ideological leanings, lead me to much the same conclusion.

From early on, my main interest in the Yankees was more in an individual player or players than in the team itself. In fact, my interest in the Yankees came of age when the great Mickey Mantle arrived in 1951. That was no surprise—everyone rooted for Mickey, and there were many reasons to admire him, including his good looks, his incredible physical skills, and later the physical adversities he had to overcome in order to continue playing. But much of my attention and adoration soon turned to a much more average player, Irv Noren, who joined the Yankees the next year and stayed until 1956. Thus began my tendency to focus on, and suffer with, marginal players (Noren was a lifetime .275 hitter, although he did hit .319 with the Yankees in 1954) on the otherwise superlative Yankees teams. This tendency was not restricted to baseball. I rooted for the New York Knicks (nothing like the dynasty the Yankees created), but mainly for marginal players such as Charlie Tyra (in his best season with the Knicks, 1959–60, he averaged a modest 12.8 points per game), who joined the team about the time Irv Noren left the Yankees and hung on for about four or five years.

Over the years my interest in sports in general, and even baseball, began to wane, largely because its "evils"—big money, big player salaries, mediatization (especially the altering of sports to accommodate the media and the creation of "schlock" sports solely for television), and so on—became increasingly abundant and obvious. However, of all sports I retained the most interest in baseball, the Yankees in particular. Even living down the road from the home of the Baltimore Orioles for the last thirty years has not swayed my allegiance in the least. However, over the last decade or two—in light of the big-spending ways of George Steinbrenner and the great financial advantage (and much higher payroll) of the Yankees over any other major-league team—it has become increasingly difficult for me to sustain and legitimize my interest in, and support for, this team. After all, here was the worst of the capitalist system that I was writing and teaching about, often from a Marxian or neo-Marxian perspective. While it's hard to see today's players as being exploited (although they clearly were in the pre-Curt Flood days; Mickey Mantle was clearly being exploited even when he was being paid what was then considered to be the highest possible salary, $100,000 a season), the success of the Yankees, and the corresponding failure of small-market, low-budget teams, makes it clear that baseball is a case of the rich getting richer and the poor poorer.

There was my dilemma, then: How, with this theoretical orientation (and others), could I possibly root for the Yankees, given that they symbolized, among other things, the fundamental unfairness and inequality of the capitalist system? As I now reflect on it, I think that it was made possible by the fact that I increasingly focused on the team's marginal players; the most proletarian of players on an otherwise highly capitalistic team not only run by a capitalist (Steinbrenner made his money in shipbuilding) but increasingly populated by superrich players (such as Alex Rodriguez, who some years ago signed a $250 million contract—still the highest in baseball history—with Texas but was traded to the Yankees because only they could afford him, to say nothing of the many other players such as Derek Jeter and Randy Johnson who are among the highest paid in baseball). Enter, in 1998, Shane Spencer. Spencer was a journeyman minor leaguer who spent eight largely mediocre years in the minors before being called up by the Yankees near the end of the 1998 season. Few players of any note have spent that much time in the minor leagues; the best players make it to the major leagues after two or three years in the minors, if that.

The Yankees were having a record-breaking year in 1998 and were running away with the pennant. They could afford to bring up a player like Spencer late in the season and give him considerable playing time both before and after they had secured the pennant. Spencer had a phenomenal September in 1998: He hit an amazing 10 home runs in only 62 at bats, knocking in 27 runs, batting .373, with a slugging percentage of .910. The first two numbers, projected over an entire season, would have translated into a record-breaking 100 home runs and 270 runs batted average, numbers far above the current records for both.

This performance generated considerable excitement, especially in me. I think the initial interest was in the fact that Spencer looked like a late bloomer and had some of the same kind of good looks as my early idol, Mickey Mantle. Everyone was aware that a player's performance in September when the pennant races were no longer in doubt may not have meant much. Spencer was batting against either marginal pitchers brought up by other teams from the minor leagues, just as he had been, or established pitchers who, because there was little on the line, were not at their best. In addition, because he was new to the league, the opposition pitchers knew little about him and his strengths (which, it turned out, was hitting fastballs) and weaknesses (hitting curveballs) as a batter. He saw—and hit—a lot of fastballs that September. It was apparent to all that Spencer was performing way beyond the level he had demonstrated in the minor leagues. However, his outstanding performance continued in the postseason, especially in the first play-off series against Texas, in which he batted .500 and had two more home runs.

However, by the next season it quickly became clear that September 1998 was the aberration all the experts thought it was. As they threw him more curveballs, and avoided fastballs as much as possible, Spencer never again approached the numbers, especially projected out over a season, that he had achieved in 1998. He was a Yankee in 1999, but a part-time player who batted a very weak .234 and hit only 8 home runs in 205 at bats. Worse, he struck out at an alarming rate—almost one in every four at bats. He continued as a part-time, mediocre player with the Yankees until 2003, when he was traded to Cleveland and then to Texas. Released by Texas, he was signed as a part-time, platoon player by the New York Mets in 2004 but was released in midseason after a series of mishaps, one involving a DWI arrest, indicated that he had a serious drinking problem. I should say that in 2003 and 2004 I spent more time following Spencer's performance with these other teams than I did following Yankees fortunes. (The Yankees did not seem to have a mediocre player who interested me and I just could not generate much enthusiasm for any of their multi-million-dollar stars.) Interestingly, the Yankees re-signed Spencer in late 2004 to a minor-league contract and he performed poorly in a few at bats with the Columbus Clippers, a Yankees farm team. He was unable to sign with a major-league team in 2005 and played, instead, in Japan (where he apparently continued to be quite mediocre). He is now burdened by history of mediocrity, a bad reputation, and the advanced age, by baseball standards, of thirty-three.

Thus being a fan of Shane Spencer's has, for the most part, been quite painful. Why do it? Why put myself through the agony year after year of suffering through his poor performance (the rewarding moments were few and far between) and, more recently, the discovery that he has some deep flaws (excessive drinking, DUIs, brawling)? (Of course, Mickey Mantle had similar flaws.) Why should a senior citizen care about a player whom he has never met and who is half his age?

Part of the answer, as indicated above, is that by rooting for him, at least in his early career, I could through him legitimate rooting for the Yankees. From any number of theoretical perspectives that I have employed over the years, the Yankees are an abomination. From a Marxian perspective, as mentioned above, they are the epitome of the capitalist enemy within the world of baseball.[1] While it is true that many other baseball owners are richer and more successful capitalists than George Steinbrenner, it is Steinbrenner who owns the richest franchise in baseball and the one that produces the greatest revenue. Like a good capitalist, Steinbrenner has plowed his profits back into the business and, in the process, made the business increasingly successful in terms of both team performance and increasing revenues.

As successful as Steinbrenner has been, however, he might have been better advised from a profit and net worth point of view to invest much of that money in other kinds of enterprises. There's a lot more money to be made in other realms, although the real profits to be made in the ownership of sports teams is obscured by murky and obscure accounting procedures. Thus, while Steinbrenner's success can be explained in capitalistic terms, I doubt his motivation was purely economic. Owning the Yankees, and making them into a perennial baseball powerhouse, brought Steinbrenner other rewards, most notably power and prestige.

This, of course, brings us more into the realm of Weberian theory, especially Weber's tripartite theory of stratification based on class, status, and power.[2] Steinbrenner's high ranking in the social stratification system is, as noted, only partially accounted for by class or economic factors. He is an elite member of society because, in addition to his wealth, and probably even more important than that, he enjoys the prestige of owning the most famous and successful team in the history of professional sports *and* exercises great power over that team and its operations. In the past, Steinbrenner has been severely criticized for meddling in the day-to-day operations of the team. He seems to have taken a more distant stance in recent years, but it is likely that he continues to exercise great power, even over the more mundane aspects of the team, its personnel, and its performance. For example, Steinbrenner is known for giving second chances to players who have had drug and alcohol problems (the best-known examples are Daryl Strawberry and Doc Gooden), and it may even be that Spencer was offered a minor-league contract late in the 2004 season because of Steinbrenner's sympathy with his alcohol problems. Thus, Steinbrenner's actions can be interpreted from a Weberian perspective as being motivated not only by economics (class) but also, and perhaps more strongly, by status and power considerations. Indeed, Steinbrenner has spent money on players that made little economic sense but were designed to enhance his (and the Yankees') status and power. From a Marxian perspective, the fact that Steinbrenner and his Yankees rank high not only on class (economic) factors but also on status and power measures gives one (me) even more reason to be wary of them, let alone root for them.

Weberian theory also sensitizes one to another reason to dislike the Yankees: They appear to run the most highly rationalized,[3] or in my terms *McDonaldized*,[4] operation in major-league baseball. The major dimensions of these concepts are efficiency, calculability, predictability, and control through nonhuman technologies. First, the Yankees certainly run a highly efficient operation. The goal of any team is to win, and ultimately in baseball to win the pennant and World Series, and each year the Yankees retool (at great expense) to achieve those goals by paying top dollar to the best available players (free agents) on the market. Year after year they go about this process, very efficiently and effectively filling in real, or imagined, holes in the team.

Second, there is great attention to factors that can be quantified—the batting averages of batters or the earned run averages of pitchers—with the objective of signing or retaining those with highest batting averages and lowest earned run averages (whatever their salary demands). Following their defeat by the Boston Red Sox in the 2004 American League play-offs, it was clear that the major problem was the aging Yankees pitching staff. Thus, in the next off season the Yankees sought, successfully, to add younger pitchers (they also added, at high cost, an aging superstar pitcher—Randy Johnson).

This continual retooling, at a very high price, is a predictable aspect of Yankees operations, as is the fact that year after year, even if they do not win the pennant and World Series, they are serious contenders for it. To achieve this goal, the Yankees predictably outspend their competitors and have by far the highest payroll in major-league baseball.

Finally, while baseball, even for Yankees, remains a highly human sport, the Yankees operate like a nonhuman technology, a well-oiled machine (greased by large salaries and a huge investment in established talent). Furthermore, the team itself is noted for its unemotional, businesslike approach to the game; on a day-to-day basis it too operates like a well-oiled machine, priding itself on things like forcing pitchers to throw many pitches to batters who are often content to take walks, and making few fielding errors. More human teams and their players are more prone to more human actions, like swinging at more balls and making more errors.

Thus, the Yankees can be seen as the best example of a rationalized or McDonaldized baseball team, but these processes always bring with them a series of irrationalities of rationality. That is, excessive rationalization/ McDonaldization always brings with it a set of negative consequences such as dehumanization. The Yankees, and their seemingly inevitable winning ways, have, as we have seen, a machinelike quality. Yankees players often seem more like automatons than genuine human beings. Indeed, Yankees (or, more accurately, Steinbrenner) policy is for players who join the team to shave off distinguishing facial hair, to cut long hair, to limit or eliminate the display of outrageous jewelry, to dress conservatively, and so on. Indeed, in the losing 2004 play-off series against the Boston Red Sox the dehumanized Yankees were pitted against a highly human Red Sox team sporting lots of long hair and facial hair of all descriptions. Most notable were the long hair and beard of series star Johnny Damon (dubbed "Mountain Man" during the year). Indeed, the fact that he was the hero seemed to be a victory of humanity over dehumanization as represented by the clean-cut Yankees team. No one who looked like Damon would have been allowed to play for the Yankees, and if a player insisted, he would likely have been traded or released.

The Yankees, in spite of the aura associated with a long tradition of victory, also seem to manifest another irrationality: They seem disenchanted. That is, there is no magic about Yankees victories; they go about winning in a methodical and matter-of-fact fashion year after year (they simply spend far more than other teams on player salaries).

As a result of all of this, perhaps the ultimate disenchantment is that experienced by the fans. The Yankees are the team fans of other teams love to hate. More important, the rationalization of the Yankees alienates some Yankees fans, including me. It is very hard to root for such a rationalized, McDonaldized "machine" that is dehumanized and disenchanted to such a high degree. Were enough fans to be alienated from the team for these reasons, fan support would decline, as would attendance at games. Thus, the idea that spending more money and rationalizing operations still further would lead to more wins and championships which would, in turn, lead to more fans and greater attendance at games might backfire, leading, in fact, to a decline in fans and attendance. Although many Yankees fans have been turned off by the team's excesses, there is no evidence of a decline in the fan base or in home attendance, which has been increasing rather than decreasing. It appears that with the Yankees as with McDonald's, highly rationalized systems seem to succeed in spite of their obvious irrationalities.

One reason, perhaps, is that side by side with idea of a rationalized machine remains a kind of magical, mystical image of the Yankees and their ability to win under any and (almost) all circumstances. A prime example of this is the legendary ability of the Yankees to prevail year after year (at least until 2004) over their arch rival, the Boston Red Sox. The Yankees always seemed to find a way to defeat the Red Sox in play-offs (e.g., Yankee Bucky Dent's legendary 1978 home run), even when the Red Sox appeared to be the better team. Just as the Yankees seemed to have a magical ability to win, the Red Sox seemed to be "cursed." Indeed, there has long been talk of the "curse of the Bambino," referring to a curse placed on the Red Sox because they traded the great Babe Ruth to the Yankees. Of course, given the victory by the Red Sox over the Yankees in the 2004 World Series, one can expect to hear (thankfully) much less about this curse.

In spite of this magic, much of it manufactured and sustained by a Yankees PR machine (another nonhuman technology), the Yankees remain the epitome of a rationalized baseball machine. Given the disenchantment associated with such a machine, it is little wonder that someone like me, so sensitized to rationalization and its evils, should turn to one of the most human, nonrational, of its cogs, a marginal player like Shane Spencer. If one *must* root for a machine, then one alternative is to root for one of its least machinelike components, a Yankee with great weaknesses as a player and as a human being. Among other things, Spencer could only hit a fastball (in his first partial season opposing pitchers hadn't learned that, but once they did his batting average and home runs dropped to the level of the mediocre) and was unable to hit a curveball, especially from a right-handed pitcher (Spencer bats right-handed, and right-handed batters are always more vulnerable to the pitches of a right-handed pitcher, especially the curveball, which tends to run away from their bats). In the parlance of baseball, there are great "holes" in his swing; in other words, if a ball was thrown in a number of places (say, low and inside, or high and away), he was pretty much rendered impotent as a batter. Pitchers learned about these holes by early in the 1999 season, and Spencer's performance as a hitter plummeted. When one adds Spencer's human frailties to his baseball weaknesses, one finds a very human player in the otherwise highly rationalized Yankees machine.

Another theoretical perspective that helps us understand my near-obsession with Spencer relates to the concept of agency in sociology.[5] A focus on agency usually involves the individual actor (although collectivities like a team can also be seen as agents) and is contrasted to, or paired with, the larger structure in which it exists. In this case, it means a focus on a player like Spencer rather than the structure (the Yankees, the American League, major-league baseball, professional sports) in which he operates. As I made clear above, it is hard to ignore the inequities and abuses in these various structures. However, they fade from view, or are easier to ignore, when one's main focus is on the agent rather than such structures.

However, the main thrust of agency-structure theory, since the two are almost always paired, is that agency and structure are dialectically related and that one cannot be meaningfully discussed without the other.[6] That is particularly clear in this case; here one cannot understand my concern for the agent, Spencer, without understanding the structures in which he existed. The Yankees organization is, of course, one such structure, but there are other structures that impact on Spencer and on my interest in him. For example, because of the Yankees' success (which largely comes down to their ability to outspend any other team, sometimes by multiples of five or more), there are teams in small-market cities (e.g., Milwaukee or Kansas City) that are virtually preordained to be also-rans year after year. Not only can they not afford to sign the best available players; they also find it hard to keep their best players, who jump ship as soon as their contracts run out and they are free to sign with the highest bidder for their services. This profound inequality in the structure of major-league baseball makes it hard (at least for someone like me) to retain an interest in it, especially its most successful team, without focusing on one of its least successful players.

Of course, there is the even larger structure of all professional sports, which shares many of the same characteristics and abuses of major-league baseball, although they are most extreme in the latter. Many other professional sports have done a better job of creating a more equitable system by, for example, taxing the richer teams better than is the case in baseball. As a result, there is nothing in other sports, especially in recent years, to parallel the Yankees' hegemony in baseball. There were dynasties in other sports (the Boston Celtics in pro basketball and the Montreal Canadiens in pro hockey, for example), but they were not reducible to the greater wealth of those teams. Even though they have done a better job than baseball, money still talks in other professional (and many "amateur") sports, making it hard, at least for me, to be interested in them, let alone retain a rooting interest in them.

Of course, the larger structure has other offensive aspects that lead in the same direction. Take, for example, the revelations about drug abuse among the stars in many sports. The recent steroid controversy has led us to doubt, if not dismiss, the exploits of not only baseball stars like Barry Bonds but also stars in other sports, such as Marion Jones in track and field. Of course, Spencer had his own problems with alcohol and for all I know may have used drugs, even steroids. Of course, in a way this all makes him even more attractive, at least to me. It makes him more human, especially if it is possible that he has been such a mediocre player even though he might have been using performance-enhancing steroids.

This leads us to the issue of the relationship among and between agents in the context of agency-structure. Here the point is that compared to the extraordinarily high-paid and glamorous players, especially on the Yankees, Spencer has always been poorly paid (by baseball standards) and is decidedly unglamorous. While I might often see the Yankees glamour players like Alex Rodriguez and especially Derek Jeter on television commercials, I have never seen Shane Spencer in any commercial, and I am not likely to, given his near-total anonymity in baseball. It is hard for me to root for players like Rodriguez and Jeter, whose annual salaries are close to, or exceed, $20 million! And this does not include additional monies from various advertisements and endorsements (needless to say, Spencer has earned relatively little from either).

Another thing that agency-structure theory points to in this context is that I, as a fan, am also an agent. The various structures in and around the Yankees should lead me to root not only for them (they are "winners," after all) but also for their much-ballyhooed and very visible media stars like Rodriguez and Jeter. The role of the media is central here, as is the degree to which baseball, and sports more generally, have been mediatized. The constant presence of the Yankees and their stars on television (even Steinbrenner and Yankees manager Joe Torre are media stars who frequently appear on commercials) is designed to lead fans to root for the team and at least one of its stars (the photogenic Derek Jeter has a huge following among fans). In spite of all this, as a fan I am an agent, and I am therefore free to ignore it all and root for someone who never received much attention from the media. While it is true that all fans are agents, the fact is that as a result of media (and other structures) more people are going to root for those like Jeter who get a great deal of media attention than someone like Spencer who is largely invisible.

In addition to agency-structure theory in general, one could also use specific agency-structure theories to think about my orientation to Spencer and the Yankees.[7] For example, Pierre Bourdieu's approach, especially his concepts of habitus and field, are particularly useful. The field in question is professional sports fans, specifically fans of professional baseball. How did I come to occupy the position I did in the latter field? Of particular importance, from Bourdieu's perspective, is my habitus (an internalized structuring structure) as it emerged in my early teen years growing up in New York City. It is no surprise that my upbringing led to a habitus that favored baseball and the Yankees, but why the simultaneous distaste for them, for their affluence and their position atop the baseball world? An important factor in this is that I was raised in a lower-middle-class background (class is of great importance to Bourdieu's thinking, especially on habitus and field) with considerable hostility toward the upper classes. In my teenage years my father was a taxi driver, and he told many stories of rich passengers, their reprehensible behavior (they often treated him as a "nonperson"),[8] and especially their propensity to undertip or not tip at all (tips were and are an important part of all taxi drivers' income). All of this played a great role in creating in me a habitus in which was embedded a distaste for the rich and successful and a corresponding appreciation of the underdog. This manifested itself in baseball in my ability to overcome my distaste for the rich Yankees by focusing on underdog players like Spencer.

I could go on with this, undoubtedly bringing even further theoretical resources to bear on the issue of how I could possibly continue to root for the Yankees. However, I think the point is clear, and in any case the reader is probably already feeling that I am overly intellectualizing a very simple and straightforward matter. Yet such is the curse of the social theorist. The fact is that I often reflect on how I can continue to be a Yankees fan in light of all of the above. In such reflections I do often utilize the theories mentioned above to explain my irrational affection for the Yankees. But enough intellectualizing; I need to return to the real world and check the Yankees home page to see if there is any indication that Shane Spencer will have the slightest chance of being on the Yankees (or any other team) in the 2006 season.

Notes

1   Karl Marx, *Capital: A Critique of Political Economy*, vol. 1 (1867; reprint, New York: International Publishers, 1967).

2   Max Weber, *Economy and Society*, 3 vols. (1921; reprint, Totowa, NJ: Bedminster Books, 1968).

3   Ibid.; Stephen Kalberg, "Max Weber's Types of Rationality: Cornerstones for the Analysis of Rationalization Processes in History," *American Journal of Sociology* 85 (1980): 1145–79.

4   George Ritzer, *The McDonaldization of Society*, rev. New Century ed. (Thousand Oaks, CA: Pine Forge Press, 2004).

5   Barry Barnes, "The Macro/Micro Problem and the Problem of Structure and Agency," in *Handbook of Social Theory*, ed. George Ritzer and Barry Smart, 339–52 (London: Sage, 2001).

6   Ibid.

7   Pierre Bourdieu, *Outline of a Theory of Practice* (London: Cambridge University Press, 1977); Anthony Giddens, *The Constitution of Society: Outline of a Theory of Structuration* (Berkeley: University of California Press, 1984).

8   Erving Goffman, *Presentation of Self in Everyday Life* (Garden City, NY: Anchor Books, 1959).

Jane Juffer

Why We Like to Lose:
On Being a Cubs Fan in the
Heterotopia of Wrigley Field

My father has been a Chicago Cubs fan since
before 1945, the last time the Cubs were in the
World Series. Throughout all these sixty years
of frustration, of seasons when "wait 'til next
year" was uttered as early as June, he has never
wavered in his devotion. He has, however, lost
his desire to watch each game that's televised.
That desire dissipated over the last two years
when the Cubs were, off and on, serious contenders, especially in 2003, when they won their
division and the first three games of the National
League championship series against the Florida
Marlins, then lost four straight. Now, my mother
says, he often leaves the room when the game is
on. The very proximity to victory is too much. At
the end of the 2004 season, my father told me,
"You know, I prefer it when we lose."

He is a connoisseur of the game, a star high
school and college pitcher, a coach for many
years, one of the many Cubs fans whose identity
was formed in the shadow of Wrigley (and in the
satellite signals of WGN) and who finds intense
pleasure in the game itself—a pleasure now
marred by the imperative to win. For my father,
as for many others, to be a Cubs fan is to live in a

The *South Atlantic Quarterly* 105:2, Spring 2006.
Copyright © 2006 by Duke University Press.

liminal zone between winning and losing; it's a space shaped by the constant deferral of desire.

What happens in this liminal zone? As my fourteen-year-old son Alex put it, "There are no expectations." One can concentrate on the game itself. My father asks Alex: "Do you think he's going to bunt or swing? Will the pitch be a curveball or changeup? Will the runner steal? Is the hit and run on?" Then there are the intricacies of keeping score, which aren't necessarily connected to winning or losing. Rather, the questions become: "What did he do last time up at bat? How many hits do the Cubs have? How many errors? Would you score that an error or a hit?" The pleasure is produced in the intensity of the moment.

Don't be mistaken: I am describing not an apathetic or lackadaisical fandom but an intensely engaged and passionate love of the game, one that is not weighed down by the final outcome.

This liminal affective space has a physical location and a historical origin: Wrigley Field. It's a place aptly described by Michel Foucault's notion of the heterotopia, an in-between space, a space of contradiction and contestation, a space that "has the curious property of being in relation with all the other sites, but in such a way as to suspect, neutralize, or invent the set of relations that they happen to designate, mirror, or reflect."[1] In terms of baseball, Wrigley exists in relation to all the other ballparks in Major League Baseball, and through that very relation, it has the capacity to render suspect that "set of relations." It is not a space of opposition so much as a space of proximity and thus denaturalization. It shares something with the other ballparks—the sense of competition, the game, the desire for a pennant. Yet it differs as well, insofar as the winning is constantly deferred (the Cubs have not won a World Series since 1908), allowing pleasure in the immediacy of the game. The contradiction revealed is that winning *does* matter, but only for a moment, and not in a way that ruins the pleasure of the game. My father doesn't want the Cubs to lose every game; he just wants freedom from the relentless demands endured by the champion. Wrigley calls into question the pressure to win not only in other baseball stadiums but also in all those other sports arenas where the only pleasure derived is that from victory. As such, Wrigley reveals the ordering of other spaces—not only sports spaces but also other capitalist arenas where the stakes are defined in terms of Us and Them.

There are different kinds of heterotopias, Foucault says, and perhaps the one that best fits Wrigley Field is his "heterotopia of deviation: those in which individuals whose behavior is deviant in relation to the required mean or norm are placed" (25). These may include rest homes, psychiatric hospitals, and prisons. This seems to me an entirely apt description of Wrigley, where on any summer afternoon, one finds a motley crew of retired people, crazy people, and criminals, all joined together in the devious and nonproductive practice of watching the Cubs lose another game. There are also the unemployed; a group of out-of-work fans named themselves the Bleacher Bums in the 1960s, and that moniker has remained to identify the beer-drinking, sun-loving patrons in left and right field.

Although many people attend Cubs games, not every one is a Cubbie fan. True Cubs stalwarts have passed *through* the heterotopic experience of self-recognition, of understanding that the pleasure of the game lies not in opposing oneself to the other team and the other fans but rather in experiencing life differently than it is experienced in other spaces. To experience Wrigley as a Cubs fan is to see oneself over there, where one lives the rest of life, caught up in the pressure to win, and then, through the experience of Wrigley, to reconstitute oneself as a subject who fully enjoys the game.

Wrigley Field

One arrives at the ballpark via the elevated train. The "El" rounds the curve from Belmont station, and Wrigley is suddenly there, rising up from the neighborhood itself. On the train, fans sport their Cubs T-shirts and caps, their shorts and sneakers, clearly standing out from the unfortunate folks who have to go to work during the day. The doors open at Addison and people spill onto the platform and file down the steps, emerging onto the street, immediately caught up in the crowd, surrounded by vendors, ticket hawkers, and ball chasers. Around the park, which is bordered by streets named Clark, Addison, Sheffield, and Waveland, there is a multiethnic neighborhood — 40,000 people live within half a mile of the stadium. Within a block, there are forty bars and restaurants, four car repair shops, three dry cleaners, three real estate offices, two car washes, two Laundromats, two convenience stores, a hair salon, a nail salon, a lighting store, a window shade store, a video store, a firehouse, and a tarot card reader.[2] Rooftops of the brownstones have been transformed into prized seats and barbecue centers. Even residents who aren't Cubs fans can't escape. In 1996, a Sammy Sosa homer broke a second-floor living room storm window at 1034 Waveland, "startling the apartment's tenant, a French immigrant named

Philippe Guichoux, who had been reading a book in the kitchen. 'I never watch baseball games,' he said" (Jacob 98).

Wrigley was built in 1914 (only Boston's Fenway Park, built in 1912, is older) and renovated in 1937, when owner P. K. Wrigley (the chewing gum magnate) had the idea to plant the now-signature ivy on the outfield walls. That was also the year the park's hand-operated scoreboard was built; still in use, it is now the only nonmechanical scoreboard in the major leagues. Three workers inside the 27-foot-high, 75-foot-wide structure update the scores of games being played throughout the league by changing five-pound green metal plates with numbers painted in white or yellow. The field didn't get lights until 1988, amid much consternation about modernization, and even now the Cubs play more day games than any team in the majors. The park is cozy; there really is no bad seat in the house.[3] In the late 1950s, an era of especially poor records, Hall of Fame shortstop Ernie Banks coined the phrase *friendly confines* to describe the park. Flying home from a dismal road trip, Banks said to his teammate Jerry Kindall, "We're going home, where people are friendly, back to the friendly confines" (quoted in Jacob 23). Despite their many losing seasons, the Cubs have a history of good attendance; in 1948, the Cubs became the first team to draw a million fans with a last-place team (Jacob 210). Although attendance faltered in the 1960s and 1970s, it picked up again in the 1980s. Between 1998 and 2003, the Cubs were in the top five major-league teams in attendance, measured as a percentage of stadium capacity.

As nearly every other team in the majors has torn down old stadiums and reconstructed new corporate-sponsored parks (PNC Park in Pittsburgh, Comerica Park in Detroit, Minute Maid in Houston, Three Comm in San Francisco, etc.), Wrigley Field has assumed a kind of mythic quality.[4] It seems to stand as a reminder of what baseball used to be, and although there is a risk here of nostalgia, there is also an important lesson to be learned through the study of Wrigley, a study Foucault called "heterotopology." The lesson is that the contestation to other spaces is both mythic and real.

Both the myth and the reality are embodied in the Curse of the Billy Goat. In 1945, a Chicago tavern owner, William Sianis, brought his pet goat to Wrigley for the World Series and was refused admittance with the goat, even though he had a ticket for his pet, because the ticket-takers were worried about the goat's smell. The story has it that Sianis cursed the Cubs; after they lost the series, "he sent a telegram to Wrigley that read 'Who stinks now?'" (Jacob 19). That was the last year the Cubs made it to the World Series. They have been close: they won the Central Division of the National League in 1984, 1989, and 2003. They won the wild-card berth in the play-offs in 1998 but lost to the San Francisco Giants. They were oh so close to the World Series in 2003, leading the Marlins 3–2 in games in the "best of seven" series and five outs away from winning Game Four to clinch the National League championship. Then a fan named Steve Bartman interfered with Cubs left fielder Moises Alou's attempt to catch a foul fly ball. After the play, the Marlins went on to score eight runs in the inning, winning that game (the sixth of the series) and then the seventh to clinch the pennant. Bartman had to be escorted from the field and received hate mail and even death threats. He had to be protected by Chicago police. Yet *most* fans didn't blame him. They blamed the Billy Goat Curse, indicating their willingness to let Bartman off the hook—and the Cubs as well, for the Cubs, after all, were the ones who lost the next game.

Because we Cubs fans don't really expect to win, we aren't so hard on the players when they lose. The boundaries between fan and player have relaxed into one of interdependence and mutual understanding rather than judgment. Boys and girls, men and women, can experience themselves as connected to the players. Players even seek advice from fans. Former Cub pitcher Mike Krukow says that "probably one of the most unique things about Wrigley Field . . . [is that it's] one of the only places in the world where if a guy comes up in September, a hitter, and you don't know anything about him, you can sit down in the bullpen and ask the fans. They'll know. That's how good and knowledgeable they are about the game" (quoted in Jacob 85).

Cubs fans will not tolerate a player who elevates himself above them. This was exhibited in the trade of Sosa to the Baltimore Orioles at the end of the 2004 season. During his thirteen years at Wrigley Field, Sosa was a beloved figure, especially after the famed home run chase for the single-season home run record with Mark McGwire in 1998. Sosa lost the race, 70–66, but won the "charisma" contest, endearing himself to fans worldwide with his energy and grace. The *Chicago Tribune*'s Skip Bayless wrote: "Strange new sports concept: a $10 million-a-year athlete who appears to be having even more fun playing than we are watching."[5] When sportswriters asked him, "Who's the man?" Sosa would answer, "He [McGwire] is the man here, and I'm the man in the Dominican Republic." Occasionally, Sosa would add, "Excuse me, Mark, but I'm the man in Chicago." He also won the Most Valuable Player award in 1998 as the Cubs won the wild-card race. Sosa hit 63 home runs in 1999, then 50 in 2000, then 64 in 2001, to become the first player to have three 60-homer seasons. In 2003, he became the first Latino to hit 500 career home runs.

But by the end of the 2004 season, Cubs fans were ready to see Sosa go. They had grown disenchanted with Sammy's ego. He blamed Manager Dusty Baker for his lackluster season (.253 batting average, with only 80 RBIs, his lowest total since the 1994 strike-shortened season). He left the last game of the season after the first pitch—cleaned out his locker and left the park. He was booed at Wrigley Field, not because he was slumping but because he was moping. A superstar who thought that he was not getting his due, he had exceeded the patience of even his devoted right-field bleacher fans. He had elevated himself above them, violating a principle of Wrigley: there can be no Us/Them division between players and fans. The bleachers in particular represent that liminal space of coming together, where super-star salaries are forgotten in the blaze of the Chicago sun and the breeze off Lake Michigan.

A heterotopia reveals the ordering of other sports spaces, the insistence on winning, with its reliance on destructive boundaries. It's like border theorist Gloria Anzaldúa says: "A counterstance locks one into a duel of oppressor and oppressed; locked in mortal combat, like the cop and the criminal, both are reduced to a common denominator of violence. . . . All reaction is limited by, and dependent on, what it is reacting against."[6] Most sports fandom continues to be predicated on clear lines of division between Us and Them, the insider and the outsider, even as the players move almost without regard to boundaries in this age of free agency and multi-million-dollar contracts. Player infidelities seem only to have solidified fan fidelities, the latter being one way to fend off the commercialization of the game. The heterotopia reveals this order, not because it exists apart from it but rather because of its closeness. Between regions, says Foucault—and we might identify these regions as "winning" and "losing"—the heterotopia "imper-ceptibly deviat[es] from the empirical orders prescribed for it by its primary codes, instituting an initial separation from them, [and] causes them to lose their original transparency." Once the "empirical orders" are revealed, it becomes possible to see another kind of order, "the unspoken order" of the heterotopia.[7]

Cubs fans want to win, as do the players, and it is this proximity to the "empirical order" that allows them to simultaneously reveal the other kind of desire to win—the desire that causes one to divert energy from the game to the result. Demonstrating that the dominant order is not "the only possible one or even the best one," Cubs fans form another kind of order—for the ritual of attending a Cubs game is nothing if not ordered. One goes to Wrigley, buys a scorecard, watches batting practice, records every pitch and every swing, cheers madly for the base hits, sings "Root, root, root for the Cubbies" during the seventh-inning-stretch rendition of "Take Me Out to the Ball Game," and usually settles in for the bottom-of-the-ninth, last-bat attempt. (As TV commentator and former Cub catcher Joe Garagiola said about his time with the team, "When you bought your ticket, you could bank on seeing the bottom of the ninth" [quoted in Jacob 82]. Other teams, when they're at home, get to stay through the top of the ninth, when their closer puts an efficient end to another victory.) At the same time, one can appreciate the skills of the opposing team. There is great joy in winning and a certain comfort and security in losing. From this vantage point, Cubs fans realize the alternate ordering of Wrigley Field.

This perspective differs from the sports norm, the fans who hate each other, who hate members of the opposing team, whose anger detracts from the complexities and nuances of the game. These fans seem unaware of the order that defines their fandom and its connection to capitalism's survival-of-the-fittest ethos. "There's a different perspective at Wrigley Field—a clearer understanding of failure as a consistent part of baseball," wrote Roy Eisenhardt, Oakland A's president, in an article in the *New Yorker* in 1986. "Because ball teams play every day, the chances for failure are always high, but the Cubs fans somehow understand that. It's a higher level of baseball culture" (quoted in Jacob 82).

Gender Bending

The Cubs have been the perfect team to follow for the mother of a boy who loves sports. Next to all the spaces where young boys learn to define their athletic identities in terms of opposition and boundary building, Wrigley teaches them that there are other ways to play the game. It's not that the pressure to win will disappear from other sports arenas, but rather that the experience of being a Cubs fan will allow the young athlete to see his "role models" as not that different from himself. The whole notion of the "role model" becomes more egalitarian as the boy understands that star athletes are not all that different from him—fallible, insecure, and caring.

How does one teach a boy to see himself in relation to others rather than in competition with them? To recognize "the potency of bonds; the relaxed boundaries of the self"?[8] As many feminists have theorized, boys are taught to think of themselves as autonomous, self-sufficient individuals, not defined through relationships. By contrast, girls come to experience themselves as less differentiated than boys; whereas the "basic feminine sense of self is connected to the world, the basic masculine sense of self is separate."[9] Many of us teach our children differently—our boys to be kind and sensitive and helping and our girls to be independent and strong while caring about others at the same time. Yet when kids leave the home, the multiple sites they traverse are often ones of more traditional gendered roles—especially, for boys, in the world of sports. There, all the old expectations remain. For eight-year-olds: Don't cry if you get hit by a pitched ball, even if it hurts like hell. Take it like a man, son. Be aggressive on the court/field. Win at all costs. Make fun of those who fall down, make an errant throw, or miss a goal kick. The contradictions between home and field can be especially challenging for boys—taught in one space that it's OK, even good, for boys to cry and in another space that if they do so, they'll be derided. Taught in one space that winning isn't that important (and maybe that competition is evil because it's the foundation of capitalism) and in another space that winning is indeed everything (maybe because competition is the foundation of capitalism). By contrast, being a Cubs fan redefines losing, suggesting that winning is produced through relationships formed with other fans and players. As Ernie Banks said, "People say I was never with a winner, but what is a winner? I was indeed with a winner because I made lifetime friends on my ball club. I won every time I stepped onto the grass at Wrigley Field because I had such a wonderful relationship with the Cubs players, the fans, and all the people of Chicago, the greatest people in the world. Not a winner? I was on a winner all my life" (quoted in Jacob 78).

I remember Alex as a four- and five-year-old, fascinated by both numbers and the Cubs, his interests converging every morning as he sat before the computer, looking up the latest Cubs stats. The most impressive numbers were the strikeouts—not by Cubs pitchers but rather by Cubs hitters. In 1997, Sosa struck out 174 times; in 1998 and 1999, 171 times each year. In 1998, his teammate José Hernandez battled him for the league lead in strikeouts, ending the year with 140. Watching the Cubs together, we would root for a home run, but the strikeout also signified, not as failure but as another component of the game. Sammy's whiffs were almost as impressive as his homers, his mighty swings turning him around in the batting box, sometimes making his helmet twist simultaneously.

America's Superstation

In 1981, Bill Wrigley, after sixty years of ownership, sold the club to the Tribune Company, owner of the *Chicago Tribune*, WGN radio, and the WGN superstation, putting the Cubs on cable and satellite and creating Cubs fans everywhere.[10] My parents, for example, live in the northwestern corner of Iowa, where you might expect more Minnesota Twins and Kansas City Royals fans than Cub supporters. Yet there they are, in the midst of the cornfields, among hundreds of Iowans rooting for their Chicago team. The televisual presence prompts Cubs fans to attend games when their team is on the road: between 1998 and 2003, the Cubs had the largest road attendance three times and were in the top three in the other two years.

This is not the Cubs of my father's youth or of my own youth, when the heroes were mainly white — Ron Santo, Bruce Sutter, Mark Grace, Ryne Sandberg, Greg Maddux — with a few African Americans — Ernie Banks in the 1950s and 1960s and Andre Dawson in the late 1980s and early 1990s. This is the Cubs of my son's youth, and so many others' youth — Sosa, Alou, Benito Santiago, Aramis Ramirez. There is a new generation of broadcasters. At Wrigley, the blustery Harry Caray with his infamous butchering of Spanish names has been replaced by his grandson Chip Caray, who has clearly studied the language. About one-third of all major leaguers are Latino or Latin American; Latin players now outnumber African Americans, and they dominate the game in terms of star status as well. In 2004, the American League's MVP was Vladimir Guerrero of the Dominican Republic, and its Cy Young (pitching) winner was Johann Santana of Venezuela. The majority of Latin players come from the Dominican Republic, like Sammy Sosa, who was born in San Pedro de Macorís, home to the multinational sugar companies that have contributed to the decimation of the Dominican Republic's economy.

Global media flows produce another aspect of the heterotopic space of Wrigley Field — the permeability of borders between the national Us and the global Them. The great American pastime is being redefined as the great Americas pastime. Dominicans in San Pedro watch Sammy and McGwire on satellite television, joined in a televisual space with Dominicans in New Jersey and Anglos in Iowa. This is the era of "second modernity," says Rob Shields, a time characterized by a "new, categorical, fuzzy logic of decidability and knowability." Drawing on the work of Bruno Latour, Shields argues that boundaries "once established a geographically- and historically-specific type of inclusion and exclusion correlated with presence and

absence. The inside was near, intimate and present. The outside was distant, foreign and absent." Globalization has made more geographically complex the idea of the other: "distant but present, once inaccessible 'others' are
now near'; they are unavoidable presences in contradiction of their spatial
remoteness."[11]

The outside and inside have become more complicated, but they are still
shaped by years of U.S. imperialism in Latin America. U.S. military and
corporate presence (now multinational) in the Dominican Republic since
it won its independence from Spain in 1898 is largely responsible for the
economic devastation that drives young men to seek entry into the major
leagues rather than playing in the Caribbean baseball leagues. U.S. interven-
tions in Puerto Rico, Cuba, and elsewhere in Latin America have had similar
effects. In his history of baseball in the Dominican Republic, Alan Klein
says that baseball is Dominicans' "best hope for the future and a leading
cause of their underdevelopment," as many young men pursue this dream
without thinking of other options. Despite the hope that baseball will offer
a way out of poverty and a redemption for the nation, it hasn't produced
those effects: "for all the success that the Dominicans have enjoyed at baseball, 80 percent of the people are unemployed or underemployed, and the
economic benefits of baseball must be negligible."[12] Much as multinational
corporations exploit the resources of vulnerable countries, widening the
gap between rich and poor, so does major league baseball exploit the Latin
American leagues, as the best players are scouted and enter MLB baseball
academies in their teens, determined to become one of the chosen few.

One would never know this history from watching baseball on television
or from visiting any ballpark. Wrigley Field has become a multiethnic
heterotopia, a space of alternate ordering because everyone seems to get
along, at least for the afternoon. On "Celebratin' Sammy" day at the end
of the 1998 season, hundreds of Dominican flags adorned the surrounding rooftops, fluttered throughout the packed stands, and were attached to
the stadium's own flagpoles. Latin music filled the air; bilingual signs were
everywhere: "Sammy es Grande," "Sosa Para Presidente," "Te Amamos,
Sammy." Dominican television announcers were in the broadcast booth,
announcing the game for fans watching in the Dominican Republic. WGN
also sent reporter Bob Jordan to San Pedro de Macorís to capture their viewing experience as well as to re-create Sosa's childhood for U.S. viewers.

Boundaries collapse and the geographical Them becomes the televisual
Us. In its ability to become a diasporic community, but one that is prem-

ised on an erasure of power differences, Wrigley offers us recourse from the messiness of globalization. It also positions Major League Baseball (MLB) as the savior of Latin players. Some heterotopias, writes Foucault, function as "spaces of compensation," like the Jesuit colonies in South America— spaces of perfect order and regulation. In their missionary zeal, the Jesuits believed they could compensate indigenous peoples for the loss of their land, religion, and culture. They constructed orderly villages and planned the day around worship: "Christianity marked the space and geography of the American world."[13] By providing Latin players with multi-million-dollar contracts, MLB can tell itself (if it cares), and its fans, that it is compensating Latin American countries for the loss of their best players, not to mention the loss of land connected to various forms of imperialism.

This space of compensation/colonization might explain why Sosa is so humble. There's not a word about U.S. imperialism or the decimation of the Caribbean leagues in his autobiography. In fact, just the opposite: He's frequently singing the praises of the United States; he could even be heard reciting the line made famous in a *Saturday Night Live* skit, "Baseball's been very, very good to me," pronouncing the *very* as *bery*. During the home run race, Sosa constantly paid homage to "America." He predicted that McGwire would be the one to break Roger Maris's record, then added, "But if I do break it, God bless America." He reminds one of Mr. Cub, Ernie Banks, one of the first two African Americans on the Cubs when he started in 1953. Banks was a humble man who never complained about racism, even when it seemed clear to other players that Manager Leo Durocher was discriminating against him. Says Banks about his philosophy of the game, "Many of the players didn't quite understand my own philosophy. I believe in forgive and forget, and keep your mouth shut and listen to whatever somebody is trying to tell you and you can learn something. . . . it was just misinterpreted that Leo disliked me."[14] This rationale seems not all that different from Sosa telling McGwire "You're the man," paying homage to the white man who most represents the American pastime.

Yet there is also an incommensurability built into the notion of compensation. It suggests an unevenness, the possibility that the dominant subject is attempting to make up for something that can't quite be replaced. Even though the former is positioned as benevolent in the desire to give, and the latter as grateful, there is nevertheless a hint of justice. Perhaps that justice is represented now in the form of the multi-million-dollar salaries many Latin ballplayers receive. In 2004, the highest-paid player and pitcher were two Dominicans: Boston Red Sox outfielder Manny Ramirez, who made $22.5 million, and Pedro Martinez, at that time also a Red Sox, who made $17.5 million.

In the space of compensation, one doesn't have to think about racism and xenophobia, about historical injustices and their present-day effects. One can seek refuge in the predictability of the game. Baseball is a game of order and regularity. At Wrigley, the gates open at 11:10 for a 1:10 game. The Cubs take batting practice and infield. The Bud man starts circulating in the bleachers. Five minutes before game time, all rise to sing the national anthem. There are three outs to every half inning, nine innings to every game. There are ninety feet between every base and sixty feet six inches between the pitching rubber and home plate. Every day, one knows what to expect, especially as a Cubs fan:

The Cubs will lose.

Notes

1   Michel Foucault, "Of Other Spaces," *Diacritics* (Spring 1986): 22–27; quote, 24. Subsequent citations are given parenthetically by page number in the text.

2   Mark Jacob, *Wrigley Field: A Celebration of the Friendly Confines* (Chicago: Contemporary Books, 2002), 95. Subsequent citations are given parenthetically by page number in the text.

3   With a capacity of 38,765, Wrigley is the third smallest stadium in the majors.

4   Chewing gum entrepreneur William Wrigley Jr. was one of a group of ten investors who bought the Cubs in 1915, and in 1920 he became majority owner of the team. In 1926, the stadium acquired the family's name. In 1981, the Tribune Company bought the team.

5   Skip Bayless, "Is Sosa Really Having More Fun Than We Are?" *Chicago Tribune*, August 13, 1998.

6   Gloria Anzaldúa, *Borderlands/La Frontera: The New Mestiza* (San Francisco: Aunt Lute Books, 1987), 78.

7   Michel Foucault, *The Order of Things: An Archeology of the Human Sciences* (New York: Vintage Books, 1971), xx.

8   Eva Kittay Feder, *Love's Labor: Essays on Women, Equality, and Dependency* (New York: Routledge, 1999), 36.

9   Nancy Chodorow, *The Reproduction of Mothering: Psychoanalysis and the Sociology of Gender* (Berkeley: University of California Press, 1978), 169.

10 The Tribune Co. consists of Tribune Broadcasting, which owns and operates twenty-two major market television stations and seven radio stations; Tribune Publishing, which owns eleven newspapers; Tribune Regional Programming, which owns two twenty-four-hour cable news channels; and Tribune Interactive. The company claims to reach 80 percent of U.S. television households. Detailed information on these holdings may be found at www.tribune.com/about/index.html (accessed April 20, 2005).

11 Rob Shields, "The Limits of Reflexive Modernization," www.spaceandculture.org/robshields/publications.html (accessed April 22, 2005).

12 Alan M. Klein, *Sugarball: The American Game, the Dominican Dream* (New Haven, CT: Yale University Press, 1991), 60.

13 Foucault, "Of Other Spaces," 27.

14 Carrie Muskat, *Banks to Sandberg to Grace: Five Decades of Love and Frustration with the Chicago Cubs* (New York: Contemporary Books, 2002), 42–43.

Grant Farred

God's Team:
The Painful Pleasure of the
Miracle on the Bosphorus

Before he was ordained a priest, and long before he became the first non-Italian pope, John Paul II was—in addition to famously being a thespian—a footballer. According to rumor, he was an amateur goalkeeper in his native Poland. There may some veracity, then, in the Vatican stories that he was a fan of Liverpool Football Club (FC). After all, it's a perfectly logical choice: the Liverpool goalie, Jerzy Dudek, is a Pole and an observant Catholic and is reported to have had an audience with His Holiness in Rome. Which is probably where all these John Paul stories got their start. Invite one Polish "Scouser" goalkeeper to the Vatican and next thing you know, the other, little-known, probably no-talent-at-all-between-the-sticks goalie, John Paul, has been a Red all his life. (Native Liverpudlians are known as "Scousers.") At the very least, you have these wonderfully crazy Koppites, the Liverpool FC fans who sit at the famous "Kop" end of the club's Anfield Road ground, producing banners saying "We've Got a Big Pole in Our Goal" for the club's 2005 EUFA Champions League final against Italy's AC Milan.

This is an unequal mixture of faiths, Liverpool FC fandom and Catholicism. Being a Pool fan is,

The *South Atlantic Quarterly* 105:2, Spring 2006.
Copyright © 2006 by Duke University Press.

with all due respect to my fellow Catholics of the lapsed, recovering, or prac-
ticing variety, a much holier, more spiritually uplifting and demanding religious experience. Supporting Liverpool is a painful pleasure because every
possibility of joy, of victory, is tempered by the recognition, borne of painful
experience, that a loss, another loss, can—yet again—break your heart. Loyalty is the most painful and pathological condition for a fan because it takes
for granted the fan's continued faith—believing, like St. Jude, in too many
lost or soon-to-be-lost causes. Loyalty is the perpetual, lifelong antidote to
"common sense." When sanity dictates that defeat, or, worse, humiliation,
be quietly accepted, painful pleasure—and, believe me, it is painful to put
yourself through this experience repeatedly; there's no pleasure, but there's
no choice, either, but to go through it one more time—demands and gets,
unequivocally, the fan's faith. Love hurts.

This essay recounts an experience of painful pleasure. Moreover, as it
charts a memorable football event, it shows that the highs, lows, and then
again the high of a single contest—a football match—is never temporally
hermetic. The event itself is always crowded in on by the past (previous victories, the memory of excruciating losses) and by how it speaks to adversaries about your prowess or failures, and by the future—how it will add
luster, how it will be the source of new pride or psychic wounds. "God's
Team" is an exercise in the peculiarly painful pleasure of a historic Liverpool triumph. It is also an unreflective, but critical, cultural undertaking:
writing passionately, unapologetically about sport by attempting to capture
in prose—as lyrically as possible—the utter joy of watching your team win,
your favorite players excelling, rising to unexpected heights, and in the process carrying you affectively along with them. This essay is about articulat-
ing the sharp, unending psychic injuries that are incurred in defeat—and
are capable of returning to haunt you in your most vulnerable moments.
In writing about the 2004–5 European Champions League final (a competition that admits only the best clubs on the continent), it demonstrates
the painful pleasure of a lifelong fan: staring your worst nightmares full
in the face and then feeling yourself elevated to a lofty height only a true
believer can experience. Finally, "painful pleasure" is a loaded metaphor,
a grasping for and toward a distinct language for sports criticism, a language—filled with rich allusions, affective excess, cultural hubris verging
on the publicly embarrassing, the articulation of politically impermissible
thoughts, the animus that approximates hatred, the kind of joy matched
only by extreme physical sensations or the birth of a child—capable of giving

voice to sport's exceptionality as a cultural, and religious, experience. Alternatively phrased, it is an idiosyncratic, self-conscious act of affective, cultural, and intellectual indulgence.

A Pole in Our Goal

In the Champions League final, Jerzy Dudek, that "Big Pole in Our Goal," was somehow more agile, gifted, lucky—one hastens to offer that "blessed" may be the appropriate adjective here—than we Liverpool fans usually know him to be. Could it be that the "other Pole" (the other "Polie Goalie"), the recently deceased pope (who died on April 1, 2005), was also in our goal on that magical, unbelievable night in Istanbul? Was Liverpool simply revealing to the world what I have always claimed to be true: that we are God's team? Or was it simply Liverpool players, the aristocrats of English and European football, with their four European Championships (the last in 1984) and eighteen national titles, remembering their illustrious history and drawing strength and inspiration from that great legacy? Was the Pole in our goal not so much (a) being blessed from up above as experiencing himself as the temporary "second coming" of the renegade Zimbabwean keeper Bruce Grobbelaar, who kept goal for Liverpool in the 1984 final? Or was it a combination of the two forces, history and faith—or, faith in history?

Whatever the case may be, all us Liverpool fans agree that the comparison with our other four championship teams is on shaky historical ground. We may even concede that the 2005 team is unworthy of the comparison, and not only because of the disparity in talent. Which is precisely, however, what makes the Istanbul final, played on the banks of the Bosphorus in the Ataturk Olympic Stadium—what else could the premier stadium in Turkey possibly have been called?—infinitely more memorable. This multinational squad (Scousers, an Irishman, a German, Spaniards, a Croatian, a Norwegian, Frenchmen, Czechs, an Australian, a Finn, and of course our Pole) was not even expected to be in Istanbul; they were certainly not expected to win. The 2004–5 side can in no way compare to its championship predecessors. The 1977, 1978, 1981, and 1984 teams were filled with stars—Kevin Keegan, Phil Thompson, Kenny Dalglish, Alan Hansen, Mark Lawrenson, Graeme Souness, Grobbelaar, take your pick, add your pick to the long lists of performers not mentioned here, and don't forget to add the name of my favorite Liverpool manager, Bob Paisley, who won Europe's premier club trophy not once but three times. They were almost always the favorites: against Borussia Moenchengladbach, against FC Bruges, against Real Madrid, against Roma. With good reason too, as those victories show. Their 2005 successors had shocked everybody, including their own captain, the native Scouser Steven Gerrard, by booking their place in the final. At the end of the group stages of the Champions League (when each team plays the three other teams in its section, home and away), Gerrard declared that this side didn't have it in them to win the competition.

I have always argued, following my logic of the divine right of European football kings, that either European competition is in your footballing genes or it isn't. Real Madrid, Bayern Munchen, AC Milan, Juventus of Turin, Ajax of Amsterdam, and Liverpool FC, we're European aristocracy. Genus Europeanus footballus, or something Latinate like that. Europe is no place for pretenders, especially not English ones. Our main foes, whatever they say, just don't have our superior genes and never will. Manchester United (two triumphs more than thirty years apart), Arsenal (who can win regularly enough in England but falter, early and often, in their European campaigns, no Champions League to their credit, and none likely, ever), and, newly flush with Russian cash, courtesy of their oil billionaire owner, Chelsea (no triumphs and, again, none likely), well, we took care of Chelsea in the semi-finals, didn't we? You have to understand and respect European competition to win there often; Europe is about tradition, a strong sense of history, of successive generations of fans who have grown up watching the magic, as the Anfield faithful call it, of "European nights" at "Fortress Anfield." This is how Liverpool's home stadium has been dubbed because visiting teams almost always struggle to win in this gray, northwestern English port city. Liverpool stands alone in England, and only a select few can match us in Europe. It is precisely because of Liverpool's genes that we, and not money-rich, tradition-poor Chelsea, were in Istanbul.

So perhaps our Stevie Gerrard, the local lad from Liverpool's impoverished neighborhood of Huyton, should have known better than caution us against our improbable ambition. After all, it was he who started us on the road to glory in Istanbul on that December 2004 Anfield night when he came back to score that cracker of a goal against Olympiakos of Greece just when our Champions League ambitions looked dead and buried. Needing to beat the Greek side by two goals, and leading only 2–1 with about three minutes left, Gerrard latched onto a loose ball outside the 18-yard box and lashed home one of the greatest goals I have ever seen, and certainly one of the best goals ever scored in European club competition. With everything riding on him, Gerrard did not hesitate for a second when presented with the opportunity: he took it in his stride, beautifully balanced, and it fairly scorched in, leaving Greek hearts broken from Athens to Los Angeles. It's the stuff greatness is made of, performing superbly in crunch matches, and our twenty-four-year-old skipper did himself and all the Koppites proud that Wednesday night in December 2004. As he demonstrated in that match, Stevie's capable of sheer brilliance—in my more thoughtful moments, I call him "God's Own Son"—though by his standards he had a less than stellar season in 2004–5. Until, that is, the last seventy-five minutes in Istanbul, the minutes that changed everything, that second half and the two fifteen-minute periods of extra time that would see Gerrard scale even higher peaks.

After Olympiakos, we dispensed with Germany's Bayer Leverkusen in grand fashion in the first knockout stage of the competition—6–2 on aggregate, after 3–1 home and away victories in which the Catalan Luis García looked like a world-beater. Liverpool, needless to say, weren't favored to go through to the quarterfinals. In that round, up against the Italian giants Juventus (soon to be crowned 2004–5 Serie A champs), it was again García who came up trumps. His goal, in a game we won 2–1 at Anfield, was stellar. He took a lofted pass from the young Frenchman Anthony Le Tallec and curled and dipped it with searing power and accuracy over the head of the Juve keeper, Gianluigi Buffon. The return match in Turin witnessed the transformation of Jamie Carragher, the other native Scouser in the team (raised in Bootle, a neighborhood even poorer than Huyton), from loyal performer into world-class central defender. With a heart as big as the Mersey, and Liverpool loyal from the part in his hair to the soles of his feet, "Carra" has always been a stalwart. Slot him in at left or right back, he's a gamer, steady and dependable, but with his insertion into the center of defense by the new manager, the Madrileno Rafael "Rafa" Benítez, he's been a revelation: a star. He was the star of a 0–0 draw ("tie") at the Stadio del Alpi in Turin.

It may be the story of this 2005 side. Especially true in Istanbul, but throughout the tournament, when the team needed something, not only did someone step up; different players were almost transubstantiated. Luis García, beloved by the Kop for his flashiness, is usually ordinary in the English Premier League. Yes, there are moments of genuine inspiration, but he is as likely to score a special goal as he is to overhit a regulation pass or, worse, fail to trap a ball you feel any twelve-year-old could master with little effort. But in Europe, he shone. He was sure and intuitive in his strikes against Leverkusen, scorer of that scintillating goal against Juve. He worked his tail off in the semis against the "Blues" of Chelsea and ran until he was knackered against Milan. Excuse me, I must be seeing things, but is that Sanz Luis García or Kop legend Kenny Dalglish? Hard to tell them apart, isn't it? There was another unlikely hero as well in the Champions League campaign. When substituting for the injured Dietmar "Didi" Hamann or Xabi Alonso or Gerrard, the blond Igor Biscan (the man I sometimes call the "Cut-and-Thrust Croat") played like he'd just been reborn as the moustachioed, curly-permed Terry McDermott. In the early to mid-1980s McDermott was then-skipper Graeme Souness's dependable, occasionally inventive, defense-protecting partner. There are Sami Hyypia, Hamann, and of course Dudek stories like this too, but let's save 'em for later.

With Carra, however, it's slightly different. When Rafa Benítez arrived from the Spanish La Liga outfit Valencia in June 2004 to replace the Frenchman Gérard Houllier, he settled upon the square-jawed, square-foreheaded Carragher as his primary central defender, breaking up and displacing the senior pairing of Hyypia and Stephan Henchoz. The Scouser warmed to his role and grew in confidence and stature as the season wore on. He was without question the pick of the Liverpool players in the 2004–5 season and arguably the only one to match his performances in Europe in the English Premier League. Every game, Carra came to play. He was immense against Juve, neutralizing their lanky Swedish striker Zlatan Ibrahimovich. Carra was everywhere, stopping attacks, cutting out through balls, heading with authority: Jamie Carragher was born in Liverpool, but "Commander Carragher" came of age on the European stage. If anything, he arguably went one better (than his Juve performance) when he almost single-handedly put paid to the arrogance of Chelsea in the Champions League semifinal. He marshaled the defense like Souness had once imperiously ruled the Liverpool midfield. Chelsea's striker, Didier Drogba, was made to look as bedraggled as a young kitten left out in the gray Liverpool rain, so ineffective was he. The much-vaunted, overpaid Chelsea midfield gave it their best, but Carra stood tall. Yes, he got help from Steve Finnan, and Xabi Alonso and Hamann put in their share of defensive work, but it was Carra who was in charge as Liverpool beat the arrogant coach Jose Mourniho's excessively hyped Chelsea — courtesy, of course, of a García goal. As the Liverpool players left the Anfield pitch after beating Chelsea, there, in front of millions of TV viewers, was

Gerrard jumping, piggyback-style, onto Carra as the Liverpool players made their way back down the Anfield tunnel to the dressing room. They'd ridden his back, all right, they had. Now that Chelsea had been dispensed with, it was on to Istanbul for Liverpool. "We're going to Istanbul," sang the Koppites to the departing Chelsea fans, after having jeered them because, as the always-savvy Scousers put it, "You've got no history." With only two English League championships for Chelsea, even if one was won in 2004–5, it was hard to argue as the Koppites booked their flights to the city on the Bosphorus, where East meets West, where Europe confronts its Other, where faith has long done battle against secularity, where Old and New Europe are always perilously entangled. Behind all this raucous energy one could hear the official Liverpool hymn—I mean, anthem: "You'll Never Walk Alone." Against Paolo Maldini's AC Milan, Stevie G. and his Reds were going to need the help of all the faithful, whether alive or recently departed.

We Came All This Way for Heartbreak . . .

By halftime at the Ataturk Stadium, it looked all over. Liverpool was down 3–0, and their opponents flush with confidence. Rightly so. It hadn't even taken long for the rot to set in. Less than a minute, in fact. Djimi Traore's a useless player—the kind of player who at once makes you understand the phrase *two left feet* and then makes you think that it's undeserved unless your name's Traore. He's the kinda guy who gives *two left feet* a bad name, a very bad name. He's the Liverpool left back, though you'd hardly mistake him for a sure tackler or a precise distributor of the ball; both these lacks were patently obvious in the opening minute of the Champions League final. In the long line of Liverpool left backs, from the imperturbable Welshman Joey Jones to the irrepressible Englishman Alan Kennedy, from the sublime skill of Jim Beglin (a career cruelly cut short by a horrendous injury, but, oh, how wonderful it was to watch you in that short moment, Jimmy Beglin) to the gangly talents of the Irishman Steve Staunton, Traore's a disgrace.

Liverpool kicked off against the AC Milan juggernaut, and within a couple of passes the ball reached Traore. True to form, he gave it away. But then it got worse. Milan immediately attacked, as any team should, against Traore's matador defense (he's in the habit of just waving attackers by). Beaten without any difficulty, he fouled a Milan player. Because Liverpool started without the German central midfielder Hammann (never a smart move), the resulting free kick curled into the heart of the Liverpool defense, where

Didi would normally be patrolling. Surprised to find himself so completely unmarked, the aged but still elegant Milan captain Maldini, within about fifty-seven seconds, got his shot on goal. Dudek remained frozen to the spot. Score one for the favorites. Less than twenty-five minutes had passed, and Benítez's gamble of playing another utterly useless signing, the Aussie Harry Kewell, backfired. Kewell is a player who spends more time on his hair than on his football. "Eye Candy" is my nickname for him—easy on the eye, corrosive to the rest of the constitution; he'll rot you from the inside before you can say "Cadbury's chocolate." After AC Milan's first goal, Kewell took his leave and was replaced by another longtime underachiever, a man I've labeled "Bloody Vladdy" Smicer. Nothing to warm the cockles of a Liverpool fan's heart, nothing to restore heart or courage. But I was soon to retract my criticism, if only for some twenty-four hours.

Still, we were only a goal down, and halftime was approaching. Outplayed, yes, but still in it. Then disaster struck, not once but twice, six minutes—remember that number—before the interval. It was delivered with a brutal swiftness that exemplified the Italians' mastery. A rare Liverpool attack broke down in the Milan penalty area and they played it out wide, on Traore's side. He was nowhere to be found, and a precise cross found the Liverpool defense in a shambles, with the Irish right back Finnan matching his flanking teammate's capacity to miss tackles. The Argentine Hernan Crespo, a Chelsea reject, tapped it home. Two down in the thirty-ninth minute, and worse was to follow very shortly. Milan's third was exquisite. With Liverpool caught napping in midfield, a slide-rule pass by the Brazilian midfielder Kaká split the defense perfectly; not even a lunging Carragher or a despairing Hyypia could get a foot to it. Crespo nipped in between the Liverpool central defenders and, at full speed, flicked the ball over Dudek's vain attempts. Crespo tucked it away neatly into Dudek's lefthand corner; it was a beautifully taken goal. Game over. So said the commentators; so thought the English bookies, who were offering 100-to-1 odds on a Liverpool victory at halftime. Who could argue?

Certainly not a Liverpool lifer, thirty-five years and counting a fan. Not me. This is what painful pleasure means. Watching a football train-wreck, and your team's the wreck—or, in the vernacular, getting wrecked, getting shredded to bits and you can't argue or rationalize because the other team is simply better than yours. I was more than sick: I could not speak. I could not form a thought. Not until the second half started, anyway. It's a frightening experience, to be so invested in your team as to have all your faculties shut down when they are not so much losing as, you feel, being humiliated. As having the extreme sense of witnessing an abomination: the public violation of your own history: the history of giants such Bill Shankly, Paisley, Ronnie Moran, Joe Fagan, Roy Evans, and Reuben Bennett, great managers and coaches all, now dishonored. Players such as Dalglish, Souness, Keegan, Hansen, Ian Rush: to have their memory shamed by this score, by this completely inept, disgraceful performance.

Restore Respectability, Please

It was all I could think as the second half began: "Restore respectability, please. Do not dishonor this football club." Do not, in other words, ride roughshod over my psychic life. Do not disgrace my past. Do not do irreparable damage to the memory of those through whom I have lived my affective life for these last three and a half decades. Do not insult my long-distance love for Liverpool. Please. One goal, I thought, and we can say that Rafa's overachieving team lost with a measure of respectability. Just that. Two goals would restore dignity. I could not conceive of a third, or imagine that we would rise from the depths of the murky Bosphorus and raise ourselves mightily into the cold Turkish night, and the early morning.

At the end of the first half I heard it. Clearly, distinctly, rising from a low, rumbling murmur to a cacophonous indictment. I heard it in Durham, North Carolina, where I was watching, coming from the suburban north end of London, from ritzy, glitzy, swanky west London, and from the outskirts of Manchester. I heard the increasingly shrill voices of Arsenal, Chelsea (north and west London clubs, respectively), and Manchester United fans, condemning us as unworthy to be in the Champions League final. I could hear it in the arrogant, unthinking tones of Chelsea's Mourinho, in the suave, bespoke-suited contemplations of Arsenal's Arsene Wenger, and it was palpable, though he would deny it, in the gruff dismissals of United's Alex Ferguson. Mourinho had been his usual ungracious self in the semifinal defeat. The best team lost, according to him. Another failed Champions League campaign for United, always a club with more hype than success. Wenger, himself a repeated Champions League failure, was surely—and in those faux philosophe terms that the Frenchman so enjoys deploying while discoursing on football—feeling vindicated now. By comparison, losing early in the competition was better than this. This humiliation. Plain, broadcast for the whole football world to see. This is what

Stevie G. would have to lead us against. Was he up to it? He, who had toyed in the summer of 2004 with swapping our history for those with no history — Chelsea. Didn't Red loyalty mean anything to him, scion of our city?

The glimmer of hope, against further damage if not revival, was the arrival of Hamann as the second half began. On he came in the place of the injured Finnan. The Liverpool defense was rearranged. Wide to the right went Carra, flanking left was Traore (why was he still on, goddammit?), anchored in a V-formation by the "Finnish Giraffe" Hyypia. With the defense now protected by Didi, Gerrard was released to play "higher up," as they say in football. He was, colloquially phrased, now relieved of some of his defensive duties, some of which were to be assumed by the sweet-passing Basque, Alonso. It looked better, except if you checked the scoreboard. Italian teams have gained a reputation in Europe for a couple of things, and they're not unrelated: their defensive prowess (they don't give up a lot of goals, and the Milan defense was loaded with veterans — Nesta, Stam, and Cafu alongside Maldini) and their notorious cynicism. They fake fouls, they tug slyly at opponents' jerseys, they complain vociferously at the officials: in short, they're expert gamesmen. None of these appellations applied to Carlo Ancelotti's side. They play football, and in that first half there was nothing to suggest that they wouldn't continue to run rampant over Rafa's ragtag outfit — which is how Liverpool looked in the opening forty-five minutes. In that opening stanza Milan defended with sureness and most often played their way out of trouble with crisp passing.

Minute Fifty-four. A newly compact Liverpool side attacked down their left flank in the person of "Perpetual Youth," the perennially boyish-looking Norwegian John Arne Risse. His first attempt at a cross was blocked, but his second effort was sure and pinpoint accurate. There to meet it, in his new role, was Stevie. It wasn't a powerful header, but it bore the imprint of a world-class player: deftly aimed, precisely met, sure. In the Milan goal the Brazilian Dida was left leaden-footed. 1–3. When Gerrard turned and ran back to the center circle, I saw something I had never seen before in the seven years (he made his Liverpool debut in 1998) I have watched him. He had an unprecedented look on his face: absolute confidence. Gerrard motioned a teammate to get the ball back for the restart and, then, in what for me is one of the most prescient, memorable moments in the history of sport, he motioned to the traveling Koppites behind Dida's goal: palms open, he dropped his hands to his knees and then raised his arms from his knees in a gesture that will live forever in Liverpool history: he implored the Kop for more than their support, which they always give; he asked for their faith. To turn the pain of the first fifty-three minutes into a pleasure for the ages. And back they roared, answering his call resoundingly, scaring the life out of the Milan fans; and now, long after the memory of that image has sharpened in my mind, I am sure they also scared the daylights out of Maldini and his teammates. Milan was never the same after Skipper Supreme scored that goal. It wasn't as spectacular as the Olympiakos one, but it struck a blow far more historic. It was the precise moment, Minute Fifty-four, that another Liverpool player joined the ranks of the Greats. Players are great not only because they are able to do exceptional things, as Alfredo Di Stefano, Gordon Banks, Pele, Johan Cruyff, and Diego Maradona routinely did, but for a more signal reason: they can see possibilities, how the game might during its very course be changed. Great players see what is not visible to anyone else, both those on the field and those watching the game. The great ones understand in a single moment how an entire contest can be turned on its head, how it is possible to go from losing to winning, how to beat your opponents because you can see what they—and your teammates—do not. Gerrard knew that, with his header and the possibilities it opened up, the 2004–5 Champions League final could now be played according to an altered way of thinking. In reaching out to the Kop, the Scouser calling out to his own, he was giving them the signal that great things were about to come. Greatness established, game on. I dropped onto my knees. It was time to join the faithful and assume an attitude of prayer.

Minute 56. Again the move originated out left, though this time worked along the ground, with Stevie and Alonso all involved in getting the ball to "Bloody Vladdy." It wasn't exactly a screamer of a shot, but it was hit with the kind of confidence no Liverpool fan had seen from Smicer in his six seasons at Liverpool. Now, with his contract at an end, and in what was guaranteed to be his last game in our shirt, this . . . this shot. Low, powerful, and skidding for the corner. His fellow Czech international, Milan Baros, obscured Dida for just a second, but that goal was all Vlad. I've never seen him smile before, let alone smile like that. It was a genuinely sweet moment, full of pathos, sadness, and unadulterated joy. For Vladimir Smicer and for all us Pool fans. "Thank you, Vladdy," we all said, from Istanbul to Prague, from the Bosphorus to the Danube. It was so saccharine I could almost swear I heard Vanessa Williams in the background crooning, "You've gone and saved the best for last." "Bloody Vladdy" certainly played his part in saving Liverpool. For an instant there he was no longer hapless Smicer, who's driven us to distraction with the promise of his talent for six years, but an invigorated blend of Jimmy Case and Dalglish. Sometimes Europe doesn't have to be in your genes, just in your history. Sometimes, as in Liverpool's case, they're the same thing. 2–3.

Minute Sixty. Through the center, this time. A gilt-edged pass from Baros that sets Gerrard free in the Milan 6-yard box and the trailing, aging-before-our-very-eyes Brazilian, the thirty-six-year-old Cafu, brings the Scouser Skipper down. Penalty. Now it's really time to get down on your knees and pray. We don't have a reliable penalty taker. This season Stevie's missed some big ones, and the one guy who relishes these, Djibril Cissé, is still on the bench. Up steps one of my favorite players: Xabi Alonso, the best passer of the ball I have ever seen. Dida looks taller and bigger than normal now, and the knot in the pit of my stomach tightens. With good reason. Xabi goes to Dida's right, and the Milan keeper gets a hand to it. A panic so momentary and excruciating it's like your closest friend just died. But no, Alonso's quickest to the rebound, and left-footed he slams the ball so hard into the roof of the net that the nylon on the underside bulges unnaturally. This game better not go to penalties. Who'd take 'em for us?

Six minutes: 3–3.

Looking bedraggled and shell-shocked after the game, Ancelotti phrased that championship-turning spell as a short period of temporary (Milan) insanity: "We had six minutes of madness in which we threw away the position we had reached until then. . . . The match was well contested and it's inexplicable because the team played well for all 120 minutes."[1] Ancelotti's not wrong about much except that those "six minutes," I believe, constitute the brilliance of a miracle on the Bosphorus. "Sei minuti di follia" is precisely what Ancelotti said. Folly, divine grace, and magic, he might have added.

Du the Dudek: Part 1

By the end of the regulation ninety minutes, Liverpool's a knackered team. Benítez shifts Stevie G. from his attacking position just behind Baros (and then Cissé, who replaced him) to wide on the right side of the midfield, with Hamann and Alonso holding in the center of the park. It's now the Skipper's job to protect his Scouser mate Carra. Out on the right flank Gerrard's all heart and intelligence, putting in one brave tackle after the next, keeping Milan at bay. Hyypia's been immense at the heart of the defense this evening, shades of the articulate 1984 captain Alan Hansen, all neat passing and sure interceptions, but Carra's feeling the pain. A groin injury had him down briefly, and he's up now, but it's obvious that he's running on empty.

On the other side Traore, much to his own surprise as well as mine, cleared the ball off the line to prevent Milan going ahead late in regulation.

The final thirty minutes, two halves of fifteen, is largely uneventful until the 118th minute. Again the cross comes from Traore's flank, and with even the "Finnish Giraffe" tiring, it lands perfectly for the Ukrainian superstar, Andriy Shevchenko, the man dubbed the "White Ronaldo" (after the white Brazilian goal-scoring maestro). He rises way above Hyypia and heads it powerfully, high toward Dudek's right. It seems certain to go in. Dudek to the rescue as up goes "Our Big Pole." Jerzy, who struggled and fumbled his way through the second half, much as he did the first, gets a glove to it. A good save. But the ball falls perfectly for Shevchenko's feet, and surely he can't miss it this time. The Ukrainian hits it low, and it looks destined to go about a meter inside the right upright. God, no. We can't lose like this. That would be so cruel, so goddamn painful. Somehow Dudek gets in the way of it rather than actually to it, gets his body in between the ball and his goal. It ricochets out, I don't remember where. It all happened so fast, and I've haven't breathed in what feels like minutes. It's less a save than a reflex, a moment of divine intervention. The TV replays show the Dudek save again and it's even more unbelievable. Maybe we do have more than one Pole in our goal; maybe this is John Paul II's last act, his message from the Great Beyond to Milan—and the rest of the footballing universe—that he is indeed a Liverpool fan and that tonight, in Istanbul, no one's going to cross him. Maybe that's what old goalkeepers who become Pope do: they look after their own from up on high. Maybe that's why he won't allow anyone, not even the "White Ronaldo," to score late against his countryman. It's more than a plausible theory—it's God's own truth, because anyone who's seen Dudek drop routine crosses and fluff back passes that my seven-year-old nephew (a Liverpool fan, Lord bless him) handles with aplomb would not believe that our Jerzy (alone, anyway) made that save. Let me rephrase: made those *saves*. Liverpool is, it can now be definitively stated, God's team. The evidence is in Jerzy Dudek's "saves." "Il Papa," as the Italians call him, gave Jerzy more than a hand or two.

Du the Dudek: Part II

Penalties. Milan goes first.

Suddenly, without any warning, in an inexplicable instant, Jerzy Dudek of Poland reappears as Bruce Grobbelaar, wildly maniacal Liverpool goalkeeper of the 1984 European championship team. A crazy showman, Grobbelaar was a veteran of the Rhodesian war against the liberation fighters led by Robert Mugabe and Joshua Nkomo. He was completely without fear, and any good sense, I often thought. But, my political misgivings apart (this guy fought for Ian Smith's UDI Rhodesia, for Christ's sake), I had a soft spot for "Grobs," as we'd taken to calling him in my apartheid neck of the African woods. In the 1984 penalty shoot-out against Italian side Roma, Grobbelaar had bent and wiggled his knees—in a playful but stunningly effective way—to psych out the opposing penalty takers. It worked to perfection as Grobbelaar's saves paved the way for Liverpool left back Alan Kennedy, a man who couldn't make a practice ground penalty, to put one surely into the Roma net for our last triumph in 1984.

It was already after midnight in Istanbul, and pathological fans like me (who know all the Liverpool minutiae) knew that it was now May 26 and officially Vladdy's thirty-second birthday. The lad from Decin was having himself a party, wasn't he? The delirious Liverpool fans, who'd somehow managed to snare as many as 40,000 of the 70,000 seats in the Ataturk Stadium, and the dumbstruck Milanese supporters (what must they have been thinking? "Why did we act so out of character? Forty-five minutes of defense and we'd be happily on our way home now") watched in fevered anticipation. But not one among them, and none watching from afar, were prepared for the rebirth of the tame, soft-spoken Dudek as the war-disturbed vet Grobbelaar. There, however, he was doing . . .

Dudek was shaking his knees, moving his hands, bopping his head. Good God, he was "du-ing the Dudek," as the dance became known. For Liverpool fans it instantly became the dance of life, the dance of joy, the dance of "Polish possession." And it worked. Up stepped yet another Brazilian, Serginho, to take the first Milan penalty, and the Dudek dance immediately worked its magic. The ball went high, wide, and so far right it eventually landed in the lap of Milan's bombastic owner, the Italian prime minister Silvio Berlusconi. (Not quite, but why not take a cheap football shot at the reprehensible Berlusconi?) In his turn, Didi calmly slotted the ball past Dida. All poise, our Didi. Andrea Pirlo was next to succumb to Dudek's dance moves. This time he saved going to his right. Cissé put Liverpool ahead 2–0. Jon Dahl Tomasson, a failure in the English Premier League, managed to evade Dudek. The Milan goal seemed to rub off badly on Risse, who had his penalty saved by Dida. Kaká did better than his countryman and equaled the score.

All the pressure was on the birthday boy, but you wouldn't have known it from the way he rattled the ball firmly past Dida. For the second time in about an hour he'd given us a glimpse of his potential. We won't exactly miss you, Vladdy, but you sure as hell gave us a rousing send-off and yourself a birthday present—or a birthday period—to remember.

3–2. Milan could not afford to miss, otherwise—who'd have believed this at halftime?—otherwise it was over. Score or the Champions League trophy was going home to where it rightly belonged: Anfield Road. Liverpool could still win with a conversion on the final kick, but it was the kind of night, or early morning, where you knew that wouldn't be the correct ending. That kind of ending wasn't in John Paul II and Jerzy's script. Determined to end this all with a dramatic flourish, the gods—of the Greek, not the goalkeeping, variety—pitted against each other two very recent adversaries who were already famous for their battles.

Dudek against Shevchenko, again. Mano a mano, these two veterans from the old Soviet bloc, going at it. Redemption of a sort, for both men. Shevchenko for the misses, and Dudek for a career whose last three seasons were strewn with embarrassing errors.

When the moment arrived it wasn't exactly anticlimactic, but it was a weak shot. Shevchenko, perhaps unnerved by his earlier misses, placed the ball and looked slightly bereft of confidence. A little like Traore. He tried the straight route, down the center of the goal, and with Dudek's body splayed like a newly gutted fish, the penalty kick looked like it had a chance. But with his right arm almost touching the ground, stretched toward his right corner, and his left leg aimed skyward, Dudek got all of his left hand to the ball. Gerrard, Risse, Alonso, García, and, yes, Smicer, came screaming toward the jubilant Dudek.

He'd done the Dudek; he'd out-"grobbed" Bruce.

At that moment, John Paul II rested. Officially and happily. His work on earth was done. Rest peacefully, Il Papa.

Shevchenko, to his credit, was gracious in defeat. He said something about "destiny." Nice lad, the Ukrainian.

Jerzy's on his own now, and it is doubtful he'll be keeping goal again for Liverpool with any regularity. Even before the final it was rumored that the Spaniard Pepe Reina was being signed to replace him. And he did. Reina's in goal these days, looking slightly crazy himself. There was also talk of Jerzy heading back to Feyenoord in the Netherlands, from whom we'd gotten him. All good and well, but if God works through his messengers, then Jerzy's got a place booked in the after(-Liverpool-)life. In any case, Dudek's at least worthy, if only for two minutes plus the penalties, of his Champions League medal. Traore, Kewell, Baros, and even Cissé (a man who rivals his fellow forward Baros for all the wrong reasons: they're both immensely quick, devoid of close control, and so selfish with the ball as to make the ball-hog Maradona look like a "pass first" player) should never show theirs in public.

In defeat, Ancelotti became Italian again: ungracious, excuse-ridden, and, most characteristically, defensive. He sounded so familiar there was good reason to mistake him for Mourinho. The hollowness of Ancelotti's rationalization, which contrasted so sharply with Shevchenko's restrained dignity, could not conceal a more resonant silence. You could hear it the second Dudek had saved that final Milan penalty. The ugly noises from London and Manchester had died to a resigned whisper. Even the pretenders know when to be quiet. Liverpool's triumph in Istanbul was a clear case of football eugenics. The Scousers had once again shown themselves to be superior. You can't argue against better (European) genes; you can fight it, but you assuredly can't beat it. Faith and hard scientific evidence, an unbeatable combination.

With John Paul II's de facto passing, Liverpool fans have good reason to be concerned. Who will protect their goal now? Who will produce, impromptu and completely unexpectedly, new demonic dances? — demonic for the Milan players, anyway. On the other hand, maybe there's not a lot to worry about. Joseph Ratzinger, the Pole's German successor (Pope Benedict XVI), is not known to be a football man. And, if he were, one couldn't imagine him being anything other than a Bayern fan — Bayern's a well-organized team, mechanistic, disciplined, almost authoritarian. Or maybe an AC Milan fan. They'd make an appropriate couple, Silvio and the cardinal who was known as "God's Rottweiler" for his doctrinaire interpretation and application of Scripture, the cardinal who gutted the radical possibilities of Vatican II. The only contact sport Ratzinger's ever played has been confined to the Church. He played, with a little too much relish, the theological "heavy," the exegetical fundamentalist, to John Paul II's populist.

God, I have it on good authority, is not kindly disposed to Rottweilers, not even his own. Besides, God knows how lucky He is to be a Liverpool fan, and if Benedict XVI has any smarts, he'll request an audience with his countryman, Herr Hamann. Look how well that tactic worked for a rank amateur Polish goalkeeper. It made him famous on Merseyside, and meeting with Didi could do wonders for a Holy Father who, quite frankly, has a few too many PR problems. That whole Nazi Youth episode, just for starters. Lord knows what stories about him could start circulating in the pubs around Anfield. So the "Rottweiler" had better be aware that God knows holiness, that He recognizes the sacred, and that He, more than anyone, comprehends the unbeatable power of red. After all, John Paul II took a long time to ascend because he had to orchestrate another Resurrection, this one worthy of Football Scripture. In any case, He doesn't want to walk alone. It is to the benefit of God's footballing acumen that he will now have John Paul II to advise him on the intricacies of Rafa's tactics, the sublimity of Xabi's passing, the value that is everywhere in Didi's graft, the loyalty that shines through Carra, and the utter joy of watching Stevie command Liverpool. Now He will never have to walk alone or struggle to find his way to Anfield. Welcome to the club, You, the Biggest of Big Guys. You, after all, know only slightly less about true faith than us Liverpool fans.

The "lesson" of Istanbul is that Red Believers are rewarded for their capacity to endure pain with their own maniacal brand of pleasure. In the annals of Liverpool Football Club's history, the Ataturk Olympic Stadium will occupy a hallowed place. Istanbul will be known, for me and countless others like me — Scousers, long-distance Scousers, wanna-be Scousers, Liverpool fans the world over — as the place where we fully experienced the pleasure of pleasure. It was a circuitous journey, from History through Pain to Pleasure. Istanbul: the place of the pleasure of pleasure after a long dalliance with pain.

Notes

This essay is dedicated to Ross Dawson, Roger Webster, and Glenda Norquay for making me feel at home in Liverpool and for their generosity during the time I spent at Liverpool's John Moores University.

1 "Ancelotti shattered after defeat," http://news.bbc.co.uk/sport2/hi/football/europe/4574893.stm (accessed May 26, 2005).

Jim Shepard

They Killed Our Grandfathers and Our Fathers
and Now the Sonsabitches Are Coming for Us

There are fans and then there are "*real* fans": the sort of people who are angry with their children for a week after play-off losses. The sort who, a year later, can still get melancholy, their faraway look in midconversation letting you know that they're back in the moment of that fumble, that strikeout, that missed free throw. There are plenty of reasons to be fans: sports are fun to watch and can be effortlessly and vicariously exhilarating. There are also plenty of reasons to be *real* fans, nearly all of those reasons being pitiable.

I have next to my desk a framed color photograph from an old issue of *Pro Football Weekly*. At the time the photograph was taken, *Pro Football Weekly* was not what one would call a high-quality magazine. None of its images were really suitable for framing. The photo in question is raggedly mounted and not the sort that would make the cover of *Sports Illustrated*. It shows Frank Pitts, Kansas City Chiefs wide receiver, and Paul Krause, Minnesota Vikings free safety, after a tackle. They're both on their rear ends, starting to get up. They're leaning into each other a little, for leverage. They look like two

The *South Atlantic Quarterly* 105:2, Spring 2006.
Copyright © 2006 by Duke University Press.

boys who aren't really friends left together in a sandbox. The image is from 1970. I'm writing this in 2005.

The photograph is as eloquent about me then as it is about me now. Consider: I framed it soon after I first saw it, to commemorate, apparently, one of the bitterest and most sorrowful moments of my life up to that point. And I still have it by my desk, thirty-five years later. Over the past thirty-five years, there have been—however rare, God knows—positive events, even *highlights*, in the Minnesota Vikings' history. Yet that's the image that I've framed. And that's the image to which, during my working day, my eyes always return.

On January 11, 1970, late in the first half of Super Bowl IV, the underdog Kansas City Chiefs, who'd been chipping away at my mental health for about an hour and a half with a steady stream of first downs culminating in field goals, finally broke the game open, as the commonplace goes, with a sucker play—a trap, designed to take advantage of the Vikings' growing desperation and defensive aggressiveness—springing old veteran Mike Garrett for a touchdown, and thereby escalating the score from a deeply worrisome 9–0 to an absolutely catastrophic 16–0. (The Vikings that year dominated, when they dominated, defensively; they featured a primitive, brutish offense poorly suited to stirring comebacks.)

The first half ended. The halftime show began. I left the television in a mental state that only Thomas Hardy or Malcolm Lowry could describe. I wandered the house. I was beside myself. I was thirteen years old.

I'd been following the Minnesota Vikings for a year. I'd watched them lose to the Baltimore Colts the year before, upset but only dimly aware of what I was letting myself in for for the next thirty-six years. The following season, leading up to the Super Bowl, had been a joyride: Crushing victories. Lopsided scores. Stirring playoff wins.

I'd had all sorts of uneasy premonitions before the game. All of them seemed confirmed during the player introductions by the visual shock of seeing the Vikings stream onto the field in their white away uniforms. Up until that point, because of the infrequency with which they were televised, I'd never seen them play in those road uniforms. Their home purple, that year for me the very visual *image* of their dominance, was gone.

The second half began. I could hear the announcers gearing up for the kickoff. Time was slipping away, and I was going to have to watch it do so. I had to *do* something. I threw myself down the stairs.

My father and brother left the game and rushed into the hallway to see what had happened. Such was the state of my commitment to the Minnesota Vikings that they didn't have to ask. My feet were in the air. My shoulder was on the bottom riser and my head was between it and the leg of a rolltop desk. I extricated myself and stood up with my knee bleeding, both elbows skinned and a disc-like pain in my back. Exasperated and frightened, my father after some ineffectual scolding followed me back to the television. He suggested turning it off. That idea didn't fly. While I sat there, dazed and arching my spine against the pain, the Vikings started running the ball with some success. They made a first down. They made a string of first downs. They marched the length of the field, for the first time, and scored. It was now 16–7.

There was, I now understood, a direct linkage: if I threw myself down the stairs, they would score.

I got up, playing with pain for the sake of the team, and left the room. My father and brother assumed that I was getting something from the kitchen, since there didn't seem particular cause to worry after a *Vikings* score. I threw myself down the stairs again.

This, as far as my family was concerned, was going too far. I was allowed back into the television room but prevented from returning to the stairs. My second tumble, meanwhile, had apparently had no effect on the Vikings' intensity. One of their cornerbacks pinched a nerve covering a simple out pattern, and the rest of the second half was like a slow-motion execution. The game ended with me lying on the floor in front of the television. The final score was 23–7, two numbers that still cause me pain when juxtaposed. Halfway through whatever program followed the postgame show, my father carried me up to my bedroom and put me to bed.

———

In the photograph the colors are dark. It's from late in the game. The gloom captures the mood that I remember viscerally, thirty-five years later, from a certain point in that greased slide of a loss. It was the late third quarter. The Vikings, who that year either won through a kind of fearsome intimidation of their opponents' traumatized offense or did not win at all, were confused and tentative. Their expressions were bewildered but game, the expressions of professionals who'd expected another outcome but saw where this was headed.

Paul Krause has that expression in the photograph. He's just tackled Pitts after yet another end-around had produced yet another demoralizing first down, and what's going on behind his eyes is a formulation that Sartre would have recognized: *Okay. So. That's the way it's going to be, then.*

He's carrying himself well in a difficult situation, in other words. The Vikings often did. I almost never did, watching them. But they certainly gave me enough chances to improve, in that regard. They lost one play-off game on Christmas Day. They lost another on a Hail Mary miracle pass on the game's final play. In the latter case, their quarterback's father, watching at home, had a heart attack and died. They played wonderful first halves and were annihilated in the second. They played miserable first halves and mounted heroic and insufficient comebacks. The one thing that's been consistent over the last thirty-five years is that their seasons have ended with a loss. They've put together great teams. They've lost countless play-off games, four NFC championship games, and four Super Bowls. They've been upset coming right out of the blocks; they've beaten great teams and then immediately lost to lesser ones. Over the last thirty-five years the Vikings have in fact been an encyclopedic workshop on losing—the cosmos taking me by the hand and murmuring, *Here are all the ways of doing it. And here are all the ways of getting through it*—and learning about losing, after all, is not a bad first step toward learning about loss. And as many before me have pointed out, loss is a seminar in which, sooner or later, we're all going to be enrolled.

―――――

That's the pious version. The high-minded one. But of course, the lunacy of being such a fan—one of those *real* fans—is not simply a matter of gaining instruction on the subjects of losing and dealing with losing. There's also something going on that's more dysfunctional and pitiable, however necessary. Being a rabid fan, as we're joltingly reminded whenever we catch a glimpse of those face-painted and bare-chested yahoos brawling in the bleachers, is not all about leading one's self toward maturity. Being miserable about the Vikings over the years was, of course, a way of not spending emotional time on—and maybe even coming to terms with—more serious issues. It was also a way, almost certainly, of focusing, or venting, more inchoate, and possibly dangerous if articulated, dissatisfactions. It was also, then, probably, a way of punishing myself, at least for the sins of omission outlined above. I was, after all, raised Catholic. Even the most rabid fan knows on some level that what he's doing is silly. And even the most self-conscious and rational fan knows that what he's doing, in a deeply pleasurable and shameful way, is mixing together, and keeping mixed, impulses toward maturity and impulses toward childishness. As well as impulses toward connection and impulses toward self-isolation and heartlessness.

It's not hard to figure out why the phenomenon of fandom is an important subject for study. It's a gigantically widespread and culturally endorsed form of behavior; and, as anyone who's been on the outside looking in—such as long-suffering spouses and relatives—can tell you, it's also bizarrely immune to anything like an emotional cost-benefit analysis. At the heart of the essential irrationality of being a rabid fan is the fact that while both the pain and the pleasure are intense, there's always more pain, and it's always more intense. I don't enjoy the pain; I never have; and yet I put myself through it. Which suggests that in some way I think I deserve it. Even at the top of the stairs that first Super Bowl Sunday, I knew that I was playing with pain for the sake of the team. I also knew, on some level, that the inverse was also true: that my family was playing with pain for the sake of me. My fanaticism hurt them and frightened them, and that gave me power. Was this only about *football*? they asked themselves. Given how he's behaving, how could it be only about *football*?

I'm not still thirteen years old, at least not in most ways, but I am, by profession, a fiction writer. I wander around in made-up worlds. I nose around trying to imagine and retrieve moments of pain and loss and revelation. That self-mortification is both high-minded and foolish. Right next to my desk, then, is a little touchstone of childhood agony—silly agony, but agony nonetheless—to give me, should I need it, that shove in the right direction.

Or at least in the direction my favorite team has always gone. I've often been asked: In the event of a Super Bowl win—a season that actually finished with a victory—would I feel a euphoria to match the devastation I feel after a loss? It's always seemed to me like a question that doesn't require an answer. As a Vikings fan, I'll probably never find out.

My loved ones have continued to consider my condition an affliction; they treat it like a drinking problem that recurs once a week for five months a year. They hold out the hope that I'll outgrow it—unlikely at this point—

or that perhaps the team will transform itself so dramatically—the Albuquerque Vikings?—that even I will register the arbitrariness of my loyalty, and drift away. But there are ominous signs to the contrary. Seven years ago, in 1998, the Vikings became an offensive juggernaut and went 15–1 over the course of the season, raising the hopes of even the most determinedly pessimistic of their fans. But if history teaches us anything, it's that one cannot be as creatively pessimistic as the situation warrants, when it comes to the Vikings. They were, it almost goes without saying, the first team to go 15–1 and *not* win the Super Bowl. Now, that seemed well within the bounds of normal negative-thinking to predict. Certainly I had been girding myself for something like that. But with the Vikings, there's always that breathtakingly unexpected and eerily sadistic twist. In the case of that year, to cite one example, their juggernaut season ended when their kicker, who had two weeks earlier become the first kicker *in NFL history* to go through the entire season—*an entire season*—without missing a field goal or extra point, missed a chip-shot field goal.

When my oldest son was seven, and he was asked what he wanted for Christmas, he led off his list with a request for a Vikings helmet. He got one, of course; a children's version. Every so often over the years I looked at it and thought, what could be a more diabolic product for children?

At such times I flashed on an anecdote related by the sportswriter Peter Gammons in his coverage of the 1986 World Series between the Boston Red Sox and the New York Mets. Gammons recounted watching the Red Sox' staggering collapse in Game Six with a group of lifelong fanatics, one of whom, streaming tears, cried out, "They killed our grandfathers and our fathers and now the sonsabitches are coming for us." Well, yes: for some of us, they are. But the news is even worse than that. We keep inviting them in.

Liz Moor

"The Buzz of Dressing":
Commodity Culture, Fraternity,
and Football Fandom

Personal histories of football fandom often provide conflicting accounts of the process of arriving at team affiliation, describing it variously as the most "natural" thing in the world, as a difficult and painful choice, and also as quite arbitrary. For the most part, however, the decision (and it is not always experienced as such) is located in, or in relation to ideas about, the home and family, and this connection with childhood seems to explain both its naturalness and its difficulty, as well as giving fandom its quality of passion and its enduring resonance. Those who do not consider themselves fans may also, however, have learned something about football in childhood, and this too may have a lasting impact. In my own case, football was rather conspicuous by its absence. Coming home from school, full of the classroom talk about Liverpool (it was the early 1980s), I would press my father on the question of his own team allegiance, and he would repeatedly deny any interest before finally shutting me up by telling me—with a knowing wink—that he preferred Everton. The local team, Portsmouth, never got a look-in, because during my childhood the club and its supporters were virtually synonymous,

The *South Atlantic Quarterly* 105:2, Spring 2006.

certainly in my family's eyes, with the 6.57 "hooligan" crew, who had strong affiliations with the National Front—an affiliation subsequently under-played by some Portsmouth fans, but clearly visible at the time in the com-bination of 6.57 and NF graffiti adorning the trains between Portsmouth and London.[1] I was often prohibited from, or at least cautioned against, going shopping in Portsmouth with friends if the team was playing at home, because fans would "greet" the day's rivals not only at the train station and outside of the ground but also in the city's main shopping district (the 6.57 crew itself often met outside one of the department stores). The nature of the threat posed by the 6.57 and the NF to a white female child was left rather vague, but in this particular variation on the theme of men going to foot-ball and women (not) going shopping, something was nonetheless learned about the lack of fit between Portsmouth Football Club and the form of femininity being cultivated in the family home.[2]

Given this history with Portsmouth, trying to approach the team again (which I have done, although from a distance) as an adult feels a lot like a return to childhood, and to a reevaluation of ways in which exclusion from some sites (imposed, in this case, not by the 6.57 but by my own parents) was linked to inclusion within others (middle-class "respectability," higher education). To put it another way, thinking about Portsmouth is a way of thinking about how the cultivation of middle-class femininity seemed to depend, at least in part, upon its separation from certain types of working-class masculinity, a separation that facilitated a beneficial class mobility at the expense of a fairly pronounced form of gender regulation. This, I think, explains some of the dismissiveness, bitterness, and even contempt that can be detected when women, particularly middle-class women, talk about foot-ball: This contempt contains an implicit recognition of some of the gender-specific exclusions involved in becoming "respectable." All of this contains, unsurprisingly, a good amount of denial too (mobility for some does, after all, depend on others being fixed in place), and the symbolic and material benefits of distance from traditionally working-class pursuits such as foot-ball tend to become obscured by a heightened sense of the "wounds" of femininity, but such a denial is itself facilitated, in the context of football, by the recognition that middle-class men historically have not been excluded to anything like the same extent. Although they may have been steered away from it, they could choose, if they wanted, to belong to the fraternity of foot-ball fans, without losing any of their class entitlement.

What one can make of these sporting connections in later life is hard to predict, and the question of what might be at stake for female fans in particular as they increasingly find themselves able to return to the game, albeit under quite complicated terms, is an interesting one. However, partly because my academic interests lie in the area of consumer culture, and partly because of this rather coincidental early link between shopping, football, and the 6.57 crew, what concerns me here is actually the relationship between football, gender, and a broader commodity culture. This is, I hope, not so willful as it might first appear.

Commenting on the capacity of commodity cultures to organize fantasy and fuse the "intimate ambitions" of a life narrative with its economic ones, Lauren Berlant questions the idea that metacultural forms such as nation or family have suffered a loss of significance in modern everyday life. She suggests instead that it is very often through commodities that such forms are negotiated and through which temporary solutions are found to the complexities they generate.[3] Whether we conceive of football as part of commodity culture—and it is increasingly so—or as part of the complex of nation that such a culture is used to confront, it is possible to argue that, in Britain at least, football too has the capacity to organize fantasy, and not only for those with a manifest passion for the sport but also for those who hover rather uncertainly around its margins and (perhaps especially) for those who profess outright antipathy. In the British context, and especially the English context, it may in fact be precisely because football has historically been so exclusionary, while insistently positioning itself as "the people's game," that it retains its capacity to overorganize various kinds of fantasies of inclusion and belonging. This may, of course, partly explain the motivations of those who now seek to reconnect with the game, having previously felt excluded from it, but Berlant's formulation also prompts us to consider how and why commodity culture might frame such a return. More recent claims to belonging sometimes choose to focus their efforts on the concrete and most easily accessible objects of football's commodity culture (e.g., club shirts and merchandise of various kinds, but also a "style" of dressing derived from football's not-so-distant past), and this fact forms part of the backdrop to the slightly more general argument that I want to make here, about the way that commodity culture itself comes, in the context of fandom, to mark relations of belonging and specify their limitations.

To explore this, however, I want to focus less on those who have historically been excluded from football fandom, and more on those who, for most of the sport's history, have sat (or stood) most comfortably within it. This is partly because these (predominantly male and almost exclusively white) fans still form the core of football's "active" support;[4] understanding their own relationship to commodity culture is therefore central to any analysis of the material culture of newer forms of fandom. At the same time, while in general terms a focus on "women and shopping" often risks naturalizing, rather than critically interrogating, that relationship, it presents very particular problems in the context of football, where discussions of football's commodification often operate as a coded way of commenting on the "problems" caused by the arrival of new (often female) fans.[5] By providing an account of the role played by commodity culture in connecting older (male) fans to each other during the 1980s, and by situating this in turn within an account of the fraternal nature of some fan groups, I hope to show how football's commodity culture is also part of its gender culture and marks a parallel relationship to *ur*-forms such as nation and family. While an exploration of such connections does have implications for the way that one might assess new forms of fandom—implications that I will try to draw out more explicitly toward the end of the essay—my main interest here is simply to outline a way of understanding the significance of material culture to earlier, but persistent, configurations of fandom against which newer fans must, in any case, define themselves.

First, though, it is worth perhaps making a few comments on the broader debates about football's commodification, and the relation of these arguments to the one made here. Debates about commodification focus, variously, on the shift to all-seater stadiums and the consequent rise in ticket prices and decline in terrace culture; the advent of satellite and pay-per-view television coverage and its relation to both the accessibility of football and its cultures of fandom; the increasing involvement in football of corporations, stock markets, and other business institutions and the effects of this shift, particularly in terms of fans' ability to either own shares in their own club or, more broadly, to exercise an influence over its future direction; the new volumes of capital provided by sports equipment manufacturers and other corporate sponsors, and the various attempts to harness, for commercial ends, fans' affective connections with teams; and, finally, an interest in the growing popularity or "fashionability" of the game, and a set of related questions about how far this is either cause or consequence of a more general trajectory of commodification.

In this essay I address the latter question, for it is here that a potential material cultural analysis of fan cultures might be located. There are relatively few works that addresses such matters explicitly, however, and in those works there is a tendency to see fandom's material culture as essentially a fairly recent feature of football support (the greater prevalence of branded commodities for fans to buy) and, more problematically, as something that characterizes newer supporters more than older ones.[6] Thus in an article by Richard Giulianotti, explicit connections are made between the (recent) "hypercommodification" of sport and the emergence of modes of spectatorship characterized by a "detached" and "consumer-oriented" demeanor. Of particular relevance to the argument I want to make here, this account reads the ownership and display of signs, logos, and things — a broader material culture of fandom, one might say — as evidence of the (negative) impact of shifts in the economic structure of the game upon its fan cultures, at the same time that it also comes to mark a particular, compromised, position in relation to established hierarchies of belonging. He notes, for example, that where the "classic supporter" has "a relationship with the club that resembles those with close family and friends," the newer "cool consumer" spectator (or "flâneur")

> belongs only to a virtual community of strollers who window-shop around clubs. In the most extreme manifestation, national allegiances may also be exchanged on the grounds of competitive successes or mediated identification with superstar celebrities. The adornment of a team's attire is in tune with a couture aesthetic, drawn to the signifier (the shirt color, the shirt design, its crest, even its sponsor logo) rather than what is signified conceptually (the specific, grounded identity of the club or the nation). The flâneur thereby avoids any personal consumption by the appended signs but instead consumes these signifiers in a disposable and cliché-like fashion, as if adopting a temporary tattoo.[7]

Leaving aside, for the moment, the questions of why some newer fans may prefer a more "virtual" relationship to football, why they might switch national allegiances, and who decides, ultimately, what is to be "signified conceptually" by particular club insignia, such an argument tends to replicate a rather romantic, and distinctly middle-class, opposition between the "authentic" and the commercial, while remaining largely indifferent to the question of what motivates certain forms of consumption practice within specific contexts. What I want to suggest, by contrast, is that consumption practices of various kinds have in fact been central to the composition and maintenance of earlier fan cultures, and that reading such practices forms an interesting adjunct to more sociological accounts of the game and its followers. Indeed, I want to suggest that if we consider consumption practices relevant only to the extent that they provide evidence of commodification within the game itself, we will miss something about the way that commodity culture has also been used as part of earlier, and more exclusionary, forms of fandom.[8]

What I am arguing, then, is that a concern among fans with consumption and aesthetics predates the structural changes in the game that occurred from the early 1990s onward and that it is therefore a mistake to see the former as merely a consequence of the latter. Moreover, if we shift from seeing the commodity culture of football only in terms of branded team goods (shirts, scarves, etc.), and focus instead on a broader set of ways in which commodities are used by fans for the purposes of adornment, it becomes clear that it is not so much the economic structures within the game that impact upon fans' behavior, but rather a broader set of social relations—instantiated both inside and outside of the game—that impact upon fans' economic activity. That these broader social relations have, in the context of football, been expressed primarily in terms of inter- or intraclass rivalry between mostly white men (the "fraternity" of football support) is, as I have already indicated, of relevance for an assessment of new cultures of fandom, but my point here, following Berlant, is that the commodity culture through which such relations are partially expressed is not separate from the apparently "traditional" forms of support based on nationality, locality, and family, but part of the way in which these are organized.

Signs of Inclusion and Belonging

I want to turn, then, to a consideration of some of the ways in which a concern with consumption, signification, adornment, and aesthetics has been evident in pre-1990 forms of football fandom. Clothes and adornment have figured in football fan cultures in a range of ways since the 1940s and 1950s, and it is relevant to my argument here that football-related fashion rivalries have such a long history,[9] but I want to focus here on the "Casual" style, which began in the late 1970s and still continues today but was especially prevalent in the 1980s.[10] This strand of football fandom, characterized in part by a preference for a specific set of designer labels and brand names (which were often interwoven with a discreet display of team affiliation through club merchandise such as scarves and lapel pins), is interesting because it predates by almost ten years the shifts that are widely held responsible for a more "consumerist" ethos among fans, yet it also provides a line of continuity to the present day, in which a similar range of brands have become central to the definition of so-called Chav culture, a resonance whose meaning will be discussed below. Although its emergence is contemporaneous with Thatcherism, and with an economic logic that laid the foundations for later structural changes in the game, the uses to which designer dressing was put by these fans suggests that the adornment of the self with brands and logos—team-based or otherwise—is not only an outcome of this more entrenched form of free-market capitalism but may also be a way of negotiating the particular configurations of masculinity that such a form of capitalism simultaneously presupposes and unsettles.

One of the informants in Paulo Hewitt and Mark Baxter's account of the relationship between football and fashion is a Cardiff supporter (and member of the "Soul Crew" of fans) called Matthew. For him, "dressing" in the 1980s was central to football fandom. Indeed, the "buzz of dressing was as good as the buzz of a football riot."[11] This pleasure has many sources. Perhaps unsurprisingly, one is linked to class: "I was attempting to shed the quintessentially British disease of deference by showing the snooty-nosed middle classes I could look smart" (195). There is a long history of using consumption as a salve for the wounds of class inequality, and although political citizenship has historically been built upon a standard of white, male embodiment, it is in fact the capacity to suppress the body, to conceal its tracks and traces, that is the real sign of power.[12] Those with white, male bodies have something of a head start in this game of public self-abstraction, but the marks of class—insofar as they take the form of various kinds of bodily disposition and adornment—tend to linger and to make the working-class body a target of conceit and stigma.[13] For this reason, practices of bodily adornment have been important sites for manipulating the way that one's body becomes visible to others and for challenging the implicit hierarchies of taste and status that reserve certain kinds of adornment for the most privileged. In this regard the particular value of publicly recognized logos and brand names may be that they tend to elicit public recognition, while also connecting their bearers to wider communities of consumers and to the capitalist public sphere itself. Thus, as Gary Armstrong notes, the clothing and fashion formats of Casual style were brand names with explicit connections to various middle- and upper-class arenas such as tennis (Tacchini, Ellesse), golf (Pringle, Slazenger), skiing (Berghaus), and country sports (Burberry, Aquascutum).[14] The adornment process seems to promise that certain signs may convert an alienable form of property into an inalienable one (a sense of self, or "self-worth") and that the objective possession of adornment may be made into a subjective sense of self-possession, a strategy that may be particularly appealing given how far the status of full personhood has historically depended on the capacity to both own property and stand in a relationship of possession to one's own body.[15] However, this adoption of the logos of middle-class leisure registers impulses that are quite complex, and sometimes contradictory. While for many fans in the 1980s (but specifically for those associated with "hooligan" activity) "passing" as middle class had a strategic value in avoiding the attentions of the police, the fact that such adornment was not usually accompanied by "middle-class college-boy looks,"[16] and indeed was often folded into a self-consciously working-class form of male embodiment, suggests an attempt to lay claim to particular (proprietary) forms of middle-class entitlement while retaining some of the advantages of the forms of power associated with the male working-class body. At the same time, as a "deep surface" that mediates between inner and outer reality, clothing also lends itself to a more complex set of identifications and disidentifications. Thus while at some points the adoption of "middle-class" logos by (largely but by no means exclusively) working-class men involves a deliberate staging of the disjunction between depth and surface, it can also register a desire to belong to a more inclusive group, or for class differences to be either obscured or eradicated.[17]

Some of these complexities can be traced in the practices described by Matthew, above, who goes on to say that another part of the "buzz" of dressing derived from the fact that "it seemed like you were trying to infiltrate an exclusive and elite bunch *within, yet beyond*, your own working-class tribe,"[18] betraying an uncertainty about whether one's dressing is motivated by a relationship, or imaginary relationship, with a group or class distinct from one's own, or with those one imagines to be similar to oneself. What stands out in many of Hewitt and Baxter's interviews is the sense of how far dressing was linked to forms of bodily competition within and between groups that would be identified as relatively similar. Thus Matthew notes that since "all rival hooligans will check your coat and your shoe leather . . . looking the part was a chance to have one over on them" (195). Equally, clothes and dressing become central to the establishment and maintenance of hierarchies *within* a group: "All the top boys had the best stuff and that's what we aspired to be—top boy. . . . All the talk was about what you had on. Where did you get it? Who made it? How much was it?" (198). That this competition may also reflect inequalities between men, and specifically between men of ostensibly the same class background, is hinted at in the way that Matthew finds himself in a form of competition with his brother over clothes and their acquisition; he says, "My brother and a select few had good jobs and could afford to indulge in very expensive clothing. . . . But for the majority, we had to scrimp and save, and to a few it was a case of smash and grab. . . . I would budget and then choose more carefully, the irony being I would find myself looking as smart or even smarter than my brother on occasion" (196). In fact, as I want to suggest below, the link between "national manhood" and capitalist citizenship is such that there is actually very little irony in men "finding themselves" in competition either with actual kin or with other men with whom they associate in fraternal networks such as those provided by the more exclusionary "crews" of fans.

Capitalist Citizenship, Fraternity, and Hierarchy

To understand the significance of this competition between men, its relationship to forms of consumption, and its implications for broader relationships of inclusion and exclusion, it is useful to take a detour via Dana Nelson's work on "national manhood."[19] Although this work emerges out of a different geographical and historical context from the one considered here, its value for my own purposes is that it highlights the ways in which forms of male rivalry such as those outlined above have historically been central to the consolidation of various kinds of fraternity. This is useful in the context of football because it allows the local or "tribal" aspects of team or crew rivalry to be understood in relation to broader national and gender-based forms of belonging.[20] Nelson argues that various types of fraternal association have historically provided men with an escape from the "agon of competition" that has been a feature of the capitalist public sphere since its inception. She suggests that where early practices of manhood located men in a thick network of obligation and duty based on family and community, the forms of "national manhood" tied to capitalism left men affectively and ideologically isolated within a structure of individual competition. While the "experientially anxious," and potentially vicious, material outcomes of capitalist citizenship contrast starkly with its ideology of "peaceful competitiveness," the dissent and conflict that these new forms of competitiveness threaten to inspire also provide a powerful incentive to cultivate and consolidate a form of "sameness" compelling enough "to take operative priority over differences that threatened the construction of national unity, without jeopardizing the economic system it prioritized" (7). While such a move is, in Nelson's account, also largely motivated by an increasing social and economic mobility on the part of (white) women, who were "testing new theories of public action, voice, and power," its consolidation into various kinds of fraternity also entailed the exercise of power over and against "an ever-expanding arena of Otherness" (15). Hence the greater significance of the category of *white* manhood, which "worked symbolically and legally to bring men together in an abstract but increasingly functional community that diverted their attention from differences between them" (6). During the period studied by Nelson, as, I think, in the period discussed here, internal differences that threaten to tear men from each other, or to find expression in political dissent, may be rerouted toward market competition and racially exclusive forms of fraternity. These in turn can be made to work corporately on behalf of the nation, but they also provide men with a comforting sense of sameness and solidarity. However, to the extent that the project of creating a unified "national manhood" is one that is fraught with problems (for it always threatens to unravel), it derives some stability from two further strategies. The first is what Nelson calls "altero-referentiality," in which a combination of "gazing at otherness and thinking about fraternity" provides men with a way to, in effect, deny their own internal differences by focusing on the alleged absolute difference of another. This altero-referentiality may take a range of forms, and the severity of its effects on others may vary,[21] but insofar as it is in essence an attempt to recapture a lost feeling of connectedness through a strategy of exclusion, it is likely to remain in thrall to those it must exclude. As Nelson puts it, "Their attempt to satisfy their own desire for human connectedness is haunted by the very human, affective foreclosures that structure their privileged spot" (18).

The second strategy, related to the first, is one in which the desire for human connectedness itself becomes rerouted via what Nelson describes as a process of "structural Oedipalization." Where civic identification with the capitalist nation requires men to "master" themselves, identification with others (with other men) must be directed not equilaterally but vertically, "toward the more powerful 'interest' that overruled 'individual' desire— nationally toward . . . idealized founding fathers, economically toward commanding men" (22). Thus although national manhood promises its (white, male) citizens the right to stand for the authority of the Father, their experience of that relationship is "not from the vantage of the father but of the son . . . vulnerable and anxious" (22). What is put in place here is a pattern of emotional anxiety in which the desire for human connectedness, and for forms of civic fraternity and equality, is in constant tension with the desire to gain exclusive recognition from the father and to seek out experiences of "loving subordination" (97). Hence, as Nelson shows in her account of John Neal's *Logan*, national manhood as an identity is "aggressively homosocial, disciplinarily heterosexual, and structurally . . . homophobic" (97) — not least because homosexuality has historically been constructed as radical equality, "a mob equivalent, a de-individualizing sameness, a dangerous construction of democracy that threatened to emerge from the ranks of citizens" (187). What homosociality provides, by contrast, is hierarchized fraternity, or "intimate inequality" (186). In various fraternal structures men are reminded to identify with male power, but the specific appeal of this power is its hierarchical ordering. Such hierarchies uphold a version of upward mobility but also provide an emotionally intense, affectively gratifying subordination to group leadership that allows the fraternal order to function in ways that satisfy the needs instilled by both national and capitalist imperatives.

This account provides a useful framework for understanding the ways in which status competition within and between "crews" of fans in the 1980s could in fact function to *contain* anxieties about differences among apparently similar men (such as those between Matthew and his brother, described above) at the same time that it provided a form of defense against real or imaginary pressures from outside.[22] In Rob Silvester's account of the 6.57 crew, for example, the rivalry and competition between Portsmouth fans and other "firms" is central to the narrative and illustrates very well the tension between a desire for fraternal equality and a deeply ingrained sense of hierarchy. This is especially evident in the relationship between Portsmouth and Millwall; describing a particularly brutal encounter between the two sets of fans in 1993, Silvester adopts a tone of loving awe: "They pursued us with such vigour, it was a compliment to us all that south London's finest would want it so badly. We are, after all, only a small city in Hampshire. Everything from pool balls to sledgehammers, scaffold poles and concrete slabs have been used when it's gone off between us. . . . they are without doubt a top mob and everyone around the country knows it. We like to think they feel the same way about us too."[23] The Portsmouth fans hope for some fraternal reciprocity or recognition from Millwall but also appear flattered that Millwall want to fight them at all; Silvester goes on to acknowledge rather ruefully that West Ham are Millwall's true "brothers" and that ultimately Portsmouth fans must settle for a position in Millwall's affections that is rather more like that of a son ("we are, after all, only a small city in Hampshire").

As I have noted above, dressing and designer labels play a significant role in marking and mediating these relationships, and they are also—in the context of these "hooligan" stories—part of how such rivalrous encounters are narrativized and remembered. To put it another way, clothes are not only used as markers of distinction within the group and as a way of challenging the "snooty-nosed middle classes"; they are also one of the most intimate ways in which symbolic hierarchies within and between groups of fans are experienced and made memorable. At another point Silvester describes the various "scuffles" that took place during a home game against Millwall in 1981, but he concludes by noting that "the thing that sticks in the mind is the change of fashion the Millwall boys showed us that day": "Walking up towards the ground alongside the escort, loads of them had walking sticks. I remember them taking the piss out of our clothes. They had sort of slouchy jumpers and Kicker boots, leather jackets with all the pockets, like hunting safari jackets. . . . We were still in flight jackets and 501s and that. I remember they went 'You scruffy cunts. Spend some money on clothes.'" While the sense of humiliation, and of the need (or desire) to be "shown" what to do, evokes some of the Oedipal quality of these relationships, elsewhere it is the complementary project of altero-referentiality that comes to the fore; thus, in another fan's account of fashion choices from the same time period: "New Balance were much fancied by a few of my mates who could dress a little and fight a little too. Nike were shite as far as I was concerned—too American, hence too commercial. Pumas were the business, as were Reebok with that British flag that reminded you that you were part of a scene that was a white working-class British phenomenon and there's fuck all wrong with that."[24] Objects, then, come to encode and fix identifications (in this case, highly defensive and exclusionary ones), while also "domesticating" experiences and encounters and facilitating their entry into personal narrative.

There are, as I have already indicated, interesting resonances between the structure outlined by Nelson and the time period considered here, in which the intensification of market-driven forms of competition under Thatcher (and the fracturing of class-based solidarity or certainty that this entailed) coincided with a greater threat to the established privileges of white British masculinity from various feminist, antiracist, and lesbian and gay political groups. In this respect Nelson's analysis is also useful in drawing our attention to the ways in which the exigencies of capitalist citizenship direct men toward forms of association that replicate power imbalances both inside and outside of that structure while naturalizing their causes and effects. This has the further advantage of showing how the fraternal structures that provide an escape from capitalist competition in fact replicate its logic of hierarchy, competition, upward mobility, and, above all, exclusion. At the same time, by drawing attention to the "affective foreclosures" that underpin such fraternity, and in particular the anxiety and ambivalence to which these give rise, Nelson's account allows us to see how such formations are always likely to hover between a compulsion to repeat themselves and a desire to change. That these fraternal structures may, from the start, be bound up with commodity culture as one of the key ways (other than fighting and team support itself) through which *both* conflict *and* connectedness can be expressed, and through which both identification and disidentification with particular class formations can be enacted, does, as I will suggest below, have implications for the extent to which such a desire to change—to be more "inclusive"— can actually be realized, and it is to the allegedly more "inclusive" context of contemporary British football fandom that I now want to turn.

Commodity Kinship

In 2003, with Portsmouth's promotion to the Premiership, Ed Vulliamy and Brian Oliver interviewed Silvester and found him pessimistic about the 6.57's prospects for causing trouble in the future (by this time he had renounced his National Front affiliations). They were, in any case, fast being replaced by their teenage sons, who organized themselves under the name "House of Burberry," chosen, apparently, "as a satire on the current fashion among young hooligans for the usually preppy checked design."[25] Regardless of whether or not it is actually satire that is intended here, this partial replacement of fathers by sons under the name of a piece of private property provides an interesting opportunity to reconsider the relationship between the forms of kinship facilitated by fraternal groups, and the commodity culture from which they have drawn symbolic and material support.

The teenage Portsmouth fans' appropriation of Burberry as the name of their "crew" is interesting, I think, for a number of reasons. Part of its appeal is no doubt, as Vulliamy and Oliver suggest, its fashionability, but this itself is linked to the fact that Burberry has, in recent years, been wrested away from its long-standing association with upper- and upper-middle-class Britishness and made into the property of a more upwardly mobile and arriviste set of celebrities drawn from the lower middle and working classes who "made it" via some of the most despised routes to material success, such as television, modeling, and football. This appropriation is not, however, entirely new, since an earlier generation of fans (including, perhaps, these boys' fathers) had also found themselves attracted to Burberry; in this sense, the adoption of the brand marks a line of connection between father and son, in which the reproduction of masculinity is coded via the trademark. Something else is going on here, though, which has to do with the fact that since the time of its initial "rewriting" by Casuals, the Burberry brand has also undergone some further interesting reinflection via its adoption by a largely metropolitan and multicultural garage music scene. It is worth considering the possibilities that this too may be part of its appeal and that what is being incorporated here is a connection not only to fathers but also to people and places that extend well beyond the realm of family or locality. Although the denigration of so-called Chav culture in the British press—a culture characterized, in part, by its consumption of brands like Burberry—tends to see its object as an exclusively white working-class phenomenon, what goes unspoken is the fact that, insofar as this group exists as a distinct entity at all, it is one that is increasingly influenced by contact with a more metropolitan, and indeed transnational, black popular culture. Although it is no doubt right to see the denigration of Chavs as the latest way for the British middle classes to deride their "inferiors" (and, in particular, those who express a desire for social mobility without acknowledging the proper middle-class ways of going about it), Chav cultural tastes in music, fashion, and especially brands reflect contact as much as separateness, and thus rather than seeing the denigration of Chavs, as some commentators have done, as the perpetration against the white working class of forms of symbolic violence that would be considered unacceptable when directed at black people (a highly conservative and disingenuous argument),[26] it may be more appropriate to see middle-class disdain for Chavs not simply as a form of class hatred but more specifically as a hatred given extra force by the fact that it undermines the middle-class capacity to accrue cultural capital through an appreciation of absolute and clearly identifiable "cultural difference."[27]

At the same time, while there is much of interest here in terms of the way that various forms of adornment (whether brands like Burberry or football shirts emblazoned with the names of an increasingly international squad) may, under specific circumstances, be read as an avowal, rather than disavowal, of forms of connectedness that exceed those permitted by normative discourses of nation and kinship (where "cultures" must be kept separate and distinct), and while such stylistic borrowings may also, perhaps, be read as signs of a more "convivial culture,"[28] it is also appropriate at this point to consider some of the factors working against such new forms of connectedness and to query the role of commodities in mediating these desires.

In Berlant's account of the relationship between commodity culture and fantasy (or "intimate ambition"), a desire to change is very liable to become stuck in "thing-oriented circuits of repetition," because what commodities offer, in effect, is the promise of transformation without any of its usual risk or pain.[29] Furthermore, the fantasy of change that becomes attached to an object is actually a fantasy of being in a space and time *"where that change has already happened"* (208; emphasis in the original), and this in turn expresses the subject's ambivalence about the very idea of change; change may be desired, but trauma is not. As she puts it, "The subject's (or a mass's) desire to move beyond whatever is dead or deadening rubs up against the comfort that the form's stability brings" (229). This desire to avoid changes that are painful or destabilizing is a critical factor in considering the tensions between those forces that serve to reproduce football fandom as an exclusionary white, male space and those that serve to interrupt it. In the context of Portsmouth, the challenges to this space (an increasingly international team, a participation—albeit partly at a distance—in a more multicultural popular culture) increasingly confront an array of forces that serve to reproduce it, organized, most notably, through the persistent presence (both metaphoric and literal) of the "fathers" of the 6.57. While it is interesting to consider the implications of Mark Simpson's claim that young men are increasingly "fathered" by popular culture and commodities,[30] I would argue that it is important not to underestimate the power of actual fathers in framing young men's engagement with ideas about family and nation. Here it is also significant, of course, that women's increasing power in the public sphere continues to provide the backdrop against which such negotiations around masculinity take place.

I hope it is clear, then, that although brands and commercial operations of various kinds increasingly seek to capitalize on the desire for new forms of human connectedness, it may not be commodities or commodification that get in the way of such a change so much as the ambivalence of subjects themselves. Commodities cannot resolve this ambivalence, they can only register it, and here it is worth noting Paul Gilroy's point that the current configuration of sports cultures in Britain may be read both as part of a national melancholia and for what it provides in terms of "fleeting, prefigurative glimpses of a different nation." At the same time, while Gilroy notes that the appeal of a "market-driven pastiche of multiculture" may derive largely from the absence of more substantial political initiatives elsewhere, he also remarks that what may be at stake in the connection between sport, commerce, and the cultural economy of "race" and nation is not so much class but questions about the "translocal integrity both of the male body and the appeal of the idea of manliness" (124). It is this connection between the commodity culture of football and very narrowly defined notions of "national manhood" that I have been trying to get at here.

Conclusion

At this point I want to return to the question of how an analysis of fans' consumption practices, and of a broader commodity culture of football, can be used to illustrate its relations of inclusion and belonging. To recap, I have argued that commodity culture is increasingly the means through which fantasy is organized and through which desired relations of inclusion and exclusion are expressed. At the same time, commodity culture is also one of the ways in which relationships to metacultural forms such as nation and family are negotiated at an everyday level, and this makes it of particular relevance to the study of football, where ideas about kinship and national belonging have historically been foregrounded. In this respect I have argued that to read fans' interest in the consumption of commodities, signs, and logos as merely evidence of the impact of commodification, or of a "flâneur-like" disposition, is to miss the very important ways in which it is also caught up with questions of inclusion and belonging and of who is—and who is not—part of the "family" of football. Although existing work in this area recognizes that the dominance of commodity culture makes it an increasingly central part of how team affiliation is expressed, it tends not to connect this to the perhaps more significant question of football's broader inclusiveness. Indeed, at its most extreme, this line of argument sees fans' consumption of football-related signs and objects as devoid of any substantive meaning at all.

I have used the example of Casual style to suggest that there is in fact a considerable degree of overlap between older and newer fan practices in terms of the way that commodity cultures come to organize fantasy. In relation to anxieties about class and status, I have suggested that the adornment of the body with brands and logos may be read as a way of protecting the body from stigma, and that this in turn needs to be understood in relation to the historical association between property and personhood. I have also suggested, however, that such adornment should be understood with reference to football's particular gender regime, and specifically that commodities operate as one of a range of ways of expressing relationships of similarity and difference among men. This in turn is an important part of how football fandom is established as a fraternity, one where internal hierarchy and competition ultimately serve to stabilize gender identity and produce a reassuring sense of masculine privilege. This project also, of necessity, involves a strategy of "altero-referentiality," and here commodities can be used to mark a range of exclusions. At the same time, because such exclusions bind fraternities to a range of necessary Others and because commodities allow ambivalence about this to be registered, under certain circumstances commodities can also work, more flexibly, as a space in which such connections may be recouped or reimagined, and through which an identification or desire for connectedness with various Others can be expressed. Some of the limits to such a strategy were outlined at the end of the previous section.

I hope this analysis has made it clear that, insofar as one is interested in the consumption practices of newer fans, these must be understood above all in relation to earlier fan practices, in which aspects of commodity culture were entwined with a practice of fandom that was almost entirely white and male. I hope it is also clear that newer fans' consumption of various branded commodities should not be read in terms of commodification alone, but rather in relation to the way that branded objects of various kinds have historically been used to mark one's inclusion in the "family of football." Viewed in this light, new fans' consumption practices may be read as claims to belonging that derive part of their power from this longer historical significance of football's material culture. I think it is also worth noting here, in relation to Giulianotti's suggestion that some newer fans are "drawn to the signifier . . . rather than what is signified conceptually," that what a team crest, logo, or indeed any other part of football's material culture "signifies" to particular fans is likely to depend very much upon the positions they have historically been able to occupy in relation to the sport, and the question of who arbitrates in these matters of signification is itself tied to such histories of belonging.

There is, I think, one final question in relation to the "objects" of football, which relates to Berlant's use of the term. Her understanding of what an object is derives in large part from Christopher Bollas's concept of the "transformational object," in which "objects" may refer not only to commodities but also to a broader range of things, people, and ideals to which subjects attach their desires and through which they seek to produce a transformation of the self. Given such a definition, we might quite reasonably ask whether football itself may be considered an "object" and, if so, what kind of object it is, and for whom. I began this essay with some personal reflections on the kind of object Portsmouth Football Club had been to me in the past, and some questions about what else I might want it to be in the future. This is a question that resonates, I think, with a wider set of actual or potential fans but that also, as I suggested at the beginning, has a rather overdetermined quality, precisely because of the historically exclusionary nature of football fan cultures in Britain. Although it is unquestionably important to persist in efforts to make British football a less exclusionary space, from the perspective of new or potential fans there are also questions about the extent to which football itself is an appropriate object for engaging with such histories of exclusion. I have already noted the sense in which, for white, middle-class female fans in particular, football may tend to evoke a sense of resentment or bitterness, and I have outlined some of the reasons for this. I am not sure where these lead, politically or practically, and experiences with football are, in any case, likely to be different for working-class white women, and for both female and male nonwhite fans (and they will almost certainly be characterized by a lesser degree of denial). Nonetheless, there remain questions about the extent to which football is an object upon which hopes for inclusion should be pinned, and about whether the desire to overcome certain conventional forms of social division might, when directed toward football, be being channeled into the most conventional of forms. Although I continue to follow Portsmouth's highs and lows in the Premiership with interest and cannot help but read them as speaking to my own preoccupations, I wonder whether it might now be time to find a new object.

Notes

Thanks to Steve Cross and Jo Littler.

1   The 6.57 was one of a number of relatively high-profile "crews" or "firms" of fans at this time. The name refers to the earliest train running from Portsmouth to Waterloo station in London, which fans took to away matches because it allowed them to be almost anywhere in the country by one o'clock. According to 6.57 diarists Cass Pennant and Rob Silvester, it "got us into enemy territory as early as possible and we could set about causing maximum mayhem" (Cass Pennant and Rob Silvester, *Rolling with the 6.57 Crew* [London: John Blake, 2004], 14). The term *hooligan* is still somewhat contentious because of its link to media mythologizing and moral panics, but broadly it refers to the loosely organized gang rivalries focused on football matches between the 1960s and late 1980s (see "Football and Football Hooliganism," Sir Norman Chester Centre for Football Research, Fact Sheet No. 1, University of Leicester).

2   Anne Coddington notes that many women did not go to football matches during the 1970s and 1980s because of their association with hooliganism (*One of the Lads* [London: HarperCollins, 1997], 96). It is taken for granted here, as in some other accounts of female fans, that (implicitly white) women will be appalled by both hooliganism and the overt racism with which it was associated. While for some women this may well be true, it ignores the wider question of white women's complicity with such racism, in both its overt and its more persistent casual and institutional forms. This in turn is part of a more general tendency to attribute racism only to a minority of fans. At the same time, there clearly are interesting questions here about the way that classed and gendered forms of regulation (even when motivated by an understandable desire to avoid violence or sexual harassment) are themselves coded through a righteous language of antiracism.

3   Lauren Berlant, "The Compulsion to Repeat Femininity," in *Giving Ground: The Politics of Propinquity*, ed. Joan Copjec and Michael Sorkin (London: Verso, 1999).

4   A survey of Premier League fans in 2000 found that 86 percent of season ticket holders were men and that 97.6 percent described themselves as "white British" ("A Profile of FA Premier League Supporters in 2000," Sir Norman Chester Centre for Football Research, Fact Sheet No. 13, University of Leicester).

5   John Williams notes that "complaints from the traditional male fans about the game's new terracotta armies are couched in terms which imply the class roots of the sport have been betrayed by the advent of a new affluent audience for the game seduced less by the sport than by its branded duvets and cuddly toys"; he goes on to ask, "Aren't these really complaints that football culture in England . . . has been unacceptably feminized?" (cited in Coddington, *One of the Lads*, 100).

6   Although Gary Armstrong's ethnographic account of Sheffield's Blades provides a useful degree of detail on the question of fans' material culture (*Football Hooligans: Knowing the Score* [Oxford: Berg, 1998]).

7   Richard Giulianotti, "Supporters, Followers, Fans and Flâneurs: A Taxonomy of Spectator Identities in Football," *Journal of Sport and Social Issues* 26.1 (2002): 25–46.

8   Part of the problem here is that surveys of fan behavior tend, of necessity, only to measure fans' consumption of team-related goods, such as replica shirts and match programs; what I am suggesting here, however, is that such goods are in fact only one part of a broader material culture of fandom and that such a narrow focus tends—for reasons I will discuss—to replicate the assumption that only *particular* groups of fans are "consumer-oriented," thereby ignoring the roots of their consumption practice in earlier fans' behavior.

9   Armstrong, *Football Hooligans.*

10   During this period (which is one of the high points of the "hooligan" problem), the Casual style of many football fans was also widely adopted by other young men who were less closely associated with the game. In this sense, the commodity culture of the Casuals is also a relay point between the specific forms of masculine association cultivated within football and a more widely dispersed "style" of masculinity. However, I want to make it clear that my focus here is on the more organized and clearly delineated "crews" of fans—sometimes known as "hooligans"—rather than either the "ordinary" fans or other young men outside of the game. While there are points of continuity between organized "crews" and other fans as forms of male association largely cut off from women, the argument made here about "fraternities" does *not* apply to all male fans; indeed, it is the defensive and exclusionary nature of these "crews," combined with their practices of rivalry and humiliation between "equals," that distinguishes them from this wider fan base.

11   Paulo Hewitt and Mark Baxter, *The Fashion of Football: From Best to Beckham, from Mod to Label Slave* (Edinburgh: Mainstream Publishing, 2004), 192.

12   Lauren Berlant, "National Brands/National Body: *Imitation of Life,*" in *The Phantom Public Sphere*, ed. Bruce Robbins (Minneapolis: University of Minnesota Press, 1993).

13   Les Back, "Inscriptions of Love," in *Cultural Bodies: Ethnography and Theory*, ed. Helen Thomas and Jamilah Ahmed (Oxford: Blackwell, 2004).

14   Armstrong, *Football Hooligans*, 166.

15   Carole Pateman, *The Sexual Contract* (Stanford: Stanford University Press, 1988).

16   Armstrong, *Football Hooligans*, 166.

17   In relation to the matter of fraternity, it is also significant that such forms of adornment may allow class distinctions within football support to be partially blurred or obscured; middle-class men in particular may benefit from this, since it allows them to strategically adopt or "perform" certain aspects of working-class male identity when it suits them but also to discard them when it does not. Needless to say, working-class men do not have the same freedom in this respect, although the fantasy of classless masculinity does, I think, allow a particular gender regime to be stabilized, if only temporarily.

18   Hewitt and Baxter, *The Fashion of Football*, 195, italics added. Subsequent citations are given parenthetically by page number in the text.

19   Dana Nelson, *National Manhood: Capitalist Citizenship and the Imagined Fraternity of White Men* (Durham, NC: Duke University Press, 1998). Subsequent citations are given parenthetically by page number in the text.

20   Accounts in this vein do, however, stress that these local or "tribal" identities involve rivalry between groups that are relatively homogeneous.

21   The historically sexist, racist, and homophobic nature of football fandom is the general context here, but it is implemented in a range of ways, from casual sexism to violent and

overt racism and homophobia. In each of these cases, however, it is hard to isolate "hooligan" activity from wider fan practice. I have not included details of the altero-referential strategies of various "crews" here, but some of the differences in how these are reported are interesting; where references to women are largely conspicuous by their absence (and this seems to be true of academic accounts as well as of books in the "hooli" genre), much of the racism of fans at this time is either downplayed or disavowed entirely, whereas homophobic violence is naturalized and even (as in Pennant and Silvester's *Rolling with the 6.57 Crew*) presented as humorous.

22 It is important to note here that while many fans in the 1980s had good jobs, mortgages, steady incomes, and easy access to credit, others were experiencing redundancy and unemployment; overall, there was clearly a great deal of variation within fan groups, with upward mobility for some and downward mobility for others. Gary Armstrong argues that the complexity of class affiliation is such that simple classifications are unhelpful and that a longer-term view of participation in fan groups is more appropriate. Especially pertinent here, he notes that the "true way" of interpreting fan identity is to see it as "bound up in the common activities of *male* leisure . . . [which are] surrounded by the symbolic, semiotic and cultural forms that give them meaning and resonance" (*Football Hooligans*, 169, my emphasis).

23 Pennant and Silvester, *Rolling with the 6.57 Crew*, 75.

24 Hewitt and Baxter, *The Fashion of Football*, 193.

25 Ed Vulliamy and Brian Oliver, "Up Pompey!" *Observer Sport Monthly*, August 3, 2003, 36.

26 Julie Burchill is the main proponent of this view. She argues that "the white indigenous English working-class [*sic*] is now the one group you can insult without feeling the breath of the Commission for Racial Equality on your neck" ("Yeah But, No But, Why I'm Proud to Be a Chav," *The Times*, February 18, 2005).

27 See Bev Skeggs, "The Wrong Sort of Authenticity: Middle-Class Paranoia in the Making of Objects of Hate" (paper presented at Making Use of Culture conference, Manchester, January 23, 2005).

28 Paul Gilroy, *After Empire: Melancholia or Convivial Culture?* (London: Routledge, 2004).

29 Berlant, "The Compulsion to Repeat Femininity," 207. Subsequent citations are given parenthetically by page number in the text.

30 Mark Simpson, cited in Steve Redhead, *Post-fandom and the Millennial Blues* (London: Routledge, 1997), 101.

Amy Bass

Objectivity Be Damned, or Why I Go to the
Olympic Games: A Hands-On Lesson in
Performative Nationalism

For historians, the question of objectivity was
supposed to have been settled back in 1988
with the publication of Peter Novick's *That Noble
Dream*. It became a must-read for all first-year
graduate students and a target for those preparing dissertation defenses. Briefly, Novick's book
takes up the idea of objectivity, arguing that it
provides not only the center for the study of
history as performed by professionals, but also
the starting point for those who want to learn
about history as a profession: "Anyone interested
in what professional historians are up to—what
they think they are doing, or ought to be doing,
when they write history—might well begin by
considering 'the objectivity question.'"[1] By and
large, per Novick's assessment, historians do not
do enough to cultivate objectivity; he calls for us
to do better, to set aside values and self-interests
in order to produce history that is, as he desires,
"found" and not "made."

The timing of Novick's book was, at the least,
interesting, emerging in the midst of the ever-
increasing influence of cultural studies on the
social sciences and the scramble to find frame-
works that worked in the post-Marxist haze. For
me, Novick's book got shoved under my desk as

The *South Atlantic Quarterly* 105:2, Spring 2006.

I approached the writing of my doctoral dissertation because it only drew attention to the fact that I was not able to reconcile my experience with my subject: As I embarked on a project on the black power movements that surrounded the Mexico City Olympic Games, I went to the Atlanta Olympics in a completely behind-the-scenes, you-are-one-of-us capacity. Objectivity be damned.

Did it have an impact? Absolutely. My dissertation, which eventually became my first book, was an exploration of the Olympic Project for Human Rights (OPHR), the organization behind the famous photo of Tommie Smith and John Carlos, black gloved fists raised above their heads, in Mexico City. I completed the dissertation in 1999. When I wrote my initial proposal in the spring of 1996, Mexico City—and Smith and Carlos—were but one part of a broader discussion that I planned regarding American citizenship, racial politics, and popular culture.

However, on my return from Atlanta that fall I transformed my project to focus solely on sports as a means to discuss the culture of civil rights, and moved Smith and Carlos to center stage. I had gone to Atlanta as a part of the National Broadcasting Company's research unit. I became involved at NBC after a phone call from a friend of my brother: NBC researchers needed help. (Full disclosure: My brother works in television news, and formerly in Olympic broadcasting.) The two gentlemen that had been working on assembling all of the information necessary for the broadcast of the Games for the two previous years needed another body, and it had to be someone with good research, communication, and writing skills—and someone who desperately needed money and would submit to what I soon found to be the tortures of working in sports television. I climbed on board in March 1996, just as I was studying for my doctoral exams and finishing the dissertation prospectus. Excellent timing. By the end of April, I was working seven days a week, averaging eighteen to twenty hours a day. It was ugly and grueling: I wrote event histories, athlete biographies, medal predictions, and so on. Few people going into Atlanta could know more about what could happen than I did.

Once in Atlanta, I spent most of my time sitting—scared stiff—on the other side of the glass from Bob Costas in what is called "The Research Room." The twenty or so people in that room find the interesting stories, make contact with the interesting people, and answer any and all potential questions in an effort to ensure that everything said on air is correct. What kinds of questions? There's the simple: How many people live in Canada?

The statistical: When was the last time, if ever, that the United States won this many golds in swimming on a single night? The interesting: Which prisoner of war camp in Germany in World War II held their own "Prisoner Olympics"? And the stupid: Will Maurice Green win tonight? It is about as tense a situation as one can imagine, but it offers an unequaled look at Olympic media culture. My Atlanta stint finished with the Closing Ceremony, where I roamed around the infield wearing an all-access badge searching for athletes that the cameras needed to focus on. Needless to say, when I returned to my dissertation that fall, everything had changed: Now that I had shaken hands with Michael Johnson and Jackie Joyner Kersee, hung out with the men's water polo team, and learned the particulars of table tennis, I only wanted to write about the Olympics. Mexico City became the focal point of my work, and Smith and Carlos my main characters.

My relationship with the Olympics continued after my dissertation was complete and I began my life as a professor at Plattsburgh State University. Within months of arriving in Plattsburgh, I audaciously asked if I could leave the following fall semester to go with NBC in a supervisor role to the Sydney Games. I was indoctrinated: I was part of a small group of highly specialized people who drop everything for several weeks during an Olympic year and gather together, working for whatever network is broadcasting the Games. It is a unique group, knowledgeable in multiple languages, geography, world politics, and specific random sports (from gymnastics to curling to judo, in which it is legal, by the way, to break your opponent's arm as a means to win). Plattsburgh graciously worked out a way for me to go, which included teaching an honors seminar—The Black Athlete— online from Sydney. I returned with more life-altering experiences: watching Marion Jones run, sitting in the bleachers as the United States beat Cuba for the baseball gold medal and listening to rumors that Castro was in the house, and again witnessing a spectacular Closing Ceremony. I reworked the dissertation after returning from Sydney, and by the time Salt Lake City rolled around, I was in the final editing phases of my book, *Not the Triumph but the Struggle: The 1968 Olympic Games and the Making of the Black Athlete*, more confident than ever of the viability of sports, especially the Olympics, as a fruitful site to examine how the world works, whether in terms of my own focus on exploring how ideas of race and nation are culturally manufactured, or the broader goals of determining where in the world politics exists.

The book, in short, argues that the Mexico City Olympics, as a forum of transnational racialized politics in the jam-packed year of 1968, represented a confluence of concerns that dominated its historical moment: the explosion of subaltern expressions of identity, student social movements, the still-mushrooming relationship between science and sports, and questions of decolonization and independence, all within an arena of ever-proliferating postwar media industries. The image that dominates the American memory of these Games, of course, is that of Tommie Smith and John Carlos, gold and bronze medals hanging around their respective necks, using their moment in front of the world to speak out against racial oppression. By examining their action and the extensive social movement behind it, the OPHR, we can understand better the degree to which black power infiltrated American culture; the centrality of television to political movements; the transnational workings of civil and/or human rights struggles; the role of an increasingly decolonized Africa within the international community; and, again, the use of sports as a site to examine racial and national identity formation in the United States in a global context.

City and Spectacle: Constructing Meanings

And the Olympic community is indeed global. Well over two hundred countries now televise the modern Olympic Games to a global audience of billions. Mexico City was the first large-scale American television broadcast of an Olympics, and it is the then-unprecedented coverage of Mexico City that makes them ripe for what the Olympics, by their very nature, cry out to do: manufacture nations and peoples. While the International Olympic Committee (IOC) claims, via the Olympic Charter, that the Games are between athletes and not between nations, the basis for any athlete to enter into competition is through a National Olympic Committee. And while the weight of such representation falls heavily on the athlete's shoulders, perhaps no entity bears what historian Eric Zolov describes as the burden of representation as much as the host.[2]

This burden impacts a city in every way imaginable, from the beginning of its campaign to become an Olympic City to the last moments of the Closing Ceremony to the problem of figuring out what to do with the sports arenas and hotels when everyone goes home. Everything within the process becomes a performance, from the way the airport staff greets Olympic visitors to the special "Olympic" traffic patterns to the wait staffs at restaurants. As one scholar summarizes, "The games are as much about the *city* as spectacle as they are about sport."[3] In Mexico City in 1968, the organizing committee had to decide upon its own image for the Games, a daunting task for any Olympic host but perhaps more so in 1968 because of the elaborate television programming, the intense political climate, and the controversies that enveloped the location itself, particularly in terms of its altitude and its burgeoning student movements against the government. Mexico opted for a modern face, designed to prove the worthiness of a "developing country" as host to the international community while strategically bolstering the image of Mexico. This strategy meant that the organizing committee had to combat internationally held stereotypes regarding Mexico and Mexicans and produce a hospitable Olympic environment, transforming itself, as Zolov explains, from the land of *mañana* to a land of modernity and harmony.[4]

Yet this modernist tone has simply not been the legacy of the Mexico City Olympics; rather, what endures is a combination of the horror of the massacre of protesters in Tlateloco, not far from Olympic Stadium, that took place just days before the Opening Ceremony, and the black power gesture by Smith and Carlos. The question of whether these events have caused the IOC to deny every subsequent Latin American bid to host the Games is not one we can answer here. All Olympics, of course, undergo complicated dramas in terms of the historical moment somewhat beyond their control. However, the host city also has the responsibility of its own legacy, honed and manufactured through pageantry, ceremony, and, of course, the cultural Olympiad, the little-known cultural accompaniment to the sporting program. The Olympic Games are, among other things, a visual spectacle, and, as Toni Morrison reminds us, "Spectacle is the best means by which an official story is formed and is a superior mechanism for guaranteeing its longevity."[5] Smith and Carlos, for example, reached approximately 400 million people worldwide with their protest, in which they confronted and resisted the American flag and anthem during the Olympic victory ceremony and effectively substituted their own symbol: the black-gloved fist. It was a strategy that played well on television, making good use of the unprecedented coverage of Mexico City by the American Broadcasting Company. Indeed, the presence of television was a critical aspect of the strategy of the OPHR because, as OPHR leader Harry Edwards emphasized, an athlete's "access at a moment's notice to the mass media" made it imperative that they "take a stand."[6]

The OPHR was not alone, of course, in recognizing the impact of television on the Olympic Games—or on any sporting event, for that matter. As David Andrews argues, network television transforms the Olympics into a cohesive, dramatic story in order to compete with other mass entertainment productions.[7] However, while Andrews astutely demonstrates how television audiences are given what he deems "an Olympic simulation manufactured to serve very definite purposes,"[8] it is important to remember that the networks alone are not doing this but are in concert with both the IOC and the host city, feeding on the ceremony and pageantry mandated and produced by both, albeit with television firmly in mind. Furthermore, it is critical to keep in mind that the reproductions—or simulations, as Andrews writes—created on television in no way make experiential discourse obsolete; rather, they force us to constantly consider mass media in how such discourse is understood, both in terms of how it is received, as Andrews notes, and in terms of how it is *created*.

Circus and Ceremony: The Example of Los Angeles

Aside from the actual moments of competition itself, which may or may not make televised air, there are three essential aspects to the televised Olympic Games: the Opening Ceremony, the Closing Ceremony, and—as Smith and Carlos so wisely used—the medal ceremony. As John J. MacAloon notes, the Opening Ceremony takes place to detach Olympic events from those of daily life. In it, specific Olympic symbols—flag, torch, flame—transform the national identity expressed by each team into a collective one. In the victory ceremonies, the individual athlete is added, representing the body itself and helping to reinforce the results of the competition. Additionally, both national and Olympic images are underlined via national flags, national anthems, and Olympic medals. The athlete, then, assumes a dual persona, because he or she stands on the dais as a member of both a nation and, as MacAloon writes, "a wider human community." The Closing Ceremony then reiterates this wider community, bringing both athletes and spectators back to everyday life by having participants march into the stadium together, rather than as members of a national team.[9]

While medal ceremonies are undoubtedly the most emotional of the three central Olympic rites, they are exclusive to less than half of the national delegations that compete in the Games. The Opening Ceremony, however, with its Parade of Nations and performative pageantry, includes all, overshadowing the Closing Ceremony which, while admirable in its emphasis on harmony and solidarity, comes at the end of an exhausting two-plus weeks, when only the very committed still have energy left to watch *more* Olympics.

The Opening Ceremony became a commercial colossus in 1984 with the Los Angeles Games. Following Montreal's disastrous $1.2 billion deficit, marking the last time a Games was funded entirely by the public,[10] the LA committee, despite a Soviet-led boycott of the Games by Eastern Bloc teams, solidified unprecedented sponsor/broadcast relationships, ensuring that the Olympics would be a financial boom, rather than bust, to its host city.[11] Without question, Los Angeles stunned its 2.5 billion viewers with its then-novel audience participation displays and the impressive eighty-four white pianos lined up to play George Gershwin's "Rhapsody in Blue." These pro-fessionally produced moments (read: Hollywood moments) worked much like the films of Leni Riefenstahl, though in a slightly ironic fashion. They performed, as Alan Tomlinson notes, to "assert the superiority of the West-ern, capitalist, free American way over the oppressive Eastern, communist, totalitarian Soviet way."[12] The LA Games also generated surplus funds of $225 million, providing the endowment that established the Amateur Ath-letic Foundation of Los Angeles (AAFLA) and adding an estimated $2.5 bil-lion to California's economy.[13]

The millions spent (and gained) in Los Angeles ensured that opening ceremonies to come would be fusions of all things theatrical, an opportu-nity for a host city to demonstrate to the world what it is most proud of. Of course, not all of these moments of spectacle and pageantry are wrapped in "Rhapsody in Blue." In the Seoul Games in 1988, for example, seventy-six-year-old Sohn Kee-Chung carried the torch into the stadium, a touching moment for this gold medalist in the 1936 Olympic marathon, who had been forced to run under a Japanese name because of the Japanese occupa-tion. However, behind the story of Sohn was that of the dozens of doves who were released into the sky to symbolize the peace and harmony expected of an Olympic Games. The doves flew straight into the Olympic cauldron, dying instantly in (for viewers in the stadium) a rather horrific display.

Playing a Part: Behind the Scenes of the Opening Ceremony

The Opening Ceremony takes up a great deal of my own time at NBC in the weeks preceding any given Olympics. The first major task of the Research Room is to determine the Opening Ceremony flag bearers for each national delegation and put together "country cards" for the writers so they can ensure that the on-air talent has something knowledgeable, fun, and global to say about each team as it enters Olympic Stadium. It remains one of my favorite parts of the job—speaking with the athletes, the *chef de missions* (delegation leaders), and the coaches about what they will wear, what it means, and what is going on back at home. It can produce heartwarming stories, or it can make you feel foolish, as when you must ask the Sudanese *chef de mission* whether the team will be wearing hats rather than asking questions about what is going on in Darfur.

In conjunction with this process, researchers also need to provide background information for the various pieces to the Opening Ceremony performances. This is difficult, of course, because many of the details of the Opening are closely guarded secrets, all of which correspond to the overarching themes and images that the Olympic host wants to present about itself. Because I am a cultural historian, the details of the Opening Ceremony quickly fascinated me, as they obviously exemplified an idea central to my own research: *performative nationalism.*[14] In terms of the Opening Ceremony, this process works both beyond and within the idea of nation, with the identity of the city itself taking priority over that of country, and the presence of *a* people—local, regional, national, cultural—dominating all. It becomes further complicated because of how the audience, for its part, operates at multiple levels, with those in the stadium presented as the local spectators, regardless of where they actually came from, pitted against those for whom the performance is ostensibly staged: the global television audience. Indeed, one of the greatest legacies of Los Angeles is how it used its audience in the stadium to help make the show look good for the folks at home. Think, for example, of the segment in which the stadium audience was asked to find the card located under each seat and hold it in the air, creating a circle of flags from each Olympic delegation in attendance (in other words, the boycotting communist countries were absent from the "global" display). The official report from thc Los Angeles Games described it this way:

> Following the "Music of America" presentation, the Coliseum announcer instructed the audience to locate the packets which had previously been placed at their seats. The plastic packets contained a colored plastic card and instructions in six different languages which requested the audience to raise their cards at a designated time. When the audience raised their cards to form the flags of every participating NOC,

it was the first time the card stunt was performed. Finding 85,000 people to test the stunt, of course, was not practical. All sections of the Coliseum, with the exception of the press section, participated in the stunt.[15]

This then-unique method of using those who were there to watch as an active part of the pageantry blurred the lines between audience and participants, ensuring that future ceremonies held those in the seats responsible for helping the host city convey its chosen image to the rest of the world.

For the Opening Ceremony of my first Olympics, Atlanta opted to appear as a center of technology, wanting to live up to its 1991 description by *Fortune* magazine as the "best city in America for business" rather than serving up portions of Dixie or the Old South. In his exploration of what he calls "the semiotics of a successful city,"[16] Drew Whitelegg shows how Atlanta (less than successfully) used the Games to cultivate its image as a conflict-free arena via corporate interests and international media. "Cities have long been associated with sports," he writes, "especially through successful teams, but a significant feature of more recent years is the way urban elites have tried to tap into the combination of image and financial boost that staging sporting events can potentially bring." This creates what Whitelegg calls "an 'entrepreneurial' approach to urban affairs."[17] The problem for Atlanta, of course, was the gap between its economic and cultural capital.[18] Debates raged, for example, over whether or not the Georgia flag, which then prominently featured the St. Andrews cross, a Confederate war symbol, should fly during the Games at events held in state-owned buildings: One politician called the flag "an American swastika," while the Sons of Confederate Veterans announced, "The state of Georgia is not today a part of the U.S. of its own free will."[19] Another site of controversy was the archery and tennis venue at Stone Mountain, which claims to be second only to Disney for popular southern tourist destinations. With its carvings of Confederate Civil War leaders and as the former home of the Venables family, the site remains one of the most powerful symbols of the Ku Klux Klan.[20] Stone Mountain would thus be difficult to market as a suitable place to welcome athletes from around the world.

Atlanta tried to overshadow this legacy by boasting that it was "one of the best-wired cities in the world for multi-media communications," with "over 150 miles of fiber-optic cable in the Olympic Village alone."[21] However, within hours of the start of competition, the IBM-designed computer system that Atlanta had promised would offer its subscribers instant results tabulations, including athlete biographies, statistics, and schedules, crashed, never to recover, so those of us on the inside had to do the work by hand for each event. Rumors (now legend) quickly circulated throughout the International Broadcast Center: According to the computers, broadcasters snickered, a fencer held the world record in the 400 meters.

Such disparities are not an uncommon feature of a host city's battle with image. As Jackie Hogan notes, there are a series of "ideological tensions inherent in the modern Olympic movement," including the tension "between tradition and change."[22] During the Atlanta Opening Ceremony, for example, the over-the-top spectacle of the thirty chrome trucks circling the infield while dancers spelled out "HOW Y'ALL DOIN?" was, of course, overshadowed by the remarkable moment of Muhammad Ali shakily lighting the flame, creating, as I have written elsewhere, a "repatriation for both a figure reviled and the nation that reviled him."[23] As *Sports Illustrated* remembers, Ali "was the picture of dignity in Atlanta," while the ceremony itself was "corporate over-kill and over-the-top glitter."[24] The power of the image created by Ali, then, ensured a positive overarching image of Atlanta, regardless of what accompanied him down on the infield. As Alan Tomlinson notes, "The dignity of the man and the sheer global charisma of the Ali personality and legend ensured that the ceremony would be greeted positively, would be hailed as a symbol of Olympic ideals, would be judged on the good-taste side of the showbiz tendency in big-time sports in the United States."[25]

In 2000, at my second Olympics, Sydney reconfigured the role of aboriginal people and culture in its history with its Opening Ceremony dramatics, paving the way for runner Cathy Freeman to become a national, rather than aboriginal, hero. Rather than give its audience the expected kangaroos and koalas, the ceremony presented an overview of Aboriginal culture, featuring some 1,200 Aboriginals from a variety of tribes; focused on its diverse landscape; and put forth "Waltzing Matilda" as its theme song, rather than the official—and much more formal—national anthem, "Advance Australia Fair." This emphasis on the local, so-called indigenous aspects of Australian culture had been an ongoing part of the Olympic movement in the country, as evidenced by the Olympic Arts Festivals that Sydney hosted in the years leading up to the Games. The first of those festivals, "The Festival of the Dreaming," according to Sydney Organizing Committee president Michael Knight, was designed to "recognize the primacy of Aboriginal culture and Aboriginal civilization . . . [and] to reach out, to give the message of reconciliation: to say that the Sydney Olympics are inclusive not exclusive, and to give the message that these are the Games for all Australians."[26] Thus, alongside the emphasis on the culture and importance of Aborigines to Australian history in a ceremony that was, according to one Aboriginal rights activist, "209 years in the making,"[27] was the attempt to ensure a national cohesiveness before the rest of the world descended upon Sydney. Doing this, of course, entailed the attempt to secure "reconciliation," the name given to "the process through which indigenous and nonindigenous people have been coming to terms with the reality of the history of white Australian settlement," Lisa Meekison notes, "and through which they have been developing terms of rapprochement."[28]

In Sydney, the Opening Ceremony also highlighted the one hundredth anniversary of women's participation in the Olympics, with Freeman taking the torch from a relay of six Australian Olympians—all women. With torch in hand, Freeman, chosen for the most important and prestigious moment in the ceremony, stood before the cauldron in the midst of a magnificent pool of water as a waterfall cascaded before her. Lighting the flame from a circle of fire in the water, designed to underline Australia's prominent sand and sea, Freeman, once considered treasonous for carrying the Aboriginal flag at the Commonwealth Games in 1994, stood before the world as the cauldron (after an embarrassing three-minute delay) slowly made its way via a belt to the top of the stadium. With this superlative display of tradition, reconciliation, and modernity, Australia shed its image as "penal colony" and became a stylish, multicultural place, one where people of all kinds— including its once "removed" Aboriginal population—resided happily.

Certainly spectacular, but not everyone was pleased. While New South Wales premier Bob Carr described the Opening Ceremony as the most important artistic achievement in Australia's history, and the *Melbourne Age* declared that the Olympic committee had "done Australia . . . proud" with a "colorful display of what Australia has been and is," John MacDonald, head of Australian art at the National Gallery of Australia (Canberra), called the Opening Ceremony "kitsch from start to finish." According to MacDonald, "Kitsch is crap with pretensions to sincerity. Kitsch takes all the emotions associated with great art, and packages them in the most compact, user-friendly fashion; editing out anything that may be disturbing or complex."[29]

However, Sydney's idea of the disturbing and complex was trumped by the situation of the Winter Games in 2002. Salt Lake City hosted the Games in a time of what many considered to be tremendous international instability, but what Walter Benjamin might have called in his "concept of history" a more familiar state of emergency.[30] Perhaps more than others, the

Salt Lake ritual constructed itself as, to borrow a phrase from Stuart Hall, a "narrative of nation." Hall defines this kind of narrative as "a set of stories, images, landscapes, scenarios, historical events, national symbols and rituals which stand for or represent the shared experiences, sorrows, and triumphs and disasters which give meaning to the nation."[31] The usual cast of American characters were there—children, immigrants, cowboys, Indians. But the Opening Ceremony presented these various groups without hinting at, as Jackie Hogan puts it, "the historical tensions and even lethal conflicts" that existed among them.[32]

From my perspective, however, perhaps more remarkable about Salt Lake was its alteration of Olympic traditions. By changing rituals prescribed by the Olympic Charter, the ceremony demonstrated how "the consciously universalist rituals of the ceremonies are," according to Hogan, "domesticated by the host nations and imbued with national meanings."[33] While the most obvious example of such a practice might be Berlin in 1936, in Salt Lake it became clear with the direct links created between the hosting of the Olympics and the then-recent events of 9/11. In the show that preceded the official beginning of the ceremony, for example, New York Police Department officer Daniel Rodriguez sang "God Bless America," a role increasingly familiar for the Brooklyn-born tenor, who became famous for singing at many 9/11 memorial events, as well as for singing the national anthem at the 2001 World Series in Yankee Stadium.[34] The drama mounted as the Opening Ceremony officially began, perhaps peaking when the Mormon Tabernacle Choir sang the "Star Spangled Banner" as the tattered World Trade Center flag entered, carried by New York police, fire, and Port Authority officers, as well as some U.S. Olympians. As the flag made its way to the center of the arena, images of other American flags flashed on the stadium's many screens. "The segment was richly layered," observes Hogan, "evoking the divine through the use of the choir; evoking the nation through its most potent symbol of nationhood, the flag; evoking the power of the state through the presence of the enforcers of law and order; and serving as homage to the victims of the September attacks."[35]

Altering Traditions: The Collision of Culture and Politics

Even more notable was the divergence by both the IOC and U.S. presidents from traditions mandated in the Olympic Charter. Predicting that the success of Salt Lake—or any Olympics, for that matter—would speak to the ability of the world to conduct itself peacefully, Jacques Rogge offered acknowledgment of 9/11 in his remarks, noting, "Your nation is overcoming a horrific tragedy—a tragedy that has affected the whole world. We stand united with you in the promotion of our common ideals, and hope for world peace." Even more significantly, amid Salt Lake's reconfigurement of Mormon migration and the Old West ("Apparently the Indians just handed the land over," an NBC colleague remarked to me while watching the stadium monitor), George W. Bush took the opportunity to deviate from the fourteen words mandated by the Olympic Charter and opened the Games with his own patriotic improv: "*On behalf of a proud, determined and grateful nation,*" he ad-libbed, "I declare open the Games of Salt Lake City, celebrating the Olympic Winter Games."[36] Finally, the lighting of the Olympic flame by the victorious 1980 U.S. hockey team, arguably the greatest cold warriors in U.S. history, supported Bush's words of national strength in this most international of forums. "The moment served," concludes Hogan, "as a symbolic assertion of American power, a promise to once again defeat its enemies."[37]

The "burden of representation" most recently fell to Athens, Greece, birthplace of the ancient Games. Like those that came before it, Athens battled with whether to put its insistent urban modernity before a more obvious emphasis on antiquity. With the return of the Olympics to the city of both its ancient (776 B.C.) and modern (1896) foundations, Athens crafted itself a face that embraced both the old and the new. Mascots Phevos and Athena, for example, were designed to resemble ancient toys on exhibit in the National Archaeological Museum. At medal ceremonies, olive wreaths were placed on each medalist's head, presenting a problem for some as they went through customs on their way home. The archery competition and the conclusion of the marathon took place at Panathianaiko Stadium, site of the first modern Games in 1896. And while most of the track-and-field events were held at the ultramodern Olympic Stadium designed by Barcelona architect Santiago Calatrava, who also had several signature installations throughout Athens Olympic Park, the shot put returned the Games to Olympia, the place where sport began. Spectators stood (no bleachers or stadium seats were built), and tickets were free. Water was the only available concession. Indeed, the only dispensation made for modern times was that women competed and the athletes were clothed. Oh, and that the women's gold medalist tested positive for stanozolol and had her medal revoked days after the historic event took place. (Cheating, of course, was not new—the sixteen remaining pedestals in Olympia were funded by fines charged to cheaters in the ancient Games—but the drug certainly was.)

Athens was fabulous. The hype of terror and traffic kept crowds away, and it was a shame. The weather was perfect, the competition was good, the positive tests were few. There were, of course, the usual controversies: for example, the soap opera drama provided by Greek sprinter Konstantinos Kenteris, and the controversy surrounding Paul Hamm's gold medal in gymnastics. Even the Opening Ceremony had its own mild storm, when details of the performances were leaked to the public several days early by British journalist Euan Stretch of the *Daily Mirror*.[38] While some members of ATHOC, the Athens Olympic Committee, claimed that Stretch had no idea what he was talking about, they proceeded to revoke his Olympic media accreditation in retaliation, allegedly in conjunction with the IOC. And it turned out he was right about almost everything.

However, Stretch's leak was not the last battle the Athens Opening Ceremony would face. Indeed, the Athens Opening Ceremony has become further entrenched in our cultural worldview, as it is now part of the ongoing Federal Communications Commission (FCC) crackdown on contemporary American culture. In December 2004, NBC turned its tapes of the Opening Ceremony over to the FCC after the federal body claimed it had received complaints of indecency, which serve as the impetus for any FCC action to be taken.[39] On December 21, 2004, the FCC announced that anyone interested could verify the complaints on its Web site, where it had posted every complaint it received regarding NBC's coverage of Athens.

As we now know, nine complaints were posted. Many of them revolved around the Opening Ceremony, particularly the part in which a gigantic white Cycladic head, representative of art from around 2700 B.C., broke into pieces to expose a replica of a Kouros, or "youth," sculpture, representative of sixth-century Greek art designed to reflect the balance of the human form. "How could NBC be allowed to show the male genitalia on national television?" one e-mail queried. "First we had to be subjected to the breast of Janet Jackson in the Superbowl an [*sic*] now an even more gratuitous display of pornography an [*sic*] indecency during what was suppose [*sic*] to be another family viewing event."

Another e-mail referenced the part of the Opening Ceremony in which a giant lake unfolded in the infield, revealing a couple playing in the water while Eros, the god of love, flew overhead, followed by a procession of figures from Greek history, including a pregnant woman with a glowing belly.

The viewer complained that this had "nothing to do with Olympic tradition." Lost on this viewer, apparently, was the careful explanation by Bob Costas and Katie Couric that the pregnant woman represented Leto, who had sex with Zeus and then, because of Hera's wrath, could not find a place to give birth to her twins, Apollo and Artemis, and eventually gave birth at the edge of a pond.

Our Year of Indecency: Contemporary Conservatisms and the Global Community

This recent scuffle over indecency and the Athens Opening Ceremony follows, of course, the infamous Superbowl "Nipplegate" scandal, for which CBS got spanked with a fine of over half a million dollars. "Nipplegate" began what *New York Times* writer Frank Rich dubbed our "year of living indecently": "The political bosses of 'family' organizations, well aware that TV's collective wisdom becomes reality whether true or not, have been emboldened ever since," Rich wrote. "They are spending their political capital like drunken sailors, redoubling their demands that the Bush administration marginalize gay people, stamp out sex education and turn pop culture into a continuous loop of 'Rebecca of Sunnybrook Farm.'"[40]

According to the FCC, it was viewer e-mail, not conservative think tanks, that inspired the government body to go after CBS. However, what the FCC never revealed, but *Mediaweek* did, was that in 2003, 99.8 percent of all "indecency complaints" to the FCC came from the conservative watchdog Parents Television Council (PTC), and the same held true for 2004.[41] In a brilliant use of the Internet, the PTC almost single-handedly ensured that complaints to the FCC went from 350 in both 2000 and 2001, to 14,000 in 2002, to 240,000 in 2003, and to 1.1 million in 2004. The FCC takes action only when there are complaints. Yet it seems that only PTC members are complaining. In 2003, then FCC head Michael Powell went to Congress to declare that there had been "a dramatic rise in public concern and outrage about what is being broadcast into their homes."[42] In response to *Mediaweek*'s research, Powell claimed that the numbers did not matter, stating that the "source of that fact does not minimize the merits of the groups' concerns."[43] *San Francisco Chronicle* columnist Tim Goodman responded:

> Yes, it does matter. Because the FCC is supposed to be a sounding board for people who view a TV show, are upset about the content and seek a place to complain outside of the network that aired it. But the

process is being hijacked by people who in all likelihood aren't even watching the shows but are responding to a group that tells them the content is wicked. Meanwhile, thinking people with minds that actually open and function are not sending in e-mails to Powell that say, "I saw something I didn't think was appropriate for my kids, so I changed the channel. I handled it. No need to start a holy war about it. I'm looking forward to 'Deadwood' on HBO. You should TiVo it if you haven't already. Anyway, have a nice day."[44]

Goodman's response to Powell exemplified the red state/blue state "values" argument that dominated the political climate at the end of 2004. Goodman's solution? That "blue-staters" should get in on the action and send Michael Powell an e-mail that says: "On my television, I like violence. I like nudity. I like guns going off. I like people having sex. I like swearing. I like shows with gay people in them. I like shows where gay people have sex. I like shows where gay people shoot guns. And swear. . . . And I know how to turn my television off."[45]

The fact that only nine e-mails professed objections to NBC's Athens coverage does not matter in terms of FCC policy. For example, in October 2004, the FCC levied fines of over $1 million against Fox because of the reality program *Married by America*, claiming that 159 viewers complained about the program's content (but not concept), which included pixilated strippers. However, the FCC could only produce 90 of those 159 complaints, and it turned out that they came from only 23 individual viewers. Fox launched a counterattack on the FCC, charging that the fines needed to be withdrawn because in its own investigation, "all but four of the complaints were identical . . . and only one . . . professed even to have watched the program."[46]

A notable voice of sanity in the FCC's attack on NBC's Athens coverage has been none other than Gianna Angelopoulos, the president of ATHOC. In a commentary piece in the *Los Angeles Times*, Angelopoulos crystallized the complexities of an Olympic television broadcast: she argued that what the FCC's Olympic investigation targeted was not in fact an American broadcast but, rather, Greek culture and history themselves. The FCC investigation, posited Angelopoulos, dragged Greece into an American culture war by paying attention to nine people who complained about profanity, male organs, breasts, and sex, out of the 3.9 billion in the global Olympic audience. "If NBC is punished for airing our opening ceremonies—which in reality depicted Greek contributions to civilization—it would, in

effect, label a presentation of our culture on your airwaves as 'indecent,'"
Angelopoulos wrote. "We resent it, and I feel duty-bound to respond."[47]

In her response, Angelopoulos emphasized the difficulties Greece faced
holding the Games: a shortened schedule, gigantic security needs, doping. Despite all, few could disagree that the Greeks threw anything but
a great party. "For 17 triumphant days," Angelopoulos crowed, "the world
saw remarkable things that its athletes and we Greeks could accomplish."[48]
And the tone was set on the first day—the Opening Ceremony—before a
seated audience of 72,000 and a televised audience of billions. Rather than
obscenity, she countered, the Opening Ceremony

> presented the Greek origins of democracy, philosophy, theater, sport
> and the Olympic Games. In this context, we represented the Greek
> sculpture people see in museums, realistic human beings as God made
> them. We also showed a couple enjoying their love of the Greek sea. . . .
> And we told the history of Eros, the god of love. Turning love, yearn-
> ing and desire into a deity is an important part of our contribution to
> civilization.[49]

While her descriptions of the meanings of the various components of the
Opening Ceremony that were under fire from the FCC likely prove more
meaningful than most that had been made before, her conclusion struck
closest to the core, reading like a veiled warning to America in a moment
when its soldiers were abroad and its dollar held little worth in Europe:

> As Americans surely are aware, there is great hostility in the world
> today to cultural domination in which a single value system created
> elsewhere diminishes and degrades local cultures. There is also a vast
> and violent global culture war raging between the forces of modern-
> ism and fundamentalism, a battle whose outcome cannot be known.
> In this context, it is astonishingly unwise for an agency of the U.S. gov-
> ernment to engage in an investigation that could label a presentation
> of the Greek origins of civilization as unfit for television viewing.
>
> It is my hope that Americans will consider this advice: Don't punish
> NBC or Greece for accurately portraying Greek culture in your living
> rooms. In the past, the U.S. has been open to the world, incorporating
> the best it has to offer into its culture. Turning away from this tradi-
> tion would bring about a close-minded, fortress mentality that would
> endanger the U.S. and its relations with other countries. Accept us as
> we are. It's the decent thing to do.[50]

Approximately 203 million people watched NBC's coverage of Athens, making it the most widely viewed non-U.S. Summer Games in Olympic broadcast history, and according to one NBC spokesman, the network received "no such indecency complaints" during the Games.[51] Thus, regardless of the critical quality of the coverage, there is no doubt that NBC considers its coverage of Athens a success. The Olympics came to the United States around the clock from seven platforms (NBC, USA, MSNBC, CNBC, Bravo, Telemundo, and HDTV), averaging 70 hours a day for a record-breaking total of 1,210 hours—more than the coverage of the past five previous Summer Games combined. In short, for an August fortnight, 86 percent of all U.S. television households were watching the Olympic Games, meaning more people were watching the Olympics than were watching all the other networks combined.[52] And while the criticism always abounds for any Olympic broadcaster, NBC did a lot of things right: for the first time in history, all twenty-eight sports on the summer program were broadcast; Telemundo's coverage was the first non-English Olympic broadcast in history (indeed, Telemundo's 169.5 hours almost surpasses NBC's entire Atlanta broadcast), securing 13 million viewers, or 51 percent of all Hispanic households; and despite the seven-hour time difference, more live coverage came from Athens than from any previous Games.

What Would Lenny Do? Taking the Offensive in Making Meanings

While such numbers indicate that few people found the Games indecent, this does not mean that the Olympics—and their coverage—should be shielded from complaint. Just as it is preposterous to assume that banning steroids in baseball will make the playing field level, it is impossible not to critique the Games, albeit in a far different way than the FCC did. There is, certainly, much to criticize, and not only in terms of the revisionist histories presented in the pageantry of opening ceremonies. The familiar, academic critique? A classic neo-Marxist examination of the Games is that rather than put forth a fair playing field on which peace and equity are represented, the Olympics underpin social inequity at a global level. In this vein, many scholars have attacked the Games as part of a larger critique of sports in general: Sport creates a physically stronger workforce; promotes commercialization; and appeases the general population via athletic spectacle.[53]

But perhaps we should take a moment and consider how the Olympics might help us better determine what is truly indecent, even offensive. When

Lenny Bruce appeared on the *Steve Allen Show* on April 5, 1959, he said he was confused as to why he was considered "offensive"; he told the audience to think about segregation and Orval Faubus before they labeled a lowly comedian offensive.[54] And while we reside in a world in which more media show up for Michael Jackson than for the people of Darfur, consider the amount of space given to a debate regarding a classical representation of the human form, rather than highlight what the Olympics actually show us. Think of Ariel Zeevi, the Israeli judoka who won a bronze medal in Athens on the same day that members of the Black September Movement had, some thirty-two years earlier, killed eleven members of the Israeli team.[55] And consider that Zeevi won his medal only a few days after an Iranian judoka—a reigning world champion—decided that he would not compete against an Israeli opponent. Before carrying Iran's flag into the stadium for the Opening Ceremony, Arash Miresmaeili declared that he would withdraw from Olympic competition because his first match pitted him against Ahud Vaks. Iran refuses to recognize the state of Israel, and Iranian policy forbids Iran's athletes from engaging in athletic competition against Israelis. The Olympics, we continue to chant, are above politics— they transcend the world that they inhabit. But we know better, of course. Athletes enter the stadium according to national identity, wear colors that subscribe to a flag, and migrate toward sports that feed national traditions: Greeks lift weights, Kenyans run, Australians swim, and Koreans can shoot arrows like nobody's business. These are the assumptions that many athletes bolster, and others work to dispel. But the one assumption that we all make, and the one that makes the Olympics themselves work, is that if an athlete comes to the Games, he or she comes to compete, rather than choose who he or she will compete against.

Despite the atmosphere of terror that preceded the Athens Games, to which Athens responded with unprecedented security—gates, fences, guards, military checkpoints—to make those of us there feel safe, the city and its people could not protect any of us from the stance of Miresmaeili, a gold-medal favorite who went home without putting forth a gold-medal effort. The Olympics, then, perhaps above all, create the time and space to think about who we are, what we do, how we perceive others, and how they perceive us. They are flawed, certainly—plagued by doping and bribery scandals, marked by elitism and aristocracy, unequivocally dominated by industrialized nations, and containing a seemingly everlasting rivalry between communist (and former communist) athletes and the rest of the world. Yet despite all of this, the Olympic Games continue to achieve a global nature that is unparalleled, and while "global" should not automatically be translated as "good," there is something to be said for the kind of global experience one gains from just taking part, whether as an athlete or a spectator or, yes, a scholar. Sport serves as a stage with the potential for tremendous symbolic power. The Olympics, in particular, force global parameters upon its audience, as the IOC is faced with considering circumstances of the geopolitical arena in terms of international athletic competition: the Taliban, South African apartheid, and the independent identities of peoples from places like Puerto Rico, East Timor, and Palestine. Via the Olympic Games and the colossal television programming that accompanies them, the world gets a sense of what it looks like for some two hundred nations, wearing something representative of their identity, to come together. Taking part in an Olympics—whether as athlete, coach, spectator, or television researcher—is an experience that can convince one that the Olympic movement must continue through its flaws. Indeed, even the most cynical of the post-Marxist critics of the Olympics admit that while the Games might "reflect and reproduce extant social hierarchies," they can also serve to "challenge" them.[56]

And while I wonder what will transpire in Beijing just a few years away, and I continue to contextualize the events of Mexico City in many ways, what I absolutely understand, regardless of how jaded my academic training has made me, is that the events that transpire in a fortnight of international athletic competition should never be underemphasized, simplified, or dismissed merely as performative pomp and circumstance.

Notes

1   Peter Novick, *The Noble Dream: The "Objectivity Question" and the American Historical Profession* (Cambridge: Cambridge University Press, 1988), 1.
2   Eric Zolov, "The Harmonizing Nation," in *In the Game: Race, Identity, and Sports in the Twentieth Century*, ed. Amy Bass (New York: Palgrave, 2005).
3   R. Fensham, "Prime-time Hyperspace: The Olympic City a Spectacle," quoted in Drew Whitelegg, "Going for Gold: Atlanta's Bid for Fame," *International Journal of Urban and Regional Research* 24.4 (December 2000): 813; emphasis mine.
4   See Zolov, "The Harmonizing Nation."
5   Toni Morrison, "The Official Story: Dead Man Golfing," in *Birth of a Nation'hood: Gaze, Script, and Spectacle in the O. J. Simpson Case*, ed. Morrison and Brodsky Lacour (New York: Pantheon, 1997), xx.
6   Quoted in Amy Bass, *Not the Triumph but the Struggle: The 1968 Olympic Games and the Making of the Black Athlete* (Minneapolis: University of Minnesota Press, 2002), 235.

7   David Andrews, "Feminizing Olympic Reality: Preliminary Dispatches from Baudrillard's Atlanta," *International Review for the Sociology of Sport* 33.1 (1998): 6. Andrews uses Jean Baudrillard's Gulf War writings, in which he formulates the idea of "instant history TV," to analyze "the mass mediated spectacles which dominate American sporting culture," with a particular focus on NBC's strategies to obtain a female viewing audience for the Atlanta Games.

8   Ibid., 6.

9   John J. MacAloon, "Double Visions: Olympic Games and American Culture," in *The Olympic Games in Transition*, ed. Jeffrey O. Segrave and Donald Chu (Champaign: Human Kinetics, 1988), 279–80. See also MacAloon, *This Great Symbol: Pierre de Coubertin and the Origins of the Modern Olympic Games* (Chicago: University of Chicago Press, 1981).

10 Whitelegg, "Going for Gold," 801–2.

11 Jackie Hogan, "Staging the Nation: Gendered and Ethnicized Discourses of National Identity in Olympic Opening Ceremonies," *Journal of Sport and Social Issues* 27.2 (May 2003): 103.

12 Alan Tomlinson, "Carrying the Torch for Whom? Symbolic Power and the Olympic Ceremony," in *The Olympics at the Millennium: Power, Politics, and the Games*, ed. Kay Schaffer and Sidonie Smith (New Brunswick, NJ: Rutgers University Press, 2000), 171.

13 The mission of the nonprofit AAFLA is to "serve youth through sport and to increase knowledge of sport and its impact on people's lives. In addition to regional outreach and programming, it includes the Paul Ziffren Sports Resource Center, which is the largest sports research library in North America. Currently, the AAFLA endowment is approximately $133 million. See www.afla.org.

14 See Bass, *Not the Triumph but the Struggle*, xx, 308–10. Perhaps the closest historical correlation to make with the Opening Ceremony of an Olympic Games would be the pageantry and performance of the turn-of-the-century world fairs or the "Wild West" shows of the nineteenth century. See Robert Rydell, *All the World's a Fair: Visions of Empire at American International Expositions, 1875–1916* (Chicago: University of Chicago Press, 1984); Richard Slotkin, "Buffalo Bill's 'Wild West' and the Mythologization of the American Empire," in *Cultures of United States Imperialism*, ed. Amy Kaplan and Donald E. Pease (Durham, NC: Duke University Press, 1993), 219–36.

15 *Official Report of the Games of XXIIIrd Olympiad, 1984*, vol. 1, www.aafla.org/6oic/Official Reports/1984/1984vi.pdf (accessed April 21, 2005), digital page 230. Many thanks to Wayne Wilson at the Amateur Athletic Foundation of Los Angeles for his help finding this information.

16 Whitelegg, "Going for Gold," 803.

17 Ibid., 801.

18 Ibid., 803.

19 Quoted in ibid., 809. Georgia changed its state flag in 2001.

20 Ibid., 809.

21 Ibid., 810.

22 Hogan, "Staging the Nation," 103.

23 Bass, *Not the Triumph but the Struggle*, 348.

24 "Showbiz, Hype Reign at Opening Ceremonies," Sports Illustrated.com, July 19, 2004.

25 Tomlinson, "Carrying the Torch for Whom?" 169.

26 Sydney Games committee president Michael Knight, quoted in Lisa Meekison, "Whose Ceremony Is It Anyway? Indigenous Interests in the Festival of the Dreaming," in *The Olympics at the Millennium*, 187.

27 Quoted in ibid., 192.

28 Ibid., 188.

29 Linda Tenenbaum, "Image and Reality in Sydney's Olympic Opening Ceremony," World Socialist Website, September 22, 2000, www.wsws.org/articles/2000/sep2000/open-s22_prn.shtml.

30 Walter Benjamin, "On the Concept of History," in *Selected Writings*, vol. 4, ed. Howard Eiland and Michael W. Jennings (Cambridge, MA: Harvard University Press, 2003).

31 Stuart Hall, "The Question of Cultural Identity," in *Modernity and Its Futures: Understanding Modern Society*, ed. Stuart Hall et al. (Cambridge: Polity Press, 1993), 293.

32 Hogan, "Staging the Nation," 116.

33 Ibid., 104.

34 Rodriguez now trains with Placido Domingo at the Young Artists Program of the Washington Opera. See www.danielrodriguezmusic.com/ (accessed September 16, 2005).

35 Hogan, "Staging the Nation," 107.

36 Quoted in Pauline Arrillaga, "Games Get Going," Associated Press, February 9, 2002; emphasis mine.

37 Hogan, "Staging the Nation," 108.

38 Euan Stretch, "Olympic Stadium to Be Flooded for Opening," *Sunday Daily Mirror*, July 25, 2004.

39 Connor Ennis, "NBC Turns Over Tapes of Olympic Opening Ceremony to FCC after Complaint," SFgate.com, December 10, 2004.

40 Frank Rich, "The Year of Living Indecently," *New York Times*, February 6, 2005.

41 Tim Goodman, "Couch Potatoes, It's Time to Drop the Remote: E-mail the FCC. Stop the Parents Television Council before It Gets Beyond the TV," *San Francisco Chronicle*, December 13, 2004.

42 Quoted in Todd Shields, "Activists Dominate Content Complaints," Mediaweek.com, December 6, 2004.

43 Quoted in ibid.

44 Goodman, "Couch Potatoes, It's Time to Drop the Remote."

45 Ibid.

46 Quoted in Shields, "Activists Dominate Content Complaints."

47 Gianna Angelopoulos-Daskalaki, "Since When Is Greece's Culture Obscene?" *Los Angeles Times*, January 16, 2004.

48 Ibid.

49 Ibid.

50 Ibid.

51 Quoted in Lisa de Moraes, "Opening Ceremony: The IX Olympic Gripes," *Washington Post*, December 22, 2004.

52 "Most Watched Non-U.S. Summer Olympics in History," NBC Olympics Press Release, September 2004.

53 See Hogan, "Staging the Nation," 100–101, for an excellent overview of this perspective.

54 Lenny Bruce, "What Offends Me," *Steve Allen Show*, April 5, 1959, on *Lenny Bruce without Tears* (DVD, 2005).

55 Much of what follows I originally wrote as part of my online Olympic Diary in August 2004. See www.cnr.edu/CNR-olympics/cnr-olympics.html.

56 Hogan, "Staging the Nation," 101.

Keya Ganguly

Of Totems and Taboos:
An Indian's Guide to Indian Chiefs and
Other Objects of Fan Fascination

Over the years, we have worked closely with the
Seminole Tribe of Florida to ensure the dignity and
propriety of the various Seminole symbols we use.
Chief Osceola, astride his appaloosa when he plants
a flaming spear on the 50-yard line, ignites a furious enthusiasm and loyalty in thousands of football
fans, but also salutes a people who have proven that
perseverance with integrity prevails.
—Dale W. Lick (former president of Florida State University), "Seminoles—Heroic Symbol at Florida State,"
USA Today, May 18, 1993

Thinking back to my first day as a graduate instructor (now almost two decades ago), I
recall having that original moment of realization
about the unpredictability of teaching. I had
wrapped up my lecture and was preparing to
leave the classroom when a student came up to
me and something like the following exchange
took place:

> Student: Would you mind my asking what
> tribe you're from?
> Me: I beg your pardon?
> Student: You introduced yourself as Indian
> so I want to know which tribe you belong to.
> Me: Oh, I get it. Sorry, I'm from India but

The *South Atlantic Quarterly* 105:2, Spring 2006.
Copyright © 2006 by Duke University Press.

you're thinking of Indians who are not—from India or, as a matter of
fact, Indian.
Student: Say what?
Me: Actually, it's all an error of cartography—mapmaking, you know.
Columbus got it wrong.
Student: I see [revealing clearly by his expression that he did not].
Me: Well, indigenous people from this country are more properly re-
ferred to as Native Americans and they are the ones who belong to spe-
cific tribes . . .

My student departed somewhat disappointed and, it seemed, without
actually seeing anything. In retrospect, he could hardly be blamed for his
confusion, one that continues to be shared by many in this land of the free
and home of the brave(s).[1] It is still not considered a problem to refer to
Native Americans as Indians, since the original cartographic slippage has
now passed from history into custom, even among Native Americans. The
dead weight of bad mapmaking no longer troubles anyone, and the issue
of cultural sensitivity is only raised if the name-calling takes a more explicitly racist turn—when indigenous Americans are referred to as Red Indians, Redskins, or Red Men, perhaps. However, within the discourse of organized sports in this country, even names like these are perfectly acceptable;
they are routinely uttered in the media as well as by fans, with no one feeling the least need to lower their voice. The stakes are simply too high and
habits too naturalized for either cartographic or racial sensitivity to matter in this arena, making it possible to recognize what Pierre Bourdieu had
so acutely observed about social mores: that concessions of politeness are
always concessions of power. Within the extravagantly orchestrated, exorbi-
tantly financed arena of sports spectacles and spectatorship—whose limits
are simultaneously set by public visibility and private (or at least privatized)
sentiment—politeness predictably reverts to power. Consequently, sensi-
tivities born out of embarrassment over geographical blindness or, for that
matter, the genocidal history of the United States do not detain anyone.
With barely a wink and a nod, ceteris can be paribus, so to speak, and things
remain the same as they always have been. In fact, for sports culture to function as an integral component of the national imaginary, it is crucial that
the past be transformed into a mythic time when all things were proper and
in place, history itself notwithstanding.

   In the cornfields of Champaign, Illinois, where I attended graduate
school, the stakes of maintaining a pristine image of the past, to go along

with the discourse of loyalty to alma mater, remain as high now as they were twenty years ago (and more); they certainly supersede any history or geography lesson, let alone ideology critique, we as teachers might offer the student/fan body. When it really matters, as it does with Fighting Illini home games (particularly in high-profile events such as football and men's basketball), the kid gloves come off and the spectacle of Chief Illiniwek comes on. The official mascot of the U of I's athletic program continues to fascinate the faithful with his leaping, jumping, cavorting rendition—in face paint and full regalia—of "his" tribal dance, rousing spectators and willing donors at halftime during games with his putatively respectful obeisance to a now-disappeared tribe. Within the university community and increasingly within the regulatory circles of the National Collegiate Athletic Association (NCAA), significant debate exists—with attendant university resolutions, court cases, and legal challenges—over the use of a racial mascot.[2] Supporters insist that Chief Illiniwek is a "symbol" of the university and, in the words of one administrator, even an "ambassador." By contrast, Illinois's Departments of Anthropology and English have issued statements that deplore the racist nature of this image, with the anthropologists remarking on the historical inaccuracy of portraying the Illini (who were mostly farmers, hunters, and traders) dressed up for a war dance in the costume of a Sioux warrior from a Plains Indian tribe. Their statement points out that this is akin to "representing Italians or Germans with someone dressed in a Scottish kilt and playing the bagpipes."[3] The total ignorance that most people evince about Native American culture is, moreover, heightened by claims that the spectacle of the "chief" honors rather than denigrates Native traditions, claims that the English department refutes in its own published position on the issue:

> We would not honor African Americans by having a Booker T. Washington imitator provide halftime entertainment; we would not honor Asian Americans by having someone in an emperor costume dance before cheering crowds; we would not honor Latina and Latino Americans by having a César Chavez imitator put on a mariachi costume and dance at athletic events; we would not honor concentration camp victims by having someone dress up as a rabbi and do splits at halftime; and we would not honor Catholics by having a student dress up as a pope and perform with miter and incense.[4]

In the to-and-fro on the politics of representation surrounding Illinois's mascot, one recognizes something peculiarly overdetermined—layering the history of imperialism, American territorial expansion, and the discourse of domination in a way that makes the hybridized and conflated image of the "Fighting Illini" peculiarly vexed. It is not the same with, say, the "Vikings," the "Spartans," or even the "Fighting Irish," even if the latter examples of mascots are no more authentic, respectful, or true to the traditions they aspire to lay claim to than the first. But "Indians," perhaps more than anybody else in this country, represent "the splinter in the eye"—the irritant that Theodor Adorno aphorized as the "best magnifying glass"—to the extent that their historical erasure from the mainstream exposes any talk of honoring their traditions as the lie that resides at the base of the ideology of pluralism.[5]

At any rate, the deployment of a figure whose antics on the sports field have less to do with Native American dances and ritual performances than with circus acts and Wild West shows has brought, in equal measure, protests from student government organizations and activists on campus as well as predictable outcries from entrenched administrators and right-wing students against "political correctness" and liberal guilt about crimes safely relegated to the past. Presumably, having committed those, it would be better simply to get on with it without worrying too much about reparations of any sort, including symbolic ones. That, at least, seems to be the thinking of the university's trustees, president, and sports boosters as well as the Illinois state legislature—all of whom have stepped in to maintain the status quo on this issue. Their often contradictory justifications shift from asserting that "Chief Illiniwek" does indeed represent an authentic "Indian" tradition to the toss-off attempt at sophistry in saying that he does not—because it would be impossible, in any case, for a representation of the university to speak on behalf of the tribe. Regardless of such fine-tunings of the rationale proffered by the institution, the rhetorical emphasis is insistently on how "honor" and "tradition" and not stereotype or debasement accompany the imagery of the chief.[6]

The question of authenticity is of course always vexed, but it is particularly charged when the traditions at stake have died out through suppression and systematic eradication. Aside from this, to pose the matter in terms of authenticity is to operate on the misplaced grounds of the real, as if the concern rested on actual and verifiable traditions that were either being observed or flouted in any particular instance of appropriation. Rather, the customs surrounding mascot worship in general (even when they do not relate to stereotypes of Native Americans) are more appropriately seen in bifurcated terms: on the one hand, in relation to the hold that fantasy and myth have on lives lived under the shadow of advertising; on the other, in terms of the displaced abjection that allows those with very little power to shore up their sense of self vis-à-vis the less fortunate, be they animals or humans—albeit these totemic figures have to be both appeased and controlled.

This is at the crux of my exploration of totems and taboos. Although it is perhaps obvious from what has already been said, I should note that my discussion here is restricted to the implications of team mascots within collegiate sports, and my references are all to examples of Division I institutions within the NCAA. This focus is shaped in part by my own amateur fascination with college sports culture in the United States and also in part by a scholarly interest in the curious disjunction in the ways that team sports and team mascots signify: as localized sites in the panoply of mass culture of the exterior and interior of life under late capitalism. For if it is amply evident that the teams themselves symbolize the outward and public face of a semiprofessional scheme of moneymaking and brand marketing for universities with highly profitable athletic programs, team mascots betoken what can only be described as interiorized and residual examples of totem worship—now equally transmogrified under the regime of the commodity into brand objects. Nevertheless, they reveal very different, even premodern styles of kinship attachments.

My point is certainly not to suggest that team mascots function as noncommodified traces of the premodern within postmodern forms of consumption; to do so would be to advance an entirely undialectical view of how the past and present congeal in the production of reified forms of value. To the contrary, my objective is to explore the reasons for psychic and social attachments to outlandish and infantile mascots—ranging from eagles, gamecocks, and blue hens to chanticleers, demons, terrapins, and warriors (as well as any number of other phantasmatic objects from the animal and spirit world). Conventionally associated with totem worship, such attachments convey something concrete about the afterlife of practices from an extinct mode of social organization no longer pertinent to existence in late capitalism. As ritual practices, these attachments now have to be reconsolidated along different ideological lines in order for them to retain a "proper," that is to say efficient or rationalized, place within contemporary life. But this ideological reconfiguration also makes a reversal of perspective possible, allowing one to turn a metropolitan preoccupation into an ethnographic object. In corollary fashion, this permits reading the all-too-familiar spectacle of sports mascots (evident in everything ranging from graphics on T-shirts and clothing to sideline performances on football fields and pep rallies) by the unfamiliar light of primitive totem worship. Nominally intended to function as little more than playful, if commercialized, emblems of team spirit and sports fandom, these mascots demonstrate not only the continuing expenditure of affective labor in the production of "normal" subjects as fans but also expose marks of the rationalization of the psyche itself.

Propositions about the commodification of consciousness have these days come to be accepted almost axiomatically, but not enough attention has been paid to the everyday mechanisms by which consciousness is so transformed. My examination of the meanings of the largely superficial though deeply felt celebrations of "mascotry" can thus be seen as an attempt to enlarge on those everyday dimensions by which mascot worship channels the tenuous hold of celebrants on the reality surrounding them into ersatz configurations of belongingness, identity, and, above all, institutional "tradition." After all, this is what it means to be a fan.

In terms of my theoretical framework, let me note that while the literature on the culture industry, commodity fetishism, or reification is entirely relevant, I will instead use Sigmund Freud's ideas about totemism to work out my propositions regarding why mascots matter.[7] One of the reasons for relying on Freud is that it allows me to emphasize the component of race and the specific repertoire of racialized imagery distinguishing Freud's own system of thinking about the past of the unconscious and the unconscious of the past. Of course, the discourse of sports mascots evinces a lot more than racialized images since, aside from braves and warriors, there are animal mascots whose names practically run the gamut of the alphabet—from anteaters to wolverines. In some cases mascots also take the form of animated objects with no resemblance (however stereotyped) to living beings. Such is the case with Duke University's Blue Devils or Wake Forest's Demon Deacons as well as with the less-well-known Angels of Meredith College in North Carolina, the Athenas of a trio of small colleges in California, or the Argonauts of West Florida. Still, the overcharged implications of using Native American imagery sharpen rather than restrict the analysis in that they serve as a modality for expressing more general dilemmas of human sociality vectored into mascot worship, and here Freud's ideas are particularly relevant in an overarching sense.

Freud's project in *Totem and Taboo* centered on reconstructing "the moment when the human animal became human," and this reconstruction was consistent with his overall arguments about the ways that religion and civilization work as forces of interdiction—preventing "man" from lapsing into both a childish and prehistoric state where only instinct and impulse rule. But the interdiction, specifically against incest and the killing of the father, is for Freud best illustrated by the recourse of "primitive peoples of Australia, America and Africa" to animated objects or totems, which only later manifest themselves within modern societies in the form of the various illusions and delusions of civilization. So, although the core of Freud's enterprise is to connect the modern with the primitive without implying a necessary value hierarchy, the fact of the matter is that racialized Others (such as his references to Polynesians, the Bantu, and Zulus) function only as the "prehistoric" if fetishized basis for his delineation of such things as the Oedipal conflict and ego formation. Indeed, the entire Freudian architecture surrounding such concepts as disavowal, fetishism, and totem worship—as well as the prohibitions they underwrite—expresses the specific nature of bourgeois, European anxieties about "the primitive," anxieties that must be managed at different levels and well into the present even though we have all been trained to accept and even celebrate "difference."

Although it is not quite a parallel matter, we have become accustomed to hearing that Marxist theories and, particularly, the Frankfurt school's analysis of the culture industry have ignored the question of race. This has been the rap against the Eurocentrism of critical theory, although the charge is less substantive than one might at first imagine (since the most influential thinkers in the Marxist tradition both within and outside the specific orbit of the Frankfurt school were, in fact, preoccupied throughout with the role of racial exploitation in capitalist development). Still, much of the analytic force, enormously substantial though it is, of theories of reification (such as that of Marx himself of Georg Lukács) or the culture industry (Adorno and Max Horkheimer, Ernst Bloch, or Herbert Marcuse) stems not so much from denying the question of racial formation as from subsuming it under the generalized category of alienation, both spiritual and material. Within this mode of analysis, existence in late capitalism represents the ongoing process of forcing human beings into different forms of slavery—racialized in some instances, but class-defined across the board.

By contrast, the "nuclear complex" that Freud proposed to uncover as the principles guiding the psychoanalysis of culture contains the ideology of race at the very heart of its elaboration of modern subject formation, although his uncovering mostly expresses itself as a double disavowal. First, Freud disavows the extent to which his self-professed "partiality for the prehistoric" could not but inflect his theorization of totem worship. For in stressing that ontogeny recapitulates phylogeny, Freud compressed human development into a linear schema; he also produced a set of structural equivalences among children, neurotics, and "primitives" whose negative charge is not disturbed even and perhaps especially given his own fascination with modernity's other. The enormous avidity with which Freud collected artifacts from the non-Western world (and which completely dominated his work space, as one can glimpse in photographs of his house in Vienna) expresses the highly personal and somewhat clandestine pleasure he derived from animated objects whose provenance inevitably remained mysterious for him. In an entirely compensatory move, he deployed these objects in a distanced and "scientific" manner to explain the structural function of pleasure and punishment in bourgeois society but without an adequate explanation for his compulsive detours through the other. This speaks to the second and more culturally determined (rather than psychological) aspect of Freud's disavowal: Nowhere does he reckon with the historical, political, and economic motivations underlying the ways that distorted views of non-European peoples and cultures completely haunt European self-understanding. And this is perhaps especially—and ironically—true when one is attempting to be reflexive about the conditions of knowledge production (as was Freud himself). Race, we might say, functions as the lever of the European cognitive apparatus despite the fact that psychoanalytic criticism has always chosen to hypostatize the role of sexuality.

Mainstream American culture, representing as it does an outgrowth of the earlier self-formation across the Atlantic, continues to replay older contradictions of ideology and the unconscious. Accordingly, contemporary mascot worship to this day teeters between the ability of its practitioners (fans, in other words) to repress their convictions about racial others and their own sanctioned though heavily circumscribed lapses into rituals associated with "primitive" peoples unshackled by the niceties of civilization. So at the very moment that the former president of a university that employs a racist symbol—a "Seminole chief"—defends the practice (as illustrated by the epigraph at the beginning), he symptomatically betrays the ways that totemic identifications and restrictions define his assertions about Florida State's commitment to cultural sensitivity. An entire complex of desires

and fears associated with underlying sexual taboos (against incest, specifically) which, in Freud's delineation, have now gone underground, reappear
in the all too revealingly named Lick's utterances about the team mascot,
"Chief Osceola" —sitting "astride his appaloosa," planting "flaming spears,"
and "igniting" enthusiasm (as well as who knows what else!).

Such incitement to energetic masculinity aside, Lick also invokes the
"dignity" and "perseverance" of the Seminole nation as a spur to inculcating habits of hard work and achievement among mainstream spectators of
the chief's performance, although one might well suggest that the goal of
learning from and about Native Americans would be better served by an academic department on campus devoted to Native American Studies (Florida
State does not have one). On its Web site the institution boasts the offices
of "Seminole Torchbearers" and "Seminole Boosters" (as well as an African Studies program, an Asian Studies program, and a Latin American and
Caribbean Studies department), but in Tallahassee, apparently, the place to
be educated about Seminole history and culture is the fifty-yard line on a
Saturday afternoon during college football season. Also, as is often the case
with university administrators who have to cater to multiple constituencies,
Lick's speech is characteristic of the sort of "spin doctoring" that accompanies cynical efforts to be seen as saying a lot without saying anything at
all. Because Lick has to address himself less to academic interlocutors (no
doubt considered burdened by liberal qualms) than to trustees, legislators,
and, above all, donors unburdened by anything other than the warm glow of
school spirit and championship trophies, his rhetoric is rendered ambiguous in ways that exceed its fetishistic undertones.

What I mean to indicate is that Lick's attempt to adduce propriety betrays
a different kind of linguistic ambiguity. In the statement quoted at the top,
he asserts that the use of the Seminole mascot "salutes a people who have
proven that perseverance with integrity prevails." But this phrase leaves
the reader puzzling over whether perseverance *and* integrity are the overarching values being advanced or whether, by contrast, integrity is in such
short supply that the folks at Florida State have to be exhorted to persevere
with it, lest it slip away. Moreover, it is unclear precisely how the chief's
appearance and performance at Florida State sporting events proves anything about perseverance or integrity. This is where the "spin" resides, since,
as in traditional forms of totem worship, the declaration about boons and
benefits—with regard to the payoff from perseverance, integrity, and so
forth—has both a constative and performative value. To put it another way,

witch doctors and university presidents alike can call on the regenerative and redemptive powers associated with totems; indeed, totemic forces need only be invoked, not proved, since there is no denying their truth or efficacy. Although here deployed as the instrument of cynical reason, Lick's statements—about why the chief's actions on a sports field amid drunken and boisterous spectators betoken the ethical and moral values of the Seminole tribe—are to be taken at face value, in the same way that animated objects are supposed, in the Freudian schema, to have functioned for traditional totem worshipers.

If we want to avoid the trap of developmentalism, we can only assume that motives of power are as relevant to a diagnosis of Lick's statements as they are to understanding totemic practices of traditional societies from the past. Although we are more apt to suspect Lick of being disingenuous (given the institutional interests he represents), there is no reason to think that earlier forms of totemic invocation and injunction were any less pressured by motivations of money and power. Even if those constraints took different forms, it is more than merely a formal analogy to suggest that totemic practices then and now are both driven by fungible values that reflect particular cultures of belief. To impute naive faith to the traditional totem clan and canny or cynical motives to today's practitioner is to lapse into a suspicious teleology based on the assumption that traditional societies and peoples are less sophisticated and more gullible than contemporary subjects disenchanted with civilization.[8] Instead, we ought to be able to say that the recalibration of the magic of words—from serving supernatural gods to corporate and commercial ones—provides the basis of the parallel between past and present. In either case, the undecidable calculation is about whether the mascot/totem is an auratic emblem of belief structures or a banal instrument of the structure of power. Or both.

Let me turn to a few more specifics of what Freud, in his elaboration of totemism, calls the "psychical continuity in the sequence of generations" (511). Such psychic regeneration is, I submit, crucial to understanding why in an age of privatized and detached existence—featuring suburban (and sometimes gated) homes, Internet banking, faceless communication, and iPod entertainment—there is an imperative to rally around a team mascot. Within college sports, public and visible rituals abound, ranging from rhythmic chants of "Let's go, Illini" to the "tomahawk chop" of the Seminole fans, not to mention the orchestrated infantilism of the "Cameron Crazies" at Duke's home games or the equally orchestrated if apparently spontaneous uniformity of clothing choices among Kentucky Wildcat and Kansas Jayhawk fans. To these examples one could add a myriad others: With very few exceptions, college sports enthusiasts seem to feel the urge to express their solidarity, continuity, and, perhaps what is ultimately curious, complete lack of differentiation from other members of the club/clan, in terms of the same predictable behaviors. Freud elaborates such behavior as follows: "In particular important circumstances the clansman seeks to emphasize his kinship with the totem by making himself resemble it externally, by dressing up in the skin of the animal, by incising a picture of the totem upon his own body, and so on" (484). This would help to explain why, in a society where everyone is compelled to declare their individualism and edge over fellow citizens (who are also their competitors), giving voice to "team spirit" involves returning to a "primitive" norm of imitation and camouflage—as if sports were the last refuge of spirit itself, an escape from the otherwise incessant demand to be different.

Needless to say, these latter-day rituals of disguising themselves as their totems no more protect their practitioners from experiencing the vicissitudes of fate—victory or defeat in a game as much as success at school or climbing the ladder at work—than did the tests of loyalty and legitimacy undertaken by totemic societies of the past. Nor do these rituals escape being reified just because they embody private attachments. Reification is, after all, the process by which one comes to accept the gradual fragmentation and division of labor within the psyche as the latter is retrained and reprogrammed to conform to the dictates of "administered life" (to echo a phrase from the lexicon of the Frankfurt school). Consequently, the intense investment in animated objects that are, on the one hand, no more than brand markers and, on the other, signs of the transgressive potential of communal longing represents the degree to which modern subjects live under the threat of being cast out as weak or inadequate, their most punctuated and voluble expressions of enjoyment tinged with the fear of not subscribing to whatever fantasy of kinship is serviced by team loyalty and mascotry. As the inimitable line from Bertolt Brecht's poem "Die neuen Zeitalter" ("New Ages") reminds us, "The new meat is eaten with the old forks," and so it is that contemporary anxieties replay superstitious compulsions that psychoanalysis would have us consign to other times and places.

In Freud's own writing on totemism, he is somewhat ambiguous about the explanation for totemic objects and the behaviors associated with worshiping them. As one might expect, at one level his primary explanation resides with the injunction against incest—members of a clan acquire an aversion to incestuous practices via the taboos against killing or harming the totem. But at another level, Freud is content to follow prior theorists of totem worship (chiefly, one Salomon Reinach) who, in 1900, proposed a "code du totémisme." In this largely sociological code, sexuality recedes from the field of vision, leaving totemism to be regarded as "nothing more than 'une hypertrophie de l'instinct social'"—as Freud quotes Reinach (486). Read along these lines, the celebration of team mascots can very well be seen as a particular manifestation of this hypertrophy of the social instinct. In the face of the atrophy of meaningful social relations outside an economy of fiscal exchange, there is little else to turn to. Such a sociological reading also makes it possible to relieve contemporary sports mascot worship of having to be understood in exclusively sexualized terms—since even for Freud (although perhaps not all his followers) the unconscious has dimensions that exceed a single source or explanation. Granting the usefulness of Reinach's argument, Freud mentions its similarity to the one proposed by Emile Durkheim (in his *Elementary Forms of Religion: The System of Totemism in Australia*, published in 1912), where the totem is "the visible representative of social religion among the races concerned; it embodies the community, which is the true object of their worship" (487).

With the idea that totems are embodiments of the community, we come closer to the core of describing both the fancifulness of totem worship as represented by sports mascots in general, and the particular shading this receives in the impulse to hold on to an image that is racially charged, but only ambivalently so. For, notwithstanding all the talk so far about clan membership, as it turns out there are no teams in the NCAA whose mascot is a Ku Klux Klansman; nor is there any group of fans whooping it up with "Niggers" or "Babes," much less a Christ figure or a rabbi. If, to recollect the statement by U of I's English department, celebrating a Native American figure in the name of honoring the past is dubious because the logic governing this practice can be shown to be so limiting and limited as to be fallacious, it is also the case that one can "safely" confess to a form of pleasure for which no sanction exists any longer. The "Indians" (at least the ones we can fantasize about) are all dead; they have been extirpated, returning only to take the forms and names of mascots, cars, and trucks (such as Chippewas, Pontiacs, or Cherokees). Obviously this is not to accept a worldview in which Native Americans no longer exist to struggle and sometimes flourish. Rather, it is to ventriloquize the inherently dominative ideology whose most racist articulation takes the form of the "joke" that the "best Indian is a dead Indian." Within the terms of this ideology, "Indians" can return as objects of attachment whose images have been cleaned up and cleaned out of any association with history—leaving behind only the aura of timelessness, speed, and guilt-free victory.[9]

In an apartheid society such as ours, cathecting onto objects that are not similarly safe and that continue to pressure the pulse of the social body requires greater revelation of fear and desire, revelations that take the guilt-free discharge of energy out of play and reinsert the subject into a zone of us and them, good and evil, right and wrong. The factual presence of unsafe objects such as Klansmen, African Americans, or homosexuals prevents them from being transformed into divine though extinct objects of affection. They risk exposing much more about that which is disavowed no less than that which is *actively prohibited*, not merely passively inhibited. The social tensions surrounding the denigration of blacks, gays, and women (to take three representatives of visible minorities in mainstream society) are simultaneously on the surface and deeply unresolved. Their power, therefore, has to do with their actuality—with a presence within the sociopolitical matrix that cannot be conjured up without reality threatening it. By contrast, braves and warriors as well as a variety of creatures from the animal kingdom and spirit world no longer inhabit the same space as those who take over their forms. Anthropomorphism thus manifests itself as anthropophagism.

I once found myself on an airplane next to a man whose company regularly sponsors the annual NCAA basketball tournament (otherwise known as "March Madness"). A privileged employee, he was flying around the country—courtesy of his employer—watching his favorite college team play against several opponents and in various venues as they went through several rounds of the men's championship (he was, as a matter of fact, from Chicago and hence an Illinois supporter, although our being seated next to each other was purely serendipitous). Judging by this man's excitement about "his team," I would have to classify him as a bona fide fan; and going by the merchandized imagery of Chief Illiniwek he sported on his clothing, he was also a mascot worshiper, his loyalty displayed without hesitation or restraint and, indeed, with pride. At the end of the day, no educated guesses are really needed as to why someone would put up with the irritations that accompany air travel, budget hotels, and fast food, not to mention traffic jams outside sporting venues, just to be able to say he was courtside, screaming and yelling on behalf of his team. For him, this represented a sanctioned reward and an escape from work—which most people find repetitious and monotonous even in the upper echelons of corporate life, making every day seem like any other, without reprieve.

The carving up of space and time in the working day attests to infinite segmentation and, somewhat paradoxically, to infinite attenuation as well (in that one's tasks do not end and are not differentiated in meaningful ways). Given a scheme of work and leisure in which there is uncertainty about where one ends and the other begins, participating in the highly orchestrated and finely calibrated spatiotemporal exercise known as "game time" may be the only way to substantially demarcate quality from quantity, renovation from repetition. So even if the rituals of spectatorship and performance that are performed at each sporting event appear the same to an outsider, to a fan the distinction resides in an actual difference collectively enacted: with a win or a loss. This represents perhaps the means and ends of the fans' fascination with teams, mascots (in whatever form), and, ultimately, themselves. Outside the discourse of sports, few arenas remain in everyday life where one can report being a loser without, as it were, a total loss of face; by the same token, winning at all costs turns out to have few rewards to satisfy one's affective needs. Both the pleasures and anxieties of being a sports fan—and of investing in ritually uninhibited acts of spectatorial excess—turn on the head of this pin, for in this realm the reality of winning and losing can be managed and accepted in ways that are denied elsewhere.

Let me return for a final look at Freud's problematic homology linking childhood, the primitive past, and neurosis, to derive some final ideas about actions and inhibitions. In keeping with the comparison he draws between primitive men and neurotics, Freud emphasizes that "the sharp contrast that *we* make between thinking and doing is absent in both of them. But neurotics are above all *inhibited* in their actions: with them the thought is a complete substitute for the deed. Primitive men, on the other hand, are *uninhibited*: thought passes directly into action. With them it is rather the deed that is a substitute for the thought" (513; emphasis in the original). If we set aside the untenable equation of neurotics and primitives (on the self-critical grounds that although we know what the former looks like, we may be hard-pressed to unearth "primitive man"), Freud's underlying proposition may still have something to offer. Neurotics, Freud says, are inhibited in their actions, living largely by avoiding action and escaping into the mind. By contrast, Freud sees primitive men as uninhibitedly driven to act. For each, there is a substitution that occurs: thought for action in the former, action for thought in the latter. Curiously enough, this represents the exact structure of motivations for teams, mascots, and fans, respectively; each is sustained by mutually identifying with the others. However, the only ones who do not act, at least in any meaningful, goal-driven way, are the fans. Rather, their expenditure of labor is mostly affective, taken up as it is almost exclusively and even obsessively just with thoughts about mimicry, celebration, winning, and losing. Active engagement in the latter two would actually demand intense physical labor as well as the kind of skill that fans can only substitute with their own energetic though inadequate forms of obeisance to the mascot and team. Thus it should come as no surprise that "we" fans (as opposed to any primitive others) are the ones akin to neurotics: In fact, we *are* the neurotics, for whom little else is available other than the dissipated and hence inactive charge of investing our hopes and fears into animated objects.

With this I come to my final observations on the discourse of sports mascots in American society. For someone such as myself (who grew up in India as an avid and passionate fan of cricket and soccer), the transfer of affection and attachment demanded by my own spectatorship of sports culture here has required a different set of ideological transformations as well. If this country's Declaration of Independence insists on "life, liberty, and the pursuit of happiness" as "inalienable rights," such a declaration is possible only in this place. And, as far as one can tell, this has not always proved to be a good thing. Nowhere else in the world do people expect happiness as a right (even if that word is only a euphemism for money and material acquisitions). Many people elsewhere expect to be unhappy; some even prefer it. This was certainly true in India (although things are changing there too in the postliberalization era) and, because one did not think that happiness was the only acceptable outcome of life, one was better prepared for the slings and arrows of outrageous fortune—even, as in the context of this discussion, when it came to sports. So it is that India, the largest democracy in the world, routinely sends contingents to the Olympics whose only glory is to have participated; so it is also that the Indian cricket team sends its fans into fits over snatching defeat from the jaws of victory; and so, moreover, is being a fan about the expectation of loss—making a win a matter of national (rather than individual) achievement. But even on its own terms, the pursuit of happiness in this country seems to override an actual expectation of it, increasingly rendering that expectation into a mere promissory note.

What I have learned is that as a fan who now resides here, my expectation about winning (and its corollary, happiness) is my right; but this is largely true of expectations alone, as actual rights continue to be eroded in the name of some other false god equally capable of producing inhibition and fear among the natives. Thus, to complete the Freudian loop, if the contemporary sports fan and mascot worshiper expects to be made happy by the actions of the team and the antics of the totem, he also expects to be inhibited in most other spheres of activity, both public and private. As we have seen all along, in spectatorship no less than in other arenas, what is safe is what is preferred; the substitution of action by thought also functions to substitute the possibility of real thinking with arrested fixations. This is what, in a completely different discussion about cricket and national culture, the Trinidadian critic C. L. R. James once described as "the welfare state of mind."[10]

Using this coinage—conflating the idea of a welfare state in which life is promised as a series of entitlements with the notion of a state of mind—James zeroes in on the difference between the experience of cricket in the West Indies (understood as a profoundly intellectual as well as proud nationalist practice) and English cricket, particularly of the 1950s and 1960s. West Indian cricket is, for James, a national cultural treasure, the West Indian crowd a sort of "collective intellectual"—what Neil Lazarus calls, in his highly suggestive explication of James's fascination with cricket, "the knowing possessor of national culture."[11] English cricket is, by contrast, characterized by vulgarity—the expectation of winning overriding every other consideration of creative stroke play, dynamic bowling, and daring field placements. A "safety first" ethic comes to define English cricket—under challenge from its former colonies—and the "welfare state of mind" sets in.[12] Although there is a great deal more to be said about national-cultural differences in analyzing global sports in ways that well exceed the scope of this discussion, there are obvious similarities as well in the structures of feeling in the imperium. So I wanted to end with this provocation of a welfare state of mind, because to the extent that the contemporary American state is moving farther and farther away from any conception of social entitlements under a welfare state (except for the rich), it promotes—through its corporate intermediaries—a passive sensibility among its sports enthusiasts. Their lives may be subject to the utter volatility of the stock market, but their fan(atic) attachments are contained safely within ceremonial shows of power, bravery, and totemic adventure.

Notes

1 Several Web sites attest to the growing debate among Native American activists (and their antagonists) over the misperception and stereotyping of Native Americans resulting from their use as sports mascots; see, for instance, www.bluecorncomics.com/mascots.htm (accessed May 25, 2005).

2 On August 5, 2005, the National Collegiate Athletic Association ruled against the use of "hostile and abusive" nicknames or imagery by teams participating in postseason championships. This ruling was immediately challenged by the institutions at whom it was directed, resulting in its retraction and modification. The debate over the meaning of mascots has thus been front-page news in recent months. One of the few instances where the representational politics of Native American mascots has been explored in detail is in C. Richard King and Charles Freuhling Springwood, eds., *Team Spirits: The Native American Mascots Controversy* (Lincoln: University of Nebraska Press, 2001).

3 This statement can be viewed at www.anthro.uiuc.edu/Department/ChiefIlliniwek.htm (accessed May 31, 2005).

4 The English department protest can be viewed at www.english.uiuc.edu/ -announcements-/statement_illiniwek.html (accessed May 31, 2005).

5 Theodor Adorno, *Minima Moralia: Reflections from Damaged Life*, trans. E. F. N. Jephcott (London: Verso, 1974 [1951]), aphorism set 29, p. 50.

6 Several news stories have featured the controversy surrounding the particular use of an "Indian" mascot by the University of Illinois. The following is an example from the student newspaper on campus: www.illinimedia.com/di/feb_99/feb5/news/feature.html (accessed May 31, 2005).

7 For my citations of Freud, I have for the sake of convenience relied on *The Freud Reader*, ed. Peter Gay (New York: W. W. Norton, 1989). The extract from *Totem and Taboo* (first published as a set of papers in 1913) appears on 481–513.

8 Johannes Fabian's *Time and the Other: How Anthropology Creates Its Object* (New York: Columbia University Press, 1983) remains the most pointed critique of developmentalist thinking, which he sees as a form of "allochronism" or the placement of objects of knowledge downstream in time.

9 Objects have always been endowed with mythological valences. The most powerful analysis of the mythologizing tendency of humans remains Roland Barthes's *Mythologies* (New York: Hill and Wang, 1995 [1957]). A more recent book that attempts to take up the cultural study of modern myth is Kristin Ross's *Fast Cars, Clean Bodies: Decolonization and the Reordering of French Culture* (Cambridge, MA: MIT Press, 1986). Ross provides a vivid analysis of the cultural transformations in post–World War II France, whose contradictions included the drive to modernization (hence fast cars, washing machines, and so on) as well as its obverse: a return to a pure culture and time not defiled by foreign contamination.

10 This is the title of a chapter in C. L. R. James, *Beyond a Boundary* (Durham, NC: Duke University Press, 1993). See also Neil Lazarus, *Nationalism and Cultural Practice in the Postcolonial World* (Cambridge: Cambridge University Press, 1999).

11 Neil Lazarus, "Cricket, Modernism, National Culture," in *Nationalism and Cultural Practice in the Postcolonial World*, 190.

12 This is mostly a paraphrase of Lazarus's arguments about the politics of cricket in ibid., 144–95.

Norman K. Denzin

Mother and Mickey

I was putting another Mickey Mantle picture up on the wall in my bedroom about the time Dad came in the front door slightly drunk. This was the summer of 1952. We were living in a little rental house on West Fourth Street in Indianola, Iowa. Dad was drinking a lot, and mother was sick. Mark stayed in his bedroom most of the time. Dad always came home after dark. I tried to stay out of his way.

Elvis Presley was singing "Blue Suede Shoes," and I had a pair. Mickey Mantle had just come up to the New York Yankees and was hitting home runs right and left. That summer it seemed like every other week his picture was on the front cover of *Time* magazine. Mickey was my idol. He could bat right- or left-handed. So could I. He could hit home runs. So could I. He had a big smile. So did I. He was happy. I wasn't. I wanted my life to be like Mickey's.

I was pretty deep into sport idols. Dad and I had a falling out and he wasn't my idol much anymore. He said I had a bad attitude. I thought he did. Mostly I looked up to old New York Yankees as my heroes—men like Babe Ruth and Lou Gehrig, but Joe DiMaggio, Yogi Berra, too; all those guys. The library in my grade school

The *South Atlantic Quarterly* 105:2, Spring 2006.
Copyright © 2006 by Duke University Press.

had a big section of books on sports heroes and other leaders of the world. I had gotten into the books on sports, and every week I checked out two or three. I branched out into football and track, and got caught up in Jim Thorpe's life story. I watched Burt Lancaster play Jim in the movie. These were stories about heroes for boys in grade school. By the time we moved to Indianola I was hooked. I was in junior high then, and pretty big stuff. I couldn't wait for Mickey's life story to come out in a book. In the meantime, I had his pictures up on my wall, along with all his statistics: runs batted in, batting average, number of home runs.

We lasted three years in Indianola. I was elected president of my seventh grade class. Our junior high team won the Warren County Basketball Tournament. I was a forward, and averaged eleven points a game. My girlfriend was a cheerleader. She'd lead a chant when I made a basket.

We had a housekeeper that Grandpa paid for. She cleaned, fixed meals, and did laundry. Dad was county agent for the Farm Bureau. He had a secretary and agents who worked for him. He got me a job as janitor. I cleaned the building three times a week before school. He was drinking more and away most of the time. They transferred him to Muscatine on the Mississippi River, forty miles away from Grandpa's farm near Iowa City. He wasn't in charge of an office anymore. He was just another life insurance salesman. But he was good. He was in the Million Dollar Club.

So in the summer of 1955 we moved back to the farm, into the two-story, four-bedroom, white wooden house on the hill where Grandpa's parents had lived. There was a hundred-foot pine tree in the front yard. Huge oaks and maples shaded the house. There were two large red barns, a grain silo, corncribs, concrete feeding lots for the hogs, a chicken house, a machine shed for a garage. A herd of fifty black Angus cows, a black bull, a hundred breed sows, sheep and chickens. A lilac hedge was on the north side of the house, next to a grape arbor that Grandma had planted, right after she and Grandpa were married. When you stepped outside the front door, and looked south, the horizon was endless. It stretched across field after field of green corn waving in the wind. If you squinted, the greenness turned to blue, as the sky bent down and touched the fields of corn.

To the north, at the bottom of the hill, was a small creek that cut the pasture in half. I could see the creek from my bedroom window. Mickey was still my hero, and he was still hitting home runs. I had his pictures up on the wall over my bed in my new bedroom.

Grandpa fixed up the house for Mother. He put on an addition, with a new kitchen and a second bathroom. Mark went to the country school three miles away. I got into University High. That fall I got a driver's permit to go back and forth to school. I'd drive to Iowa City, and Dad drove to Muscatine. We didn't see much of each other. We didn't seem to have much money, or else mother wasn't a good cook. We ate a lot of chipped beef and gravy on white bread.

Dad was drinking more and coming home later every night. I think this was causing problems between Mom and Dad, but I never heard them talk about it. There was a lot of fighting going on, though. These were silent fights, the ones where people ignore each other when they walk through a room. Everybody was ignoring everybody. I never saw Dad touch Mother when he was angry. If he was really mad he would just yell at her. When he did that, Mark and I would leave the room.

This all changed the night Dad took out after me. We were finishing up another dinner of chipped beef and gravy. It was pretty clear Dad had been drinking. I could smell beer on his breath. I hadn't cleaned my plate. Nobody was talking. Mark was trying to eat and read a book. Mother was crying. It was kind of a typical meal for that summer. I got up and said I had to go outside. Dad would have none of this. "Sit down and finish your dinner," he shouted.

I got up and took my plate to the kitchen sink and started doing dishes. "Did you hear me?" he shouted. "Yes," I said, "You don't have to yell." "Don't talk back to me, young man!" He got up from the table and came toward me. Mother yelled, "Kenneth, sit down!" "Shut up," he said.

I slammed a pan down in the sink and ran out of the kitchen. The door banged shut behind me. Dad yelled, "Get back in here and sit down!" I kept walking, past the oak tree in the yard, down toward the machine shed. I stopped next to the gate that led to the feed lot. I turned back to the house. Mother came running out of the house. Dad was following her. He ran right past Mother and caught up with me at the gate. He grabbed my shoulder and spun me around. I turned and looked at him. I was shaking all over. I was sweating. My pulse was racing. I pushed him back. "Get your hands off of me." Mother pushed between us. "Don't touch my son!" she screamed. "Get out of my way," Dad shouted, and he threw me to the ground. Mother flew at him. She spit at him. She scratched his face. "You monster," she said, "You're no father."

Dad swore, "Dammit, Betty! I'll show you," and he bent slightly at the waist, and put his arms around her body. As he raised up, he hit her head with his chin. Her shoulders fell back across his arms. He lifted Mother off the ground as if she was as light as a feather. He tried to throw her over the gate. She kicked against the top board and scratched Dad's eyes with her bright red fingernails. Blood ran down his check.

Mark came running from down the hill. "Daddy, Daddy, stop hurting Mommy. Mommy, are you all right, Mommy, I love you."

I jumped on Dad's back. He fell to the ground, dropping Mother. She got up and kicked him. Mark ran over and kicked him too. Then Mark put his arms around Mother and hugged her. She kissed him and she turned to me. She stood between the two of us and said, "Here are the real men in my life. These are the men who love me." Arm in arm, the three of us walked back to the house.

I looked back at Dad. He was walking slowly into the garage. A few minutes later I heard the car go roaring out of the barnyard. I ran to the dining room window. The car disappeared in a cloud of dust at the bottom of the hill. Dad didn't come home that night.

I went upstairs to my bedroom and started looking at Mickey Mantle on the wall. Mother came in and sat on the edge of my bed. She looked at Mickey with me. "You like him, don't you?" she said. I said "Yes, I do." She said, "He seems like a nice gentle man."

Five years after this fight, Dad left for good. That was the summer of 1960. By that time he had joined AA. About a month after Dad left, Leon, his AA sponsor, came out to the house one Sunday afternoon. He took me to the side and said, "I've heard from your dad. He's not coming home. He told me to tell you." I looked down at the ground. I started to cry. Leon continued, "I don't think you knew that your father was fooling around with a woman who was also in AA. Well, he was, and he left with her."

I wanted to hit Leon for telling me this. Every night I waited for Dad's footsteps to come up the stairway. I looked for his shadow to fall across the hallway. Those were the things that said he was home. Now Leon said these things were never going to happen again.

Three years after Dad left, Mom got a divorce. Over the years Mother and I talked about many things, but never about the night she and Dad and I and Mark fought in the barnyard. Dad and I eventually got back together. And he never brought this fight up either.

Dad died five years ago, and Mother died a year later. Three summers ago Mickey Mantle died. It turned out his life had not been a bed of roses either. People talked of his carousing and his alcoholism, and the pain he caused his family, especially his wife and his sons. Mickey had stopped being my hero sometime after Dad left us. Around that time, I lost faith in heroes more generally.

Five days after Mickey died, Bob Costas, the NBC sports analyst, spoke at a memorial service for the Mantle family. He talked in glowing terms about Mickey: about the high arc of the ball when he hit home runs; about Mickey being a switch-hitter; about his grace and elegance on the field; about the poetry in his movements when he caught a ball, stole a base, or made a throw to home plate; about Mickey being a man who lived a hard life and paid for it; about Mickey as a man who got a second chance and turned some things around.

I thought about all these things as I listened to Bob Costas eulogize Mickey. I was with my wife in our rented car in Red Lodge, Montana. We were up on the West Bench, above town, watching the sun set on the Beartooth Mountains. The sky was a beautiful orange, and purple and deep blue, and the mountain seemed to glow. If you squinted it looked like a Chinese landscape, mountain peaks and soft white clouds touching each other. Then it got dark.

I came between Mother and Dad that night because of Mickey. He was my hero, and he would not let this happen. Today, I think of the four of us as a group. Mother thought Mickey was a gentle man. But Mother was married to a man who could be violent when he had too much to drink. Mother never knew the dark side of Mickey. Nor did I.

Annie Paul

Body Wisdom: The Way of Karate

Why do I learn karate? In this essay I want to answer that question and to convey a reasonably vivid sense of the way karate is less a sport than a system of living and a philosophy. For more than how to act, karate teaches how to react, or, frequently, how *not* to react. And curiously karate achieves this mastery of the mind and spirit through vigorous training and preparation of the body.

I certainly had no idea of all this when I joined the Kingston, Jamaica, branch of Seido karate in the year 2000. You could even say that I joined for the most ignoble of reasons. A man I had recently met and liked was never available on weekday evenings because he had "karate class." When I finally responded to his invitations to come and watch a class, I discovered that he not only taught karate; he was the head of the school. This was, so to speak, his dojo.[1] His rank was *Kyoshi* or "senior teacher."

Why didn't I try out a class or two, he suggested. I would be a white belt, and white belts received separate instruction until they were ready to participate in the general class, so I wouldn't have to worry about keeping up with the rest. I found the very idea of joining

The *South Atlantic Quarterly* 105:2, Spring 2006.

such an activity faintly terrifying and somewhat amusing. After all, I was no lithe young thing anymore but a forty-four-year-old who in India would be considered a matron. I doubted that my limbs would accommodate the sorts of contortions I saw in front of me. But I agreed to try a class, thinking that this was one way to be in the general vicinity of the object of my affections. I expected that after one or two sessions the novelty would wear off and I would tire of such exertions, and whenever that happened I would stop.

Instead, I was hooked from the very start. At first the thing I most enjoyed about karate was simply the experience of being a student again; to be placed at my age in the bottommost class, the equivalent of a nursery, was in itself a novelty. As a beginning student with no natural aptitude for the subject at hand, I received individualized instruction for a longer period than most, learning slowly but surely from each of the black belts. One of the things that impressed me about the dojo was the sheer number of female black belts in it. At least half of the class members were women. There was little or no sense of being in a "male" space; my comfort level was high.

As a schoolchild I had felt profoundly alienated from the learning process I was offered in an Indian convent school. I had in effect never had the experience of being a willing and enthusiastic student. By the time I reached university, my learning faculties were quite blunted. Obviously I must have learned something, but the process itself was unpleasant and not conducive to spiritual growth. Worse, very few of my teachers were individuals I could relate to or feel much respect for.

The dojo offered me a completely different learning experience. It felt as if I was being given a second chance to correct something fundamental. I fully succumbed to the discipline of karate, opening every pore of myself to this fascinating new way of knowing and being. It was a frustrating but rewarding process—frustrating because I had spent a lifetime treating my body as an insignificant appendage to my head. Sport was something you watched, often on television, not something you actually did. Thanks to this mind-set, my body had been systematically deprived of attention. Most of my time was spent reading; the only activity I sometimes indulged in was a brisk walk around the Mona Dam.

I often joke that when I approached forty my body finally delivered an ultimatum: I was to start treating it with due respect or else. For once I listened and promised to give it an equal say in all matters; after all, the decisions I made affected it profoundly, and it was clearly tired of being a sleeping partner, as it were, in my existence. Of course, making a promise is one thing, keeping it is another; and while I tried my best to keep my word, the years were passing without any significant change having taken place in my modus operandi.

Until I started to do karate. The joyous response from my body is the other factor that kept me going back. In fact, I became so obedient now to my body that I hated to miss a class and rarely even arrived late during those first two years. I could barely do push-ups, and latecomers had to do ten of these before they could enter the dojo. While I made immense progress in all respects, push-ups were the one thing that continued to defeat me. Even today it remains an area of underdevelopment. As for doing push-ups on one's knuckles, I have an exaggerated respect for those who can do this. In Seido, knuckle push-ups are required of all black belts and brown belts.

The Pedagogy of Karate

To watch the female green belts perform their katas was breathtaking. Their grace and control was balletic, something I admired intensely and never hoped to attain. Admiration for one's teachers is crucial to the learning process. As I started learning karate and participating in the life of the dojo, I began to appreciate the ritual Japanese regimentation that structured this ancient martial art. I had always rebelled against the tyranny of unnecessary ritual, but now I routinely participated in it.

More than anything I was struck by karate's pedagogy. Our classes were never repetitive, and there was something to be said for having so many different teachers, for each white belt class was assigned to a different black belt or senior belt. All of them had their own style of teaching and their own idea of what they thought white belts should learn.

I had been the sort of person for whom even walking from one end of a room to the other in front of an audience was an excruciating experience. Now I had to submit myself to the torture of performing entire sequences of movements ineptly and clumsily in front of a critical audience, some of whom tried in vain to hide their amusement at my pathetic rendition of the most basic katas. Fortunately the atmosphere was fundamentally friendly, and my anxiety soon evaporated in the rough-and-tumble of the daily routine of karate. Criticism and correction of posture and form were laced with affection and the kind of rude teasing that characterizes interaction in a large family.

Before I knew it I lost my self-consciousness. This had the most unexpected benefits, for among other things, one of the activities that had always terrified me was public speaking. Within a few months I had grown a healthy shell and no longer quivered anxiously in my thin skin before what I imagined were derisory stares. I was astonished at how comfortable I felt now with myself, with my body, with other people. I started walking differently, talking differently, thinking differently. I no longer burst into tears at the slightest thing and was able to hold my own in disagreeable situations.

Classes took place three times a week, in the evenings. Mondays were a test of endurance; our bodies were pushed to their limits by doing hundreds of sit-ups, push-ups, leg raises, and the like. Wednesday class, according to Kyoshi, was the best one, fighting class, where we were initiated into kumite, or self-defense. We all put on boxing gear and sparred with one another. I still remember that initially I had thought that I would skip Wednesday classes, so alien was the thought of fighting. There was absolutely nothing about it that attracted me. "Listen, don't underestimate the pleasure of being able to hit men as hard as you want when they can't hit you back with all their strength because you're a white belt," one of the female black belts told me.

I couldn't imagine what she was talking about. The thought of punching anyone didn't appeal to me. But more than that, what put me off was the fear of being hit. Why on earth would I want that to happen? But I soon realized that karate wasn't like your neighborhood gym classes that you could sign up for based on your personal whims and desires. Karate was the whole package; especially in the foundation years, you had to participate in all the classes. That was your training as a *karateka*. There was no question of not going to fighting class.

Fighting didn't come intuitively to me, and I went to it reluctantly, but I hope I can begin to describe the exhilaration of physical combat, the cut and thrust not of debate or scholarly argument but of actual physical interaction. I suffered a lot until I learned to block the kicks and striking fists. In fact, that is how I realized I was making progress. Fighting is as much about feinting, dodging, and blocking blows as it is about striking, kicking, and punching. I used to come home with impressive bruises, especially in the stomach area, but that hasn't happened in a long time. I wouldn't describe myself as an outstanding fighter, but I'm no pushover either.

I suppose physical contact is a prominent feature of most sport. Physical contact with a group of human beings is probably rare for those who don't participate in group sports. Other than immediate family (and even that is not as common as one might think, especially in traditional societies), one doesn't engage too many people in a physical way. And if one does, this grows less and less frequent the older one gets. (I am not here talking about "swinging" couples, "players," and the like, whose experience for obvious reasons may be different.)

Kata was taught on Thursdays. This rapidly became my favorite class; kata consists of a series of choreographed fighting techniques arranged in distinct patterns. Technically kata teaches you to defend yourself from an imaginary attack coming from different directions. Although each movement is preset, kata actually allows for and depends on an individual's expression and rendition of these movements. How an individual puts it all together in performance of the kata counts for a lot; the display of control, grace, strength, and timing are more important than getting the kata letter-perfect, so to speak. In this respect kata is like singing. Even in performing ancient ragas or operatic movements, singers imbue the exercise with their own individual personality.

It was in the process of learning kata that I realized what an abominable sense of coordination I had. If I was asked to put my right foot out, I was seized with panic: Which foot was my right foot? While everyone else had mastered this step and several more, I would still be wavering with indecision. It must have taken immense patience to teach me the basics. It took twice as long as anyone else for my body to learn the full sequence of movements. Nothing came intuitively.

Karate's Practice

Miraculously, however, while I had trouble with remembering sequences I was good at getting each position right. More than once I overheard senior belts commenting that I had good form. This boosted my confidence immensely, and one day, on hearing a black belt say that the easiest stage at which to win a prize was as a white belt, I resolved to make a serious attempt to win the white belt kata event at our upcoming tournament.

I decided to perform Tai Kyoku kata, the most basic kata we had been taught but one which I knew thoroughly. The tournament was not restricted to Seido but included tae kwon do, Shotokan karate, and many other martial art forms. Kyoshis and Sihans from the New York and London Seido schools had come for the event. This was my very first tournament. I was nervous but determined.

When the time came, I gave it my best, but there was a tae kwon do white belt who was very good too. We tied and had to perform our katas again and again. Dispirited by her confidence and persistence, I was on the verge of giving up when suddenly the judges decided in my favor. I beat my opponent narrowly, but I was elated. It felt incredibly good to be going home with this trophy. The Kyoshis and other black belts were thrilled on my behalf, particularly Kyoshi Gregory, who had taken pains to teach me good form.

Alas, this happy circumstance has never repeated itself. But then again, not since then have I put in as much effort and determination as I did during that first tournament. Winning the trophy was fantastic, but as we were told over and over again, karate is not about triumph in competition; rather, it is about developing one's spirit and approach to life. Although I failed to place at the next tournament, it gave me great pleasure when two older women said to me afterward, "Hush, you didn't win but you did your kata so beautifully. We enjoyed watching you."

The dojo delivers its lessons in different ways. Our membership was wide and varied and included people from a cross section of society across the class and color divide. Immersed in the middle-class existence of the University of the West Indies, I rarely met or interacted with people from other backgrounds. Now I was part of a group that included security guards, nurses, soldiers, doctors, lawyers, and individuals from completely different worlds than my own. I found this very stimulating.

In the dojo status is ascribed purely on the basis of merit, unlike the secular world, where it's often based on caste, age, gender, wealth, and other variables. This meant that as a forty-four-year-old white belt you might find yourself facing a twelve-year-old brown or black belt. Regardless of his or her age you would be expected to bow, show respect, and generally defer to the black belt in every way. This wasn't as difficult as you might think, for by the time one becomes a brown or black belt, one learns enough to command the respect of one's juniors. Similarly, you could be a rich businessperson starting karate under the tutelage of black belts who were delivery men or security guards. Often you will encounter senior belts in real life and find that they are in subservient positions to your own, but it requires no effort to bow and acknowledge the others' seniority, for they have earned it by their superior knowledge and practice of karate.

What the rest of the world thinks karate is about—self-defense and a mode of fighting—is a reduction of this grand sport to its basest elements. What I have learned from karate is the kind of presence of body and mind required in times of attack: not to overpower the enemy but to outwit them. Karate is not only thinking on one's feet, it is also thinking *with* one's feet. A precept often stressed in the dojo is this: If confronted with an attack, turn and walk away if possible; run if necessary. Avoid a confrontation at all costs; attack only if there is no other option, and use only as much violence as is necessary to deflect the attack.

In his novel "The Last Jet Engine Laugh," Ruchir Joshi tells a memorable story that illustrates this aspect of karate well. The protagonist, Paresh, who plans "to represent India in karate by the year 1979," is one day confronted with a situation in which his father comes under attack. It is his father's tongue, adept and vicious as a knife, that gets him into trouble ("I thought my father often used his tongue like my karate teacher used the side of his hand for a chop"): after a meeting, two targets of his vitriol attack him in an alley. Paresh happens to be nearby and witnesses the onset. He intervenes. Later, after breaking the arm of one of the knife-wielding attackers, trying to gouge out the eyes of the other, and generally demolishing both men and rescuing his father, Paresh is unable to salvage any memory of the fight.

> From what I could then recount of the fight, little, almost none, of my karate training had come of any use. When I reported what I had done to the men, my teacher confirmed that.
>
> Being old-fashioned, he prided himself on teaching his pupils control. While I took little pleasure from the fact that both men probably went to hospital, I was happy that I had saved my father from being beaten up badly. But my teacher was disappointed that I had not been able to repel the attack with minimum effort and without losing my temper.
>
> Later, in class he took this up as an example. "In your head you were talking to them," he said, "arguing with them."
>
> I stood head down looking at the knot in my belt. The evening sun threw rectangles of light on to the mats. Other students from the advanced class stood in a row, arms clasped behind their backs, quiet. My teacher stood facing me as if about to demonstrate something, both of us in profile to the other. I could hear the baying of a small crowd watching a football match in the stadium nearby. I could hear the evening traffic on Mayo Road.
>
> "By shouting at them you lost the argument with your sadhana, with your karate. You turned your body into a babbling tongue—and a tongue is never strong in a fight. These boys were obviously street

thugs, new to the job. Had they been more experienced, you would be dead." With which he reached across and untied my orange belt and gave me a green one, the next lower.

"You still have a lot to learn," he said."[2]

The Group as Teacher

Perhaps the most profound lesson I've learned from karate is the value of community. Again, community had always signified oppression for me; I had always distrusted groups and what I thought of as groupthink. But one of the great pleasures of karate was slowly realizing that this multifaceted body-based practice of living and form of knowledge came from the so-called East, from a traditional society not unlike the one I had been born in.

For even though I had been born in India, I was the product of a class and culture profoundly influenced by the West. My immediate family was highly Westernized, my father having done his PhD in the States in the 1950s. I grew up closed to the cultures closest to me and open to the distant but powerful culture of the West. In that respect I was a more than willing "conscript of modernity."[3] Therefore it wasn't until I started doing karate that I was actually exposed to the ingenuity of Eastern culture in such a meaningful way. Here was a countermodernity so powerful that it had permeated not only the West but the entire world with its seductive combination of action and thought, its participatory nature, its focus on the body, its effective harnessing of human potential. Here was a product of Eastern culture that had globalized itself successfully long before other exports such as yoga and transcendental meditation.

Our dojo is an example of how a healthy, well-functioning group reproduces itself, how it perpetuates its knowledge and passes it down, not encoded in books but in active bodily form. Our activities as a group are not limited to the dojo either; every now and then we get together at a member's house to play board games such as Guesstures, Outburst, or Pictionary. We have beach training and go on hikes to the Blue Mountains, and we occasionally go to plays.

As a confirmed bookworm and individualist, all of this was new to me. Belonging to such a focused group was new. Before I started karate, Kyoshi Tony had described the Seido school, with its branches all over the world, as being similar to a church. In a way I didn't know what he meant by that, for churches were quite alien to my life; I generally gave them a wide berth.

Now I understand much better what Kyoshi Tony meant, though I suspect that half the reason churches are so popular is for the very same feeling of community they foster. Life in the West is too atomized; there is a deeply felt need to belong, to congregate, to cling together. And in places like Jamaica, churches would have provided a population recovering from the experience of slavery with survival skills and identity.

Thinking with the Body?

There is a wonderful story called "The Transposed Heads," an Indian story retold by Thomas Mann, in which two friends fall in love with the same woman.[4] The friends are practically inseparable, though they are quite different from one another. Sridhaman, Brahmin-like, leads a sedentary life, reading religious and philosophical texts, while Nanda, a shepherd, cares little for "things of the mind." As a result their bodies are quite different: whereas Nanda has a "well-set up body," Sridhaman's is "clerkly, with a rather soft, narrow breast and some fat on the little belly." According to the narrator, "It was a body proper to serve as adjunct and appendage to a noble and knowledgeable head-piece, that was of course head and front of the whole, whereas with the whole Nanda the body was, so to speak, the main thing, and the head merely a pleasing appendage."

Sita, the object of their affections, becomes the wife of Sridhaman, whom she loves, though she longs to experience the far manlier arms of Nanda. By a bizarre twist of fate, both men behead themselves in a desolate Kali temple in the forest, and when Sita discovers the bodies, she is inconsolable and tries to hang herself from a tree. An irate Kali orders her to take her neck out of the noose, saying that she has had enough of intemperate human beings sacrificing themselves to her. Instead she orders Sita to place the two heads on their respective bodies, promising to bring them back to life. In the darkness, however, Sita mistakenly transposes the heads: Each friend now has the other's body.

After the initial shock, Sita is overjoyed, as she can legitimately enjoy Nanda's body now that it is attached to her husband's head. Sridhaman, too, is happy, having been aware of Sita's longings and having long coveted a body like Nanda's. His former body, however, now attached to Nanda's head, is left out in the cold. Nanda decides to banish himself to a distant forest and become a hermit rather than stay and witness the impassioned union of the other two.

Within a few years Sridhaman's new Nanda body becomes a shadow of what it once was, for the Sridhaman head continues to live like a Brahmin, sitting down all day surrounded by books. Nanda, on the other hand, now a hermit in the forest, continues to lead a physical life, chopping wood, plowing the earth, and so on. The soft, pudgy body he had acquired becomes hard and strong. Sita is once again disconsolate. The story continues to its disconcerting end, but what I find striking about it is the belief in the dominance of the head over the body.

My experience of karate makes me wonder if it isn't humanly possible to challenge this dominance, this traditional dichotomy between mind and body. The latter is often associated with a lack of thought, an exclusive orientation toward action. But even though it is the body that is often accused of "hotheadedness," I wonder if it isn't actually the head which is at fault. It is the head that takes offense, wreaks vengeance, and demands false respect; a body that has been nurtured, loved, and treated as an equal rather than an inferior is rarely so self-centered.

When trained through karate, that body becomes a receptacle of wisdom, a living, breathing, thinking entity capable of sidestepping the head's importunate demands instead of enacting them. From karate the body learns to appreciate and love community. It knows the value of community through living it in the dojo, for karate cannot be learned from an individual; it is the kind of knowledge that can be imparted only by a group.

The Kingston branch of Seido is a multiple-award-winning sports organization, the most successful one of its kind in the Caribbean and many other places. Our team spirit and karate are so strong that we tend to dominate international meets that we attend. What is remarkable about this is that our training is not focused on winning tournaments or dominating others at all; our victories are simply a by-product of the spirit of our dojo.

I didn't realize quite how special our dojo was until Michael Hanchard, the MacArthur Fellow from Illinois, was in Kingston doing research and needed a place to practice his boxing. I introduced him to our dojo so that he could spar with the black belts; he later told me that I was lucky to belong to such a group. Hanchard had experienced many sporting organizations, but rarely had he come across one as cohesive and healthy-spirited as ours. This is undoubtedly due to the leadership and example of Kyoshi Tony Robinson, who heads our dojo.

Seido karate is also special in that its founder, Grandmaster Tadashi Nakamura ("Kaicho" to us), has always emphasized accessibility to all. We therefore have a number of students with physical handicaps of various sorts. In the dojo we are all equal, and it is an awe-inspiring experience to see someone overcome their handicaps and achieve the heights of the higher belts.

It would be appropriate to end by quoting Kaicho himself:

> If karate only exists for the purpose of winning at tournaments and to create physical strength, then karate will end up being only accessible to that small segment of society that is both young and strong. If karate is only concerned with winning and losing, then karate will end up excluding those who are physically weak or unable to perform well at tournaments.
>
> The karate that is really needed in our society today is one in which strength can be sought equally by those who are physically weak, and even by those who are physically handicapped.
>
> It should not be a karate where we fight with each other to become strong, but karate where each person can become just a little bit stronger each day than the day before. A karate where each person cooperates with those around him or her, everyone working together to become strong.
>
> A karate where the individual works with others to help each other to improve—that is the goal and desire that I have for Seido Juku Karate.[5]

I hope I have absorbed some of the lessons karate has to offer. Sometimes I wonder if it is ever possible to stop learning from karate. I am a green belt now and am determined to reproduce the grace and strength I saw in those first green belts I encountered. People who started after me are now brown belts, but I'm not in a hurry. Getting a black belt is not my highest priority; I'll get there when I get there.

Notes

1 *Dojo* refers to the martial arts training hall and comes from a word meaning "place of enlightenment."
2 Ruchir Joshi, "My Father's Tongue," in *The Last Jet Engine Laugh* (New Delhi: Harper-Collins India, 2001), 27. *Sadhana* means "devotion" or "practice."
3 David Scott, *Conscripts of Modernity: The Tragedy of Colonial Enlightenment* (Durham, NC: Duke University Press, 2004).
4 Thomas Mann, *Stories of a Lifetime* (London: Secker and Warburg, 1961).
5 Tadashi Nakamura, *Karate Kyohon* (Tokyo: Shufunomoto, 2001), 11.

John Hartley

Sync or Swim? Plebiscitary Sport, Synchronized
Voting, and the Shift from Mars to Venus

New things are happening at the interface of
sport and media that may barely be visible from
the perspective of regular sport, whether you're
a player, a fan, or a spectator. If your sporting pleasures are mainstream—if, for instance,
they involve any combination of men, a ball,
and a team—then you might want to insist that
an activity from which men are excluded, that
requires smiling, a flamboyant costume, and trying as hard as possible to appear *exactly the same*
as everyone else involved, can't be a "real" sport.
But while that seems obvious today, the days of
ball-assisted male combat as the ideal type of
sport may be numbered.

Instead, growing up unnoticed in the thick-
ets of popular entertainment and "reality" TV
are new sporting attributes. They celebrate
not individual heroics but spectator-oriented
teamwork, where no matter how strenuous
the performance, it must look effortless and
stylish. Instead of objective measurements—
"faster, higher, stronger," as the Olympic motto
puts it—winners are picked by how they look
to a panel of judges; by consumer choice, as it
were. Sporting values are feminizing.

Sport and media are converging and integrat-

The *South Atlantic Quarterly* 105:2, Spring 2006.
Copyright © 2006 by Duke University Press.

ing. As they do so, what counts as sport, why it is valued, and what it symbolizes for contemporary culture are all changing. I take these changes to be emblematic of something emergent in the culture at large. The modernist paradigm—four hundred years in the making—is shifting toward a new consumerist paradigm, and this is symbolized in new sports, of which the paradigmatic example is synchronized swimming.

Mars to Venus

I think I was the first scholar of cultural and media studies, possibly of any sort, to publish an analysis of synchronized swimming, in my 1992 book *The Politics of Pictures*.[1] That book's cover features a production still from a famous Hollywood film celebrating—perhaps originating—this most unlikely sport. It shows Esther Williams, surrounded by mermettes, at the climax of *The Million Dollar Mermaid* (1952).[2] In other words, in my book, whose subtitle is "The Creation of the Public in the Age of Popular Media," synchronized swimming is literally taken as the *emblem* of the contemporary mediated public.

In this context, one aspect of a strange sport stands out as especially peculiar—compulsory smiling. I made it stand for other contemporary jobs in which smiling is compulsory, ranging from PR and TV presenters to retail assistants. Synchronized swimmers are an appropriate metaphor for the "smiling professions"; modern professionals in media, marketing, and the services who *represent the public to itself*. The smiling professions address and call into being, and also personify and embody, "the public" for large, diverse societies where the community can no longer experience itself as self-present. They do the work of holding together—by strenuous but invisible effort—the Andersonian "imagined community." They turn work into spectacle, competition into desirability, the imagined community into smiling faces. Synchronized swimming is their sport.[3] But like synchronized swimming, which suffers a "reputation deficit" compared with ball-centered sports, the smiling professions are among the most despised of all contemporary occupations. In both cases the put-downs bear no relation to the levels of training, skill, and dedication required to perform the job well. Socially, the reputation deficit also masks how important the smiling professions are to the daily functioning of hyperdemocratized societies, just as the jocular dismissal of synchronized swimming masks the extent to which combat models of sport may be under threat from apparently weaker forces as sporting values migrate from Mars to Venus.

It was Robert Kagan who coined the memorable line about Americans being from Mars and Europeans from Venus:

> On the all-important question of power . . . American and European perspectives are diverging. . . . On major strategic and international questions today, Americans are from Mars and Europeans are from Venus: they agree on little and understand one another less and less.[4]

Of course this is a simplification, and it refers to strategic rather than sporting power. Nevertheless, as Kagan says, "the caricatures do capture an essential truth." He draws attention to two divergent models of strategic policy: one based on unconstrained power (Mars), the other on the arts of *weakness*: "negotiation, diplomacy, and commercial ties, on international law over the use of force, on seduction over coercion, on multilateralism over unilateralism" (Venus).

In Kagan's analysis, Europe has embraced Venus (miraculously, the "German lion has lain down with the French lamb"), while, since the Second World War, the United States has taken over the Martial mantle from imperial ("Old") Europe. Kagan's own interest is confined to strategic power — military supremacy and the willingness to use it on the world stage. He does not expand his analysis to include other spheres, including culture. But a parting of the ways has occurred in that sphere as well. Some countries — notably France — want to protect their national culture by using the Venusian arts of negotiation and law (diplomacy, negotiation, "seduction, not coercion"). Others — notably the United States — see culture in market terms, and market strength has become a metaphor for military might, following a "Hobbesian" model of power where competition produces winners and winner takes all. From this perspective it's easy to see the values of Venus as illusory. But equally, many countries and individuals across the world reject the "power" model of competition in favor of the "law" model. It seems to me that the same forces are at work in sport. Here the distinction between Mars and Venus is drawn not along national borders but in the differences between different types of sporting endeavor. To put it simply, there is hegemonic, modern, power sport, and there are "seductive," postmodern, law sports.[5] It's the difference between football and synchronized swimming.

Why should we care? My argument is that the turn from Mars to Venus in sport is an instance of more general changes, amounting to a paradigm shift. What interests me here is the "reputation deficit" that emergent forms suffer at the hands of those whose values they may be supplanting. I'm making synchronized swimming a metaphor for other forms that have suffered, and continue to suffer, a reputation deficit, namely the smiling professions and the popular media they serve. Compared to the world of official (political) power, popular media are Venusian synchronized swimmers. But just as the Venusian value of "seduction, not coercion"—despite its apparent weakness—is challenging Martial notions of power, so the popular media are a challenge to existing political and intellectual elites.

A Sprinkler System

Many of the components of what we recognize as modernity were assembled during the seventeenth century, including secular science based on reason and the theory of the modern state. A leading theorist in both of these endeavors was Thomas Hobbes, whose great work *Leviathan* was published in 1651.[6] Hobbes thought the natural condition of humankind was "war of each against all" and that only a strong state—Leviathan—could maintain order. Hobbes was interested in power; like Kagan, he was on the side of Mars, not Venus.

However, it was Hobbes himself who identified—by their very absence—the need for the smiling professions and popular media within his constitutional arrangements for the modern state. He imagined their political and cultural *functions*, the need for some sort of societywide mediating system to teach the lay public the political and moral truths of the day, long before technology or a suitably trained profession were available to deliver them.

Hobbes was obsessed by the inadequacy of the only mechanism available in his own day to teach civil and moral doctrine to the population at large, namely the universities. He saw the universities as fountains not of truth but of error (papism and sophistry). He could only conclude *Leviathan* with this rather forlorn hope: "For seeing the Universities are the Fountains of Civill, and Morall Doctrine, from whence the Preachers, and the Gentry, drawing such water as they find, use to sprinkle the same (both from the Pulpit, and in their Conversation) upon the People, there ought certainly to be great care taken, to have it pure" (728).

A fountainhead from which both *professionals and opinion leaders* (preachers and gentry) drew *ideological principles* (civil and moral doctrine) to use for *teaching* the lay population (sprinkled upon the people): This is a succinct description of the social-cultural function of mass media in modern nation-states. Hobbes just lacked the technology. He was very skeptical about universities. They weren't up to the job; they were more likely to define themselves *against* the authority Hobbes wanted people to "obey" in order to achieve "concord" in the body politic (380). Hobbes thought the universities were inclined to papism, to which he objected not on theological but on political grounds because it fostered allegiance to a foreign prince. He also criticized "Aristotelity" (scholasticism or sophistry) in the universities, in contrast to what would now be recognized as modern empirical science based on mathematics and observation (708, 688). Thus, at the very outset of modernity, there was perceived to be a tension between the *need* for popular instruction in the service of a state of "concord," and the *means* to deliver it. Formal (university) education was divergent from necessary civic and moral education.

It was exactly this gap that popular media came to fill, starting during the same early modern period with popular entertainments like the theater (including bearbaiting) and various forms of news—from juicy murders to constitutional debates—circulating via print and song. As industrialization kicked in, the media developed "mass" forms, from the radical "pauper press" to the commercial media empires that dominated the twentieth century. Such media were popular not because of the purity of their doctrine, however, but because they proved good at storytelling and spectacle; they often found a way to couch the great questions of turbulent times in a popular idiom, and by no means always to the advantage of the government of the day. Media professionals were not endowed with the authority of the state— quite the reverse in many cases—but this may have made them seem more trustworthy to laypeople, even when their commercial might rivaled that of countries.

While Hobbes despaired of the official institutions for the mediation of ideas, the popular media were establishing a new "fountainhead" from which the population came to draw ideological water because they *liked* it. Media professionals had to strive above all to maintain people's goodwill toward the media themselves, their stories and sights, to keep them coming back for more not out of "obedience" but "concord." Because there was no compulsion, popular media had to seek approval from their users ahead of the political and ideological authorities. Perhaps this is why Hobbes missed them—he was a modernist, concerned with political theory, government, and the state, not with "smiling." Of "doctrine" he only thought that it should be "*pure.*" It did not occur to him to make it *palatable* too, even though he understood that Leviathan (i.e., the monarchical state) depended not on the mere *existence* or mere assertion of the rights or powers of the king, but on the people accepting those rights and obeying authority in "concord" (380). This failure to connect "concord" with consent, and consent with communicative media that people liked and trusted, left Hobbes's political theory incomplete at the end of *Leviathan* and perhaps made his vision of the modern state much more authoritarian in the matter of popular instruction than it needed to be.

Leviathan was never put into practice as Hobbes imagined it. Instead, two independent systems for the creation and control of "the public" grew up across the span of modernity. One was the formal domain of politics and learning (including the tensions between them). The other was the informal arena of popular entertainment. The latter was essential to the constitution but intensely disliked by the denizens of the former.[7] Perhaps this explains why "civil and moral" teaching, using a popular idiom to "sprinkle" ideas on the people, remains despised by institutionally placed political, civic, and moral professionals. The popular media are disliked (by cause-effect rationalists especially) precisely because they are *media*—they come *between* political purpose and its object. They can be fun and they can't be directly controlled, and what's more, they reach another part of the body politic that the authorities can't control—the hearts and minds of laypeople.

Reputation Deficit

Popular mediation as go-between, both connecting and disconnecting power and people, also offends the Protestant work ethic, another invention of the seventeenth century, because "consuming" media is taken to be part of the world of private pleasure, not public affairs. Compared with sober public duty and the industrious creation of wealth, taking pleasure in stories and spectacle, the dissembling arts of acting, the seductions of music and rhetoric, and the necessary lies of fiction seemed literally sinful, especially when such means were used to convey weighty public truths in the vehicle of entertainment. How, in short, could bearbaiting teach citizenship?

This vein of Puritan suspicion of the most popular media remains. It is manifest in the endless game of invidious comparisons where there's a reputation deficit on one side of any given pair of terms: quality versus trash, art versus entertainment, production versus consumption, serious versus sensational, and so on. There's a hint of the same in the disciplinary sus-picion expressed by some social science or political economy approaches (where media are *work*, a problem of control) toward the humanities (where media are *culture*, a source of pleasure).

Since Hobbes's time and especially since the nineteenth century, when the press became fully industrialized, the media themselves have grown and prospered, and some of them have become an accepted part of the governmental administration of life. The "deficit" model also operates here to distinguish the sheep from the goats; invidious comparisons are designed to accord "official" status to serious outlets and approved modes of address and to label *disapproved* versions (often the most popular) as aesthetically, educationally, politically, and/or morally deficient.

From within this modernist/workerist tradition that values power over rhetoric, decisions over drama, comes a strongly expressed disapproval for mediation of any sort. The same mental settings are evident in sport. Modern sport celebrates power, so it can't deal with a sport based on aesthetics—like synchronized swimming. The response is standard: Many within the system refuse even to recognize it *as* sport, or they treat it with dismissive humor:

> Swimmer: I get really annoyed watching Roy and HG and the Olympics. . . . I feel that they don't really appreciate what we do. They'd never do that to the swimmers or the track athletes, they'd never criticize them the way they criticize us; but I think it's just being a little bit naïve, I guess, because they don't really understand what goes on behind the scenes. . . . here we are making it look easy when actually it is really, really hard and it takes years and years of training to get it to look easy.[8]

Leviathan to Mermaid

But times are changing again. Industrial society has evolved beyond the need for strong states and territorial loyalty (nations and their national games), while media have evolved beyond the broadcast era. The "business plan" of modernity, based on power and control and on one-to-many, "read-only" ideological communication, is drawing toward the end of its useful life. The Hobbesian model of social life as "war of each against all" is shifting to a new model of Venusian, *feminized* competitiveness. New sports are emerging to symbolize the change.

Economic and symbolic emphasis has shifted down the value chain toward the consumer. This is part of a much more general process that can be observed across many cultural sites and communicative contexts, along what I've called the "value chain of meaning."[9] The "behavioral" consumer of the long-dominant "media effects" model of communication—the despised or vulnerable feminized figure who for most of the twentieth century stood passive and manipulated at the supermarket shelf or in the polling booth, responding to commercial and political campaigning designed to make her behave as causal agents farther up the value chain wanted her to—is giving way, even in marketing literature, to a new model of the consumer as "action." This much more interesting figure is the *user*, who is able to make as well as consume and write as well as read, who interacts with peers and organizations, and who drives innovation and co-creation in many dynamic sectors of the cultural and information economy from the open source movement to games and online journalism.

It does seem to me that symbolic meanings can be associated with this historic shift down the value chain. For instance, the modern era differed strongly from the premodern or medieval period, when the source of meaning was thought to be divine and unarguable and truth was *revealed* as an article of faith. In contrast, *realism*, whether factual (journalism) or fictional (the novel, screen drama), suits the *modern* era's preoccupation with locating the source of meaning in objects—as, for instance, scientific observation of the properties of things in themselves, documentary evidence in law and history, the primacy of the text in literature and philosophy. But now it seems that an epochal change is under way again, in which the modern certainty that the source of meaning is to be found in objects, texts, and evidence is undergoing attrition. In the *contemporary* ("globalized") era, realism is shifting to *"reality."* Instead of one scarce truth, there are plenty. Instead of one type of subjectivity, there is difference and diversity.[10] There's a kind of hyperdemocratization of meaning going on. Instead of investigating objects to determine what they mean, we ask consumers. The more who buy, vote, or choose, the more something is worth. Instead of using criticism and aesthetic judgment of the internal qualities of an object, artwork, or text to determine its value, we use the plebiscite.

Symbolic values associated with sport are not immune to change. The long-term historical drift in the location of the source of meaning can be discerned in sports. They are drifting toward "reality," consumer-plenitude, and the plebiscite. Some developments that seem pertinent:

> · *Synchronized* sports—where choreographed collaboration within a team is prioritized, and where teams don't play each other as they do in many ball-centered sports (here the difference between synchro-

nized swimming and water polo may be instructive). A telling example is formation skydiving: The current women's world record, where 151 skydivers held a pinwheel formation for 4.8 seconds, is held by a group called "jumpforthecause.com," which gained the record in aid of breast cancer research.[11]

· *Feminized* sports—there's a drift from male solo combat hero to female collaborative competitive being-looked-at, a shift from Mars to Venus.

· *Plebiscitary* sports—where winning is an outcome of voting, not defeating an opposition directly but impressing spectators. An extension of such sports from the era of "realism" to the era of "reality" is the practice of throwing open voting from empaneled experts to spectators at large. Consumers determine the winner. Here ballroom dancing leads the way.[12]

· *Consumer-integrated* sports—where, for example, fashion (the costume) is *integral*—as in ballroom dancing and synchronized swimming, of course, but also and increasingly in tennis, women's beach volleyball, surfing, and so on. Consumer integration extends to sports where merchandising and mediation are pivotal, possibly primary, although this may apply to all sport now.

Synchronized, feminized, plebiscitary, consumer-integrated sports include ice-skating (figure skating/ice-dancing), rhythmic and artistic gymnastics, trampoline, diving, synchronized swimming, ballroom dancing, surfing, and equestrian dressage.

Fascism to Fashion

Synchronized sports should not be confused with *regimented* fitness. I vaguely remember people talking about calisthenics in my youth, and despite the fact that calisthenics had its origins in ladies' colleges in the mid–nineteenth century—the word comes from the Greek for "beauty" (*kallos*) plus "strength" (*sthanos*)—the dominant image is of mass physical exercises on parade grounds.[13] Such displays were "synchronized," but on an industrial scale: regimented and standardized. The type of new possibilities being explored in synchronized sports is evident in the difference between those 1984-style proletarian triumphs of the will and synchronized swimming itself, where makeup, hair gel, music, and nose clips are specified equipment. Economic dynamism has shifted from production to consumption, from industry to services, from work to entertainment. Media have begun to open up to interactive, DIY, user-led, or consumer-cocreated inputs. The spheres of public politics and learning are both migrating away from traditional institutions and professions, toward private identity and the self. Perhaps there's less of a structural imperative now for adversarial combat sport, for masculine heroics and outdoor collective militaristic bonding.

The integration of sport into consumer culture is not just a matter of persuading teenagers to buy each season's upgrade of their team's kit. Fashion values as well as marketing gumption are at stake when sporting icons swap shorts for gowns, and fashion icons swap gowns for swimsuits. For instance, tennis champion Serena Williams has launched her own fashion label, Aneres (which is *Serena* reversed).[14] Or, in a stunning transformation where all trace of "sport" seems to have been erased, fashion photographer Daniela Federici has taken Olympian athlete Cathy Freeman—a world icon of power sport (Mars)—and made her over *as* Venus for Charlie Brown's winter 2004 collection (fig. 1).[15]

We've become so used to seeing fashion models in swimwear that it's hard to remember a time when sportswear was not regarded as fashion apparel. But when fashion was "modern," sportswear rarely if ever featured on the catwalk or in *Vogue*. Those days are long gone. Fashion and sport are so integrated that you can't see the seam where they join. For instance (not quite at random; but no one origin can be offered from distributive media like magazines), witness recent sets featuring fashion icon Kate Moss, who has no sporting background. She starred on the cover of an issue of *Vogue* (Paris) that was devoted to the proposition "Mode/Sport" (by Mario Testino).[16] Her set showed her on the athletics track in starting blocks; throwing a javelin; being handled by a trainer; looking almost antifashion in running shorts and tracksuit. Soon afterward she appeared for *W* magazine in the United States as "Glamazon" (by Mert Alas and Marcus Piggott), variously modeling sumptuous gowns and swimwear, sometimes indistinguishably, as in a shot of an Yves Saint Laurent jacket worn over an Eres bathing suit.[17] Throughout the set her hair is coiled, synchronized swimming–style. And so on, throughout the distributive media.

It is noteworthy that while sports and fashion are integrating, many of the sports in the "synchronized" category are at or beyond the edge of what is accepted as a "proper" sport. Synchronized swimming in particular seems to attract uncomprehending teasing from the locker-room jocks of competitive team contact sport. Like rhythmic gymnastics, it is also one of the few women-only sports to have achieved Olympic status. There's more than a

Figure 1. Photo of Cathy Freeman for the Charlie Brown (fashion house) Winter 2004 collection, by Daniela Federici. Courtesy Daniela Federici

whiff of gender politics in the refusal to see a women-only event as a sport at all, especially one where compulsory smiling and fashion-linked costumes and makeup emphasize what some see as feminine traits rather than sporting prowess. In terms of reputation deficit, the feminized and spectator-oriented style of synchronized swimming is to masculine combat-contact sports as popular media entertainment is to serious politics.

Airbrushed, or History?

So where did such a strange fish come from? It transpires that the origins of synchronized, feminized, plebiscitary, consumer-integrated sport go back to just one person, and an Australian at that. She was identified in her own day as *Venus*. Her name was Annette Kellerman:[18]

> Kellerman was Australia's aquanaut, the beauty who—long before Elle Macpherson—was known as The Perfect Woman. The self-promoter who—long before Madonna—got herself arrested, knowing the com-

mercial value of sensation. The thespian who—long before Nicole Kidman—was a Queen of the Screen. The fitness guru who—long before Jane Fonda—showed middle-aged women how to stay sexy.[19]

This catalogue of claims may seem hyperbolic, applied as it is to someone who is now largely forgotten even in the country of her birth. But in fact even this list falls well short of what Kellerman achieved. Not only was she the contemporary equal of Macpherson, Madonna, Kidman, and Fonda, but she was also a world champion sportswoman in both swimming and diving, and she was a sporting innovator, developing what was known at the time as "water ballet"—the precursor to synchronized swimming—and popularizing it worldwide via stage, screen, and stunt. As if all that wasn't enough, Kellerman is also credited with the invention and popularization of the one-piece swimsuit for women, making her an icon of fashion history too. And there's more. It is likely, however, that more people today have heard of the film made about her life than have heard of her. For the film was Esther Williams's *Million Dollar Mermaid* (1952), which, as we've seen, is itself the very emblem of the contemporary mediated public.

Esther Williams herself admired Kellerman as "a pioneer of women's rights." Williams told an interviewer in 2004:

> She knew there was more to being a woman than being kept in corsets. She wasn't content to float. She was determined to swim. . . . She was a woman who had a different opinion of what women could achieve. . . . Women have told me they learned to swim because they saw *Million Dollar Mermaid*. I loved that, and I know Annette would have loved it too. What she did was to persuade women to get in the water. I'm a continuum of that.[20]

Williams met Kellerman (then in her sixties) while she was making *Million Dollar Mermaid*. She asked her:

> "Do you like the idea of me playing you in the movie?" because I was a champion swimmer and a dedicated athlete like she was. She told me: "I wish you could have been Australian." I replied: "Annette, I'm all you've got. I'm the only swimmer in the movies. There won't be another one. So let's see what we can do with an American girl playing an Australian."

Kellerman was born in Marrickville, New South Wales, in 1886, suffering rickets (some accounts say it was 1887, and polio), for which she had to wear

Figure 2. Costume worn by Annette
Kellerman, Object number 2000/66,
Powerhouse Museum (Gift of the
Denis Wolanski Library, Sydney Opera
House, 2000)

leg braces until she was seven. She took up swimming to overcome this condition. She began to break records in her midteens. It was her swimming
prowess that opened up the possibility of a career as a professional swim-
mer, an opportunity she took by sailing for England in 1904. She worked
in Britain and Europe for the next few years, with three attempts to swim
the English Channel; river races on the Thames, Seine, and Danube; and a
coastal swim from Dover to Ramsgate. She emerged as a world champion in
both distance swimming and high diving. While still in her teens, according
to the citation in the International Swimming Hall of Fame, she attracted
the "largest live audience ever to see a swim race": Half a million Parisians
watched her race seventeen men down the Seine.[21] Then she went to the
United States, where she became the "million dollar mermaid" (fig. 2).[22]
And the rest is history.

To the Macpherson-Madonna-Kidman-Fonda list must therefore be added
one more name to signify her *sporting* renown and influence, which far

exceeded that of Australia's current greatest swimming hero, Ian Thorpe. But where Ian Thorpe is famous for swimming (and big feet), it remains the case that Kellerman was *also* famous as a beauty (Macpherson), self-promoter (Madonna), film star (Kidman), and fitness guru (Fonda).

Her reputation for beauty is based partly on her contribution to *fashion* — the invention of the one-piece swimsuit. This innovation also explains the reference to Madonna-like self-promotion. It was this garment — or lack of very much of it at all — that attracted the attention of both the Prince of Wales and Lord Northcliffe (owner of the *Daily Mirror*, which sponsored her appearances) while Kellerman was in the United Kingdom. The Power-house Museum marks the moment:

> At a time when female swimmers wore restrictive, cumbersome bath-ing costumes, Kellerman came up with the idea of a more practical one-piece swimsuit. When invited to give an exhibition of swimming and diving before members of the Royal Family at London's Bath Club, she was forbidden to show any bare leg. Her solution was to buy a long pair of black stockings and sew them onto a boy's short racing swim-suit. The women's one-piece swimsuit had arrived.[23]

After she went to the United States in about 1910, it was this garment (boy's shorts, with or without sewn-in stockings) that got her newsworthily arrested on a Boston beach. In turn that incident attracted academic atten-tion, leading to her reputation as "The Perfect Woman." Her biographer Emily Gibson tells the story:

> [Harvard professor Dr. Dudley Sargent] actually heard about her be-cause she was doing a swim from Revere beach in Boston, and she went down in her Australian boy's bathing suit, and was arrested for indecent exposure because nobody liked seeing legs in those days. So it was in the papers and Dr. Sargent heard about her and asked her to come along to Harvard where he measured her. Before her he'd measured thousands of women, which I don't think would have been such a bad job for a Harvard professor. What his standard was, was the Venus de Milo, and none of them had even come close to those mea-surements; and Annette Kellerman did. He even measured Annette's wrists. There are wrist measurements in Dr. Dudley Sargent's little jot-tings, and the Venus de Milo, as we know, didn't have any wrists, but anyway.[24]

Annette Kellerman had one more claim to fame up her sleeve: she prefigured the exercise video (Fonda). In 1918 she published a book called *Physical Beauty—How to Keep It*, and later in life ran a business called Physical Instruction by Mail.[25]

The International Swimming Hall of Fame makes it clear that her place in history was secured because of the all-too-corporeal nature of her swimming achievements:

> Annette Kellerman starred in motion pictures such as the *Diving Venus, Queen of the Mermaids, A Daughter of the Gods,* and *Neptune's Daughter.* She crisscrossed the US and circled the world in the famed "Annette Kellerman black one-piece suit" which *made swimming attractive to men and liberated for women.* She performed stunts and dives which made her first among the fore-runners to synchronized swimming and women's high diving.[26]

She commented on her own fame later in life: "I come from a nation of swimmers but no one remembers me now, yet I was once one of the most famous women in all the world. *They called me the 'diving Venus,'* the perfect woman, a daughter of the gods."[27] Officially modeled on the goddess Venus, attractive to men, liberated for women, world champion, star of stage and screen (and river), inventor of a film genre, progenitor of two sports (synchronized swimming and women's high diving), inventor of the one-piece swimsuit, inventor of home-fitness instruction—and forgotten. The modernist era of sport didn't know how to deal with an attractive celebrity entertainer who contributed to fashion, films, and female fitness. Kellerman was ahead of her time. That time has come.

Synchronized Voting

The combination of publicity, showbiz, skimpy costumes, and a perfect body, masking but also popularizing world-class athleticism and female achievement, was too much for traditional sporting culture to handle. But now we are witness to the integration of all such values into sport. Synchronized sports are on the rise.

Here the shift from sports based on Mars (power, victory) to Venus (law; "seduction, not coercion") is complete. The "law" component comes into play in the mechanism used to decide winners. Instead of literally beating the opposition, sports like ice-skating, diving, and synchronized swimming require a choice to be made in a rule-governed environment. Judges are understood to be partial, so they too are multiplied, up to seven from different nationalities, whose scores are combined and sometimes discounted, to ensure that national interest or hegemonic power does not prevail. The mode of scoring brings such sports into the realm of media, where the arts of Venus, performance, look, style—and smiling—can carry the day.

Somewhere beyond what we currently recognize as sport lies "reality" TV, some of which is strongly based on sports values. *Plebiscitary sports* are beginning to draw from "reality" TV the image of consumer choice as the ultimate arbiter of sporting achievement. These not-quite sports represent a dispersal of competitiveness itself from the individual combative hero to the feminized image of the consumer. For a taste of things to come, behold *synchronized dancing.*

The progenitor of this emergent form is one of the oldest and longest-running shows on international television: the BBC's *Come Dancing*, which debuted in 1949 and lasted until 1995.[28] Its demise was short-lived, however, for in 2004 the BBC replaced it with *Strictly Come Dancing*.[29] The title borrows a bit of glam from Baz Luhrmann's 1992 movie comedy *Strictly Ballroom* to enliven the rather naff image of *Come Dancing*.[30] It worked wonders. The show immediately became a major hit in the United Kingdom and internationally. It has been spun off and reversioned ruthlessly by the BBC, making it one of the corporation's biggest export earners.[31] In Australia it topped the ratings as *Dancing with the Stars*.[32] In Italy it scorched the floor as *Ballando con le Stelle*.[33] It has been bought by Belgium, Poland, Denmark, and New Zealand. There's a children's version called *Dance Factory*,[34] and there's an amateur-only version called *Strictly Dance Fever*.[35] There are one-off specials like *Strictly Ice Dancing* (a Christmas show) and *Strictly African Dancing*.[36] The latter was screened in July 2005 to coincide with Live8 and the G8, as part of the BBC's "Year of Africa." It featured sporting and showbiz celebrities of Afro-Caribbean background, paired with traditional African dance troupes. After training and visiting Africa to see where the dances came from, each one performed their dance live in front of a studio audience, with a panel of experts judging their skills while viewers could vote for their favorites.

Finally, the ultimate citadel has fallen—*Dancing with the Stars* has conquered the United States.[37] The Disney-owned ABC bought it to rival *American Idol* on Fox. It became the surprise summer hit of 2005—a surprise because no one in the United States thought it could succeed. The ABC even had to bring over the original BBC team to make the local version:

"I am fully aware that this may sound like the craziest show anyone in the US has ever heard of," Andrea Wong, ABC's vice-president, said. . . . Ms Wong said: "In a world where it's easier for reality series to imitate than innovate, I just love how fresh this format is. And the show's global success demonstrates how audiences around the world find it surprising and, undeniably, fun."[38]

In all of these versions the basic proposition is the same: viewers get to see someone who can't necessarily dance being put through their paces, in synchronized competition with other pairs who are eliminated by a combination of expert judges and viewer plebiscite until a winner emerges at the end of the series. The format is usually a celebrity paired with a dance professional (*Strictly Dance Fever* used all-amateur couples). Often the viewers' vote is at odds with the judges' score. It seems that viewers enjoy watching people who dance as badly as they do, so frequently an incompetent but plucky celeb will survive long after rivals who can dance.

Voting is a matter of public interest. In Australia a major national scandal broke out when teen celebrity Nikki Webster was eliminated from the 2005 series of *Dancing with the Stars*.[39] Webster shot to international fame in 2000 as the thirteen-year-old in a sundress who aerially guided 4 billion TV viewers through the Sydney Olympics opening ceremony. But she was booted out of *Dancing with the Stars* when a judge on the show awarded her tango a score of one out of ten—too low to be offset by the other judges' scores or viewers' vote. A tabloid feeding frenzy ensued.[40] Ratings soared.

Competitive dancing is not new (*They Shoot Horses, Don't They?* is a vision of dancing as Mars, not Venus),[41] but as a *plebiscitary sport*, the *Strictly/Stars* format is a pioneer. Whatever the version, the key to commercial (if not competitive) success is consumer choice. Elimination is achieved not by brute endurance but by the extent to which skill, attractiveness, fashion, and the human appeal of flawed celebrity or plucky amateur combine into an SMS-able vote. Given the controversy surrounding judging panels in both accredited sports and reality TV, can we be very far away from the *plebiscitary Olympics*, where the winners will be made in the image of the feminized viewing-voting consumer-citizen? Conversely, when can we expect politics to abandon Martial Leviathan and embrace Venusian synchronicity? When will we see *Strictly Come Voting*, where politicians waltz in an election special? At the moment that's only a spoof imagined by some wag at *The Times*.[42] But it can't be long before it becomes politico-sporting "reality."

Notes

1 John Hartley, *The Politics of Pictures: The Creation of the Public in the Age of Popular Media* (London: Routledge, 1992), 136–39.

2 For more information on *The Million Dollar Mermaid*, see www.imdb.com/title/ tt0044903/ and wwwmcc.murdoch.edu.au/ReadingRoom/6.2/Lucy.html (both accessed September 21, 2005).

3 Hartley, *The Politics of Pictures*, 137. Tom Streeter notes my "description of the growth of the 'smiling professions' in the twentieth century. . . . Hartley wittily uses synchronized swimming—a strenuous, highly skilled activity performed with a contrived smile—to illustrate the internal character, artfulness, and improbability of this new form of professionalism." Thomas Streeter, *Historical Journal of Film, Radio and Television* (June 1996), available at www.findarticles.com/p/articles/mi_m2584/is_n2_v16/ai_18897276 (accessed September 21, 2005).

4 Robert Kagan, *Paradise and Power: America and Europe in the New World Order* (London: Atlantic Books, 2003), 3; see also www.policyreview.org/JUN02/kagan.html and idg.communication.utexas.edu/flow/?jot=view&id=814 (both accessed September 21, 2005).

5 See Robert Cooper on the difference between premodern, modern, and postmodern countries: Robert Cooper, "Why We Still Need Empires," *Guardian*, April 7, 2002, available at observer.guardian.co.uk/worldview/story/0,11581,680095,00.html.

6 Thomas Hobbes, *Leviathan* (1651; Harmondsworth: Penguin, 1968), 378–86, 728; see also Hartley, *The Politics of Pictures*, 122–30.

7 A situation that remains; see Stephen Coleman's comparison of PJs and BBs—"political junkies" and fans of *Big Brother*—in Stephen Coleman, *A Tale of Two Houses* (London: Hansard Society, 2003), also available at www.hansardsociety.org.uk/node/view/21 (accessed September 21, 2005).

8 Sarah Bombell and Eloise Amberger, Queensland champion duet in synchronized swimming, interviewed on *The Sports Factor* (Mick O'Regan), ABC Radio National, May 27, 2005: www.abc.net.au/rn/talks/8.30/sportsf/stories/s1376333.htm. "Roy and HG" refers to a comedy sports commentator duo with a cult following in Australia.

9 John Hartley, "The 'Value Chain of Meaning' and the New Economy," *International Journal of Cultural Studies* 7.1 (2004): 129–41.

10 John Hartley, *A Short History of Cultural Studies* (London: Sage Publications, 2003), 3–5.

11 The women's skydiving world record was set September 30, 2005. See jumpforthecause .com/2005_wwr.html (accessed December 3, 2005). Thanks to Christi Stanforth for this reference.

12 Ballroom dancing is already a world sport: see dancesportinfo.net/ and www.dancesport .uk.com/world.htm (both accessed September 21, 2005).

13 Like this from West Point: www.usma.edu/PublicAffairs/Press_Kit_files/Cadet%20 Calisthenics%20in%20the%20Courtyard.jpg. The Nazis loved calisthenics too: www .ushmm.org/museum/exhibit/online/olympics/zcb016.htm. Now it is beloved by police youth clubs: www.afp.gov.au/afp/page/Kids/YouthResources/PCYC/Programs/ Callisthenics.htm (all accessed September 21, 2005).

14 For more information on Serena Williams's fashion label, see www.aneresdesigns.com/ aneres.html (accessed September 21, 2005).

15 For more information see Charlie Brown fashion house: www.charliebrown.com.au/ (click on front door; wardrobe; catalogue/clothes rack; Winter 2004); and for more information on photographer Daniela Federici see www.danielafederici.com/ (both accessed September 21, 2005).

16 *Vogue Paris*, November 2004 (no. 852).

17 *W*, March 2005; also edited for www.style.com/w/feat_story/020205 (accessed September 21, 2005).

18 Kellerman's surname was often rendered "Kellermann" in her own day, especially in the United States; see www.stairstars.com/dyn/detail.php?listingid=20 and www.whitehat .com.au/Sydney/People/Kellerman.asp (accessed December 4, 2005). The sport's governing body in Canada claims that "ornamental swimming" was invented by Canadian water polo player and diver Margaret Sellers in the 1920s, but they also concede chronological primacy to Annette Kellerman: www.synchro.ca/history.htm (accessed September 21, 2005).

19 From a review of the documentary *The Original Mermaid*, *Sydney Morning Herald*, April 14, 2004: www.smh.com.au/articles/2004/04/13/1081838727299.html.

20 Quoted in Steve Meacham, "Beauty Who Swam in the Big Pool," *Sydney Morning Herald*, April 14, 2004: www.smh.com.au/articles/2004/04/13/1081838727299.html.

21 International Swimming Hall of Fame: www.ishof.org/74akellerman.html (accessed September 21, 2005).

22 See the biopic *The Original Mermaid*, dir. Michael Cordell, screened SBS April 15, 2004, for sale at www.abc.net.au/abccontentsales/s1132527.htm. Video available at www .roninfilms.com.au/video/1886377/30/2387690942; ATOM Study guide at www.ronin films.com.au/related/2387690942-0.pdf (both accessed September 21, 2005).

23 Kellerman biography, Powerhouse Museum Sydney, www.powerhousemuseum.com/ opac/2000-66.asp (accessed September 21, 2005).

24 Emily Gibson, interviewed on *The Sports Factor* (Mick O'Regan), ABC Radio National, May 27, 2005: www.abc.net.au/rn/talks/8.30/sportsf/stories/s1376333.htm; and see also Emily Gibson with Barbara Firth, *The Original Million Dollar Mermaid* (Sydney: Pavilion/Allen & Unwin, 2005), and John Lucas, "Making a Statement: Annette Kellerman Advances the Worlds of Swimming, Diving, and Entertainment," in *Sporting Traditions* (Los Angeles: Amateur Athletic Foundation of Los Angeles, 2004): www.aafla.org/ SportsLibrary/SportingTraditions/1998/st1402/st1402e.pdf (accessed July 2005); and for information on Dudley Sargent see the Iowa Health and Physical Readiness Alliance: www.ihpra.org/dudley_sargent.htm (accessed July 2005).

25 "Geoff Howe's Inner West History" (2000): www.sydneyhistory.com.au/kellerman.html; and see also www.smh.com.au/articles/2004/04/13/1081838727299.html (both accessed September 21, 2005).

26 Kellerman biography, International Swimming Hall of Fame (Fort Lauderdale, FL): www .ishof.org/74akellerman.html (accessed September 21, 2005), my emphasis.

27 Quoted in *The Sports Factor* (Mick O'Regan), ABC Radio National, May 27, 2005: www .abc.net.au/rn/talks/8.30/sportsf/stories/s1376333.htm, my emphasis.

28 For more information on *Come Dancing*, see www.ukgameshows.com/index.php/Come_ Dancing; en.wikipedia.org/wiki/Come_Dancing; www.nostalgiacentral.com/tv/variety/ comedancing.htm (all accessed September 21, 2005).

29 For more information on *Strictly Come Dancing*, see en.wikipedia.org/wiki/Strictly_Come _Dancing (accessed September 21, 2005).

30 The Oxford English Dictionary defines *naff* as "unfashionable, vulgar; lacking in style, inept; worthless, faulty." For more information on *Strictly Ballroom*, see www.imdb.com/ title/tt0105488/ (accessed September 21, 2005).

31 Adam Sherwin, "Come Dancing Set to Have a Twirl on American Television," *Times Online*, March 24, 2005: www.timesonline.co.uk/article/0,,2-1538643,00.html.

32 For more information on *Dancing with the Stars*, Channel Seven Australia, see seven.com .au/seven/041005_dancing_FAQ (accessed September 21, 2005).

33 "BBC Worldwide and ABC Dance with the Stars in the U.S.," BBC Press Office: www.bbc .co.uk/pressoffice/commercial/worldwidestories/pressreleases/2005/03_march/strictly _us.shtml (accessed September 21, 2005).

34 Brand Republic, "BBC to Extend Successful Strictly Come Dancing Brand with Children's Edition," *Media Bulletin*, March 21, 2005: www.brandrepublic.com/bulletins/media/ article/467330/bbc-extend-successful-strictly-dancing-brand-childrens-edition.

35 For more information on *Strictly Dance Fever*, see www.bbc.co.uk/strictlydancefever/ dancefever/news/2005/06/04/19761.shtml (accessed September 21, 2005).

36 For more information on *Strictly African Dancing*, see www.bbc.co.uk/pressoffice/ pressreleases/stories/2005/06_june/20/dancing.shtml (accessed September 21, 2005).

37 For more information on the U.S. version, *Dancing with the Stars*, see abc.go.com/ primetime/dancing/vote.html (accessed September 21, 2005).

38 Quoted in Sherwin, "Come Dancing Set to Have a Twirl on American Television."

39 For more information on Nikki Webster, see en.wikipedia.org/wiki/Nikki_Webster (accessed September 21, 2005).

40 "Dancing Controversy," *The Age*, March 17, 2005: www.theage.com.au/news/TV — Radio/ Dancing-controversy/2005/03/16/1110913657005.html; see also Channel Seven: seven .com.au/seven/dancing_webster (accessed September 21, 2005).

41 For more information on *They Shoot Horses Don't They?* see en.wikipedia.org/wiki/ Horace_McCoy and see imdb.com/title/tt0065088/ (both accessed September 21, 2005).

42 Sherwin, "Come Dancing Set to Have a Twirl on American Television."

Kenneth Surin

Fandom: Colin "Pine Tree" Meads

> They once asked him [Meads] why British forwards
> were no good in his era. "Too many sweatbands, not
> enough sweat," he growled.
> —Stephen Jones, "Not Enough English Lions," En-
> glish Rugby Union Web site, www.rfu.com/index.cfm/
> fuseaction/RFUHome.News_Detail/StoryID/10145

There are three primary ways of understanding or producing the concept of being a fan. One is the more typical notion, which hinges on the notion of a decisive identification with a player or team that is invariably constructed along binary lines. Thus one is for Manchester United and hence against Liverpool in English soccer (and vice versa), for Serena Williams and against Lindsay Davenport in women's tennis (and vice versa), for the Detroit Pistons and against the San Antonio Spurs in American basketball (and vice versa), for Michelle Kwan and against Sasha Cohen in women's ice-skating (and vice versa), and so on. This kind of identification can be understood in broadly psychoanalytic terms, involving an idealization of one's "own" team or player, and with a corresponding abjection of the supposedly adversarial team or figure. Being a fan is something like belonging to a tribe, and

The *South Atlantic Quarterly* 105:2, Spring 2006.
Copyright © 2006 by Duke University Press.

one's affinity for the team or player in question is apt to be the outcome of a mythopoesis—the goal scored by X surpassed all excellence, the performance of Y in the championship is never going to be equaled, Z is the best hockey player of all time, and so forth. The performer thus idealized might as well be said to commune with the gods, a state of affairs reflected in the frequently publicized "excesses" of some fans—the bedroom that is festooned from floor to ceiling with pictures and memorabilia of just this one sports figure, the parents who gave their hapless newborn child the names of all eleven players of a championship-winning English soccer team, and the horrific incident in which a besotted Steffi Graf fan stabbed Graf's archrival Monica Seles in the shoulder in an effort to destroy (literally) the adversary of his idealized object. This notion of "fandom" is relatively easy to theorize, since our widely prevalent celebrity culture provides analogous figures in other cultural spheres such as pop music and the movies and television. For every Michael Jordan there is a Will Smith, for every David Beckham there is a Brad Pitt, and for every Annika Sundstrom there is an Angelina Jolie. Sometimes the fields of media culture and sport even get blurred, as when Anna Kournikova, the tennis player who never won a tournament, nevertheless became a celebrity with an income from endorsements and advertisements that dwarfed the earnings of other vastly more talented players, thanks to her photogenic appearance. It is of course easy to dismiss and even to sneer at this way of constituting one's "fanhood," if one happens to be a fan, but given the importance of such identifications for the sheer living of one's daily life, why should a "cathexis" or identification with Tiger Woods, say, be any less well regarded than a similar psychic identification with the late Pope John Paul II, whose decision to prohibit condom use in the context of the AIDS pandemic probably resulted in vastly more deaths than Woods would accomplish if he walked golf courses with a bag full of live hand grenades instead of a set of golf clubs? We'll return to this question later.

A second way of constructing the notion of fanhood relies on criteria that are perhaps best described as "ethical" (provided the notion of the ethical is fairly broadly construed). An athlete is beloved for his or her "sturdiness" or "resoluteness" (one thinks here of Michelle Akers, the American soccer player who never achieved the celebrity of the much better-known Mia Hamm); or "astuteness" (here someone like the quarterback Joe Montana comes readily to mind, since it is hard to recall any memorable individual move or play made by Montana, except that he was unerringly right in his choice of passing options in game after important game); or "indomitability" (English soccer fans would refer here to someone like the defenders Tommy Smith of Liverpool or Nobby Stiles of Manchester United, much less athletically gifted than their respective teammates Kenny Dalglish or Bobby Charlton, but nonetheless absolutely indispensable to their teams' successes over nearly two decades). One could of course multiply the list of these putative moral qualities. Their import for the notion of fanhood is not susceptible to generalization: one encounters sports aficionados who profess to "hate" the "overrated" Tommy Smith or Nobby Stiles in a way that would be impossible to associate with Dalglish or Charlton (who are rarely accused of being "overrated," even by opposing fans), and one doubts that there ever was an official Tommy Smith fan club outside of Liverpool and its environs that survived long after his career was over, though given the passion of Liverpool's supporters, even those who are expatriates, it would be no surprise if there were such a club. But there is at least one Tommy Smith fan in the world, to wit, this particular author (who would much rather belong to a fan club for Tommy Smith than one for David Beckham — here's the kind of barbed partiality that typifies the true fan!), and there will be pubs in Liverpool where no doubt a pint is still raised to the dourly indomitable Tommy Smith from time to time.

It is true, of course, that such putatively "moral" qualities can quickly be reduced to the level of cliché and platitude, as when a sports commentator says that "the great ones always know how to elevate their game," a slogan now being used in a television advertising campaign by the petroleum company Philips-Concoco. One has to be a relativist here, since with a few notable exceptions, such qualities tend overwhelmingly to exist in the eyes of the beholder (i.e., the fan) and few others. The exceptions are constituted by the "truly great," about whom there is often no consensus, though here one could pretty much get away with designating as "great" such athletes as Wayne Gretzsky (ice hockey), Donald Bradman and Garfield Sobers (cricket), Walter Payton (American football), Martina Navratilova and Pete Sampras (tennis), Mia Hamm and Pele (soccer), Emil Zatopek and Edwin Moses (track), Gareth Edwards (rugby), "Marvellous" Marvin Hagler (boxing), and Rudy Hartono (badminton — but what is it to be truly "great" in a much, but wrongly, denigrated sport like badminton?). However, the fact remains that sports fans do evaluate their idols in terms of such moral categories, amorphous and slippery though these categories happen to be. The "truly great" tend to be those whose claims to such paramountcy are much less likely to be challenged by the mass of fans in that sport — although when it comes to making a positive specification of the qualities that inhere in the supposedly great athlete for that sport, a consensus is much more difficult to establish. But fandom becomes interesting and quirky not so much when someone professes to be a fan of Mia Hamm and Pele (such fans tend to be rather boring, and more interested in the pursuit of celebrities than anything else) as when someone turns out to be a partisan of some obscure toiler playing for a club like Doncaster Rovers or Plymouth Albion in the bottom rungs of the English soccer league, or some largely stationary and square-jawed lineman in American football whose name eludes even the expert commentators. Fans of Manchester United are a dime a dozen, but truly special is the fan of a club like Plymouth Albion, who gives his or her support year-in and year-out to a team of no-hopers, as opposed to the glitzy multimillionaires who play for Manchester United and who expect to win at least one major trophy every season.

A third way of understanding the notion of fanhood is actually a way of destabilizing the notion, though it involves a process that probably only the fan can undergo. The core of this process is a form of *memoire involontaire*, a fleeting recollection of the sight, on television or film or at an actual game, of some sporting moment. I am mowing the lawn and there is a sudden flash-back to Björn Borg fiddling nervously with his racket strings just before he receives John McEnroe's serve in a Wimbledon final; I am driving between Blacksburg and Durham, and there is a similar momentary recollection of the great West Indian fast bowler Wesley Hall, tearing in to bowl off his long run, shirt unbuttoned and gold crucifix flying, as he unleashes a fear-somely fast ball at a Malaysian batter in 1963; I am walking to the university library slowly, with a big pile of books, when I suddenly recall the incredible last lap of the 10,000 meters in the 1971 European Championships, when Juha "the Cruel" Vaatainen, the Finn who ran the entire distance with spike wounds in both his shins, produced an electrifying final lap of 53.8 seconds, then thought impossible in 10,000-meter running, in a race where five runners broke the 28-minute barrier for the first time at this distance; I am eating dinner when I see a mental image of the New York Giants linebacker Lawrence Taylor vaulting a covering player to sack the opposing quarter-back with a ferocity that made me pause as I ate; and so forth. Most fans, I believe, have such involuntary experiences, just the way in which a gardener who loves roses, which I am, will have a similar involuntary image of a certain kind of rose when writing an essay for *SAQ*. But what is it about such images that makes the person who undergoes them a fan? If the walls of my bedroom were covered in pictures of Borg or of Vaatainen (in his prime, at any rate—today, in his fifties, he is a bespectacled, bald, plump figure who would not easily be identified as someone who had once been a world-class runner of long distances, even thirty-five years ago), then I would be more easily recognized as a fan. To wear the visible emblems of fanhood is one thing; to be submitted to involuntary images of the sporting figures one may happen to treasure, that is quite another. But to have such sport-ing images float capriciously and frequently before one's mind is surely a matter of significance: What exactly can these images be said to indicate for the putative sports fan, or what is it about them that is likely to suggest that one is somehow a sports fan?

There are of course no easy answers to such questions. The crux of the issues raised by these questions is that there is for the sports fan something absolutely "essential" about one's veneration of a team or sports figure, yet when it comes to being the subject of an "involuntary memory," one may not even consider oneself to be a fan of the sport in question. After all, I do not consider myself to be a tennis fan, yet I do have these fleeting and involuntary, but recurring, images of Borg and McEnroe playing those won-derful championship games in their prime. I consider myself to be a fan, a true fan, of rugby and cricket, and in an obvious and predictable way, I check scores in these sports with a passion that I simply do not have for other sports like basketball or tennis. But I am still subject to the involun-tary memories of events and personages in sports for which I do not have an overt and evident affinity. In these episodes of involuntary memory, I am able to visualize every step of the bowling stride of the great West Indian cricketer Michael Holding, even though he ended his international career in 1987. At the same time, I can also visualize, from time to time and also inadvertently, the stride pattern of the great American hurdler Ed Moses, even though his last Olympic competition was in the 1988 Seoul Games, and I am not as interested in track-and-field as I am in cricket. These things just happen to some sports fans, as my conversations with many of them indicate.

But are such phenomena as the ones occurring in involuntary memory enough to signal "fandom" or "fanhood"? Here we have to address, no mat-ter how cursorily, some of the distinctive features that attend these occur-rences of involuntary memory. The most notable of these qualities is that the recollected event becomes suddenly contemporaneous for the person whose memory it is. This is depicted with exquisite clarity in what is almost certainly the most famous literary rendition of the phenomenon of involuntary memory, namely, the famous madeleine scene in Proust's *À la recherche du temps perdu*:

> And suddenly the memory revealed itself. The taste was that of the little piece of madeleine which on Sunday mornings at Combray (because on those mornings I did not go out before mass), when I went to say good morning to her in her bedroom, my aunt Léonie used to give me, dipping it first in her own cup of tea or tisane. The sight of the little madeleine had recalled nothing to my mind before I tasted it; perhaps because I had so often seen such things in the meantime, without tasting them, on the trays in pastry-cooks' windows, that their image had dissociated itself from those Combray days to take its place among others more recent; perhaps because of those memories, so long abandoned and put out of mind, nothing now survived, everything was scattered; the shapes of things, including that of the little scallop-shell of pastry, so richly sensual under its severe, religious folds, were either obliterated or had been so long dormant as to have lost the power of expansion which would have allowed them to resume their place in my consciousness. But when from a long-distant past nothing subsists, after the people are dead, after the things are broken and scattered, taste and smell alone, more fragile but more enduring, more unsubstantial, more persistent, more faithful, remain poised a long time, like souls, remembering, waiting, hoping, amid the ruins of all the rest; and bear unflinchingly, in the tiny and almost impalpable drop of their essence, the vast structure of recollection.
>
> And as soon as I had recognized the taste of the piece of madeleine soaked in her decoction of lime-blossom which my aunt used to give me (although I did not yet know and must long postpone the discovery of why this memory made me so happy) immediately the old grey house upon the street, where her room was, rose up like a stage set to attach itself to the little pavilion opening on to the garden which had been built out behind it for my parents (the isolated segment which until that moment had been all that I could see); and with the house the town, from morning to night and in all weathers, the Square where I used to be sent before lunch, the streets along which I used to run errands, the country roads we took when it was fine. And as in the game wherein the Japanese amuse themselves by filling a porcelain bowl with water and steeping in it little pieces of paper which until then are without character or form, but, the moment they become wet, stretch

and twist and take on colour and distinctive shape, become flowers or houses or people, solid and recognizable, so in that moment all the flowers in our garden and in M. Swann's park, and the water-lilies on the Vivonne and the good folk of the village and their little dwellings and the parish church and the whole of Combray and its surroundings, taking shape and solidity, sprang into being, town and gardens alike, from my cup of tea.[1]

As depicted by Proust, the focal point of the recollection, in this case the taste and scent of the tea-soaked madeleine, opens up an entire universe from Marcel's childhood, rendering it present in the process. It is, however, a process over which the narrator has no control—everything occurs as in a swift and unexpected flood. This aspect of involuntary memory also marks the recollections of the sports fan who has his or her "Proustean moments." One does not just recollect the goal or try or basket that wins the game, but also the untied shoelace, the stray bead of sweat, the color of the sweatband, the specific and distinctive yell and the grunt, the limp that occurs at no other point in the game, and so on. This can happen even when one is self-avowedly not a fan of the player in question: I have involuntary recollections of the now-retired American tennis player Jimmy Connors, with his ferocious grunts and demented fist-pumping, even though he has never been a favorite of mine; quite the opposite, in fact. I find myself recollecting him more than I do Björn Borg, my favorite tennis player. The upshot of this is an effective repositioning and complication of my admiration for the great Swedish tennis player—not a diminution of my affinity for his great playing record, but the dawning insight that one's sensibility as enshrined in memory is trying to tell a different story. Or, at any rate, to allow the possibility that a different story may be heard. But how is a different story regarding one's "fanhood" going to be heard and constructed? The rest of this essay will focus on the central but not ultimately determinative role of involuntary memory in the constitution of "fanhood," and then on the object of my own "fanhood," the great New Zealand rugby player Colin Meads.

Memory, especially involuntary memory, is a psychological state par excellence, and it would be quite misleading to reduce "fanhood" to this kind of state. More, much more than psychology accounts for the character of being a fan.

Involuntary memory is of course only one dimension of memory, and it can be understood only when contrasted with its counterpart, voluntary memory. Unlike involuntary memory, voluntary memory follows the "arrow of time" and extends from an actual present, the *now* of chronological time, to a present which "once was," that is, an event that once was present but is now no longer in "the present." For Gilles Deleuze, therefore, the past of voluntary memory is relative in two senses: (1) to the present which it had once been, but also (2) to the present, the *now*, with regard to which it can only be the past. Voluntary memory is not able to access the past directly; it can only reconstitute it with different "now" times. Thus, the severe hamstring injury in 1971 that ended my college rugby season was retrieved as a memory in 1990 in relation to the now that was 1990, and again in 2004 in relation to the now that was 2004, and so forth. At each of these times, 1990 and 2004 and so on ad infinitum, 1971 is an inert "past present" refracted through the prism of a 1990, a 2004, and so on, so that 1990 and 2004 represent a kind of photo image of my various pasts, similar to the way in which the pictures of myself in the family album show me as a baby in 1948, a toddler in 1950, a teenager in 1963, a young man in 1975, a middle-aged person in 1990, and so on. Each time, my hamstring injury is a kind of residue from the past which comes to perturb, albeit now only very gently, my various present times, in 1972, 1973, 1984, 1985 up to . . . But it does not make the actual present any different, no more than does my recollection (whether in 1972, 1982, 1992, or 2002, and so on) of the sensational save made by the England goalkeeper Gordon Banks from Pele's header in the 1970 World Cup game between Brazil and England, make any difference to my actual presents as they were in 1972, 1982, 1992, or 2002, and so on. There is nothing transformative about this kind of voluntary memory, even though I happen to be a great admirer of Gordon Banks, who with the Russian Lev Yashin was surely one of the two greatest goalkeepers in the history of soccer.[2] The same is true, alas, of involuntary memory—were my recollection of Banks's spectacular save to occur as an involuntary memory as I was watering my flower beds or pushing the cart in my local supermarket last month or this week, it would still make no difference to the "now" of these times, no more than it would if, in quest of a voluntary memory, I replayed this evening my videotape of that wonderful 1970 England-Brazil game and used it as the vehicle to recall Banks's save as I saw it on the BBC live transmission in 1970. The sheer fact of the matter is that subjective identification, of the kind that pivots on the "great moments" associated with this or that sporting event or figure, is not in the end the way to approach "fanhood." Granted, the conventional wisdom may grasp "fanhood" exclusively in terms of subjective identification ("those fanatical cheese-heads who support the Green Bay Packers," "those crazy Millwall soccer fans," "Sachin Tendulkar is my cricketing idol," etc.), but it may be more productive to look for other theoretical instruments and resources for producing the fanhood concept.

Let us turn here once more to Deleuze's reading of Proust for some clues regarding an approach that places less emphasis on the forms of subjective identification. Deleuze insists that "Proust's work is not oriented to the past and the discoveries of memory, but to the future and the progress of an apprenticeship. What is important is that the hero does not know certain things at the start, gradually learns them, and finally receives an ultimate revelation. Necessarily, then, he suffers disappointments: he 'believed,' he suffered under illusions; the world vacillates in the course of apprenticeship" (25). In *À la recherche du temps perdu*, Deleuze argues, Marcel undergoes an "apprenticeship of signs" (4).

In what follows, I want to explore the possibility that "fanhood" is a similar apprenticeship in signs, one that cannot hinge ultimately on subjective associations and identifications but that must in the end be connected in some way with the truth. This is the only way I can explain my own "fandom" where Colin Meads is concerned, since I never was a fan of his while he played, and it took nearly two decades after his retirement for me to see that he was a truly great rugby player, one who perhaps more than any other embodied for me the "essence" of the game. Let's begin with Deleuze's elaboration of Proust's use of signs in *À la recherche du temps perdu*.[3]

The madeleine, the sign of involuntary memory, however par excellence, is only one of four kinds of signs Deleuze believed to be found in *À la recherche du temps perdu*. The *signs of worldliness* belong to the world of social norms, manners, bourgeois etiquette, customary practices of "decency and decorum," and so on. All signs are hieroglyphs, concealing even as they inform, and worldly signs are no exception. It is, for example, a mystery of social life why X should belong to the circle of upper-class wastrels around Prince Harry, but not Y, who is just as privileged, "posh," anti-intellectual, oafish, and superficial as X (and indeed Harry himself). Equally, it is a mystery why a seemingly banal remark will make someone cringe with embarrassment or appear hurt, and so on. Or why such a meaningful look should be exchanged between two colleagues at just this point in an aimless conversation at the faculty start-of-year party. Where Deleuze is concerned, worldly signs lack any direct reference; they serve only as the placeholders of our ideas and deeds.[4] They are relatively trivial and meaningless, the very stuff of convention and ritual (7). Very little in the world would change if Y and not X belonged to Prince Harry's circle, or if one's two colleagues had not exchanged a meaningful look at just that point in the party, and so forth.

The *signs of love* constitute the second kind of Proustian sign. The signs of the one who is loved expresses a mysterious world. In Deleuze's words, "the loved one implicates, envelops, imprisons a world that must be deciphered, that is, interpreted" (7). The one who is loved embodies a multiplicity of worlds, and the task and challenge extended to the one who loves is to become involved with these mysterious worlds and the signs that express them. But this is a huge and momentous undertaking, and the worlds of the loved one can often remain opaque to the one seeking to decipher these signs. These signs therefore often serve as an incitement to jealousy and the frequently unruly passions that afflict many forms of love. These passions and their accompanying language—the language of half-truths, red herrings, enticements, and sudden withdrawals with no ultimate purpose in mind, if not outright deception—are integral components of the erotic relationship. As Deleuze puts it, "The interpretation of amorous signs is necessarily the interpretation of lies" (9).

Sensuous signs represent the third kind of Proustian sign. The madeleine, the uneven stones in the baptistery of St. Mark's Church in Venice, the ringing doorbell are the famous signs of involuntary memory in *À la recherche du temps perdu*. In the sensuous sign, an entire world, implicated in the sign, unfolds as a result of a spontaneous experience associated with the act of dunking the madeleine, tripping over the baptistery steps, and so on. Thus, in the passage quoted above, Marcel says that dipping the madeleine led to an experience in which "in a moment all the flowers in our garden and in M. Swann's park, and the water-lilies on the Vivonne and the good folk of the village and their little dwellings and the parish church and the whole of Combray and its surroundings, taking shape and solidity, sprang into being, towns and gardens alike, from my cup of tea."[5] Sensuous signs are suffused with affect, and administer a jolt to the mechanisms, given that they require the world implicated in them to be explicated and interpreted. Unlike voluntary memory, in which recollection is steered by the conscious will of the one who recollects, the sensuous signs of involuntary memory reveal the essence of the world opened up by the recollected object (Combray, Venice, etc.). In voluntary memory the goals and purposes of the individual having the recollection superintend the recollected object, thereby deflecting awareness from its essence. Involuntary memory, by contrast, precisely because spontaneity subverts the directionality supplied by the will, is able to open itself to the essence of the thing and the world implicated in it. This world goes beyond the sensuous sign (there is much more to the childhood world of Marcel in Combray than the madeleine itself betokens), but the sensuous sign itself is always material. At the same time there is an evanescent and gratuitous quality to the sensuous sign, which makes it difficult to sustain as a vehicle of interpretation where the essence of a world is concerned.

The sensuous sign has thus to yield to the fourth kind of sign, the *sign of art*, in which the essence is freed from its material base and can become less unstable because less susceptible to the vagaries of mere sensuousness. Sensuous signs are indispensable, but they do not have primacy over the signs of art, which enable essences to be anchored in the truth itself. If this looks startlingly like a form of Platonism, then Deleuze is a Platonist, albeit a "reversed Platonist"—the signs that Deleuze discerns in *À la recherche du temps perdu* reveal truth, but the truth in this case functions as the subverter of tranquillity, and it steers the subject in what is potentially a new direction. There is an irruptive dimension to Proustian (and Deleuzean) truth, which surges forth from the sign itself to push its recipient in some new and unanticipated direction.

What has all this to do with "fandom"? Well, "fandom" is an apprenticeship in signs, though it does of course have its own distinctive logic and myths. One of these myths is that of the "lifelong" fan, and the great merit of being able to view "fanhood" as a kind of apprenticeship in interpretation is that it allows for the evanescences and also the permanent loyalties that contend with each other in fans' minds and hearts. This is true of my own "fanhood" with regard to Colin Meads (1936–), the great New Zealand rugby player, voted in a 1999 poll that country's greatest-ever rugby player, and given that country's preeminence in the world game, certainly one of the world's truly great players. (It would be hyperbole to call Meads the greatest player the game has ever known, rugby not lending itself to the way in which a single player, e.g., Pele, can dominate a team sport like soccer.)

Colin Earl Meads, known throughout the rugby world as "Pine Tree," played fifty-five international matches (or "tests" as they are called in rugby parlance) for the New Zealand All Blacks between 1957 and 1971 (the All Blacks lost only ten of these games). In all, "Pine Tree" Meads appeared

Figure 1. Meads playing against Wales in 1969

a record 133 times for New Zealand. It should be noted that he played in an amateur era—rugby became professional in 1995—when international competition was restricted to many fewer countries than it is today. Nowadays New Zealand plays internationally against countries like Samoa, Fiji, Tonga, Japan, Argentina, Romania, Italy, and so on, something that did not occur in Meads's playing days. Had there been as many international matches in his time as there are today, he would easily have been capped (i.e., he would have played) at least one hundred times. Meads played in the second row of the forwards or scrum, and the nearest equivalent in American football would be offensive lineman, though this is a somewhat misleading approximation, since apart from the centrality of physical contact, the scoring of touchdowns, and the oval-shaped ball, the two sports have little in common. But the easiest and most accurate way to convey his playing ethos to those not familiar with rugby would be to characterize him as rugby's incomparable "enforcer"[6]—the recurring adjective used to characterize his play is "uncompromising," and in my research for this essay it surprised me just how often sportswriters used this term in connection with Meads.

I have to admit that although I saw him play twice "in the flesh," and numerous times on television, I was not a fan of Meads during his playing days. Meads was only six feet three inches or at most six feet four inches in height and 220 pounds in weight, a stature that would be regarded as too small for someone playing in his position today. Besides, he was not really preeminent in any one specific aspect of the game—as a second-row forward, Meads's contemporary, the Welshman Delme Thomas, is widely regarded as the supreme line-out jumper of that time, and in the open field

of play, the consensus is that Frik du Preez of South Africa and the Frenchman Benoit Dauga were preeminent among those who were second-row
forwards. But Meads seemed to be an absolute colossus on the field, playing every game with a ferocity invariably unmatched by anyone else (he
occasionally threw punches, often in retaliation, and did commit a hand-
ful of very hard fouls, but was not generally regarded as a "dirty" player).
Tony O'Reilly, the Irish international, humorist, and (after rugby retirement) CEO of Heinz Foods, who played against Meads, described him this
way: "Colin Meads is the kind of player you expect to see emerging from a
ruck [scrimmage] with the remains of a jockstrap between his teeth." The
stories about Meads, some no doubt apocryphal, are numerous: He trained
by running up hills on his farm with a sheep under each arm, he made a
point of refusing treatment for injuries on the field, and there is the well-
known story involving Kel Tremain, Meads's teammate in the national team
but rival in the New Zealand interprovincial tournament:

> One famous story is told by Kel Tremain, that magnificent All Black
> flanker, who happened on this occasion to be captaining Hawkes Bay
> against Meads' King Country outfit during the inter-provincial cham-
> pionship. Meads was operating with his customary brutish efficiency,
> and the Hawkes Bay forwards were taking a pounding. "Hey, Ref," Tre-
> main cried out in exasperation, "I think you'd better count the players.
> I think Meads ate one of them."[7]

Meads was a sheep farmer from a small country, even today widely regarded as a distant and culturally isolated former British colony in the southern hemisphere, and in some ways was a throwback even for his own time. It
was difficult for someone like me, of the baby-boomer generation, to relate
to someone like Meads during my playing days at a British university in
the late 1960s and early 1970s,, even if I stood in awe of him as a player.
Somewhat more personally appealing to my own echelon of players and fans
were very talented players of a somewhat countercultural disposition, such
as Jean-Pierre Rives of France, who turned out to be a highly gifted sculp-
tor after his retirement from the game, and the mercurial Gerald Davies
of Wales, of whom that greatest of all rugby commentators, Bill MacLaren,
said that "he had a side-step like a shaft of lightning" and who became a successful journalist after retiring from rugby. Both Rives and Davies often feature prominently in polls for the "all world rugby team of all time," so their
rugby abilities are beyond question. But journalism for *The Times* of Lon-

Figure 2. Meads in 2004

don? And sculpting? Meads was certainly of no such disposition, and given his relentless (some would say ruthless) but always unspectacular effectiveness on the field ("as hard as the hobs of hell," according to Willie John McBride, Meads's great Irish and British Lions rival), one had to undergo an apprenticeship of signs to appreciate him for the kind of rugby player he was.

The game had to change, and so did I, before someone like me could learn to be a lasting fan of Meads. With the introduction of professionalism the game did of course change radically. There were important rule changes to make the game more appealing for television viewers, to enhance the "entertainment" aspects of rugby, and both players and coaches felt obliged to espouse a "scientific" approach to training and playing strategy as they became full-time professionals. The British Lions rugby team touring New Zealand as I write is accompanied by an army of coaches (including a "visual awareness" coach; when Meads heard about this he commented that the hardest player he ever played against was the one-eyed South African Martin Telser); a medical staff of doctors, trainers, and masseurs; video technicians; a legal consultant; its own cooking staff; and a PR team headed by Tony Blair's former spin doctor, the notorious Alastair Campbell.[8] The British Lions team of forty-five players and twenty-seven staff has an estimated tour budget of British £10 million, and Meads himself has warned that such sums of money could not be matched by the less wealthy rugby-playing nations and will probably spell the death of international rugby there.[9] Players today have individually tailored dietary and fitness regimens, and there is a hilarious account, typifying the changed nature of today's game, of Meads's conflict with a team dietician when he was manager of the New Zealand team in the 1990s. The team dietician had ordered the players not to eat meat for two days before a test match. Meads's response to this directive is reported thus by Donald McRae in *The Guardian*:

> Meads told her [the dietician] that on Test mornings he ate steak and eggs for breakfast—with lashings of cold meat and mashed potatoes at lunchtime. "Jesus, I used to get my mashed potatoes and put a big blob of butter in, wait until it melted, stir it all up and . . ." Well, she stopped me and said, "You don't know how good a player you could have been . . ."[10]

The idea of "Pine Tree" subsisting on a vegetarian diet two days before an important game is of course utterly incongruous, and the notion that anyone in Mead's time could have played any better is just as fanciful (though this is something that Meads himself would never have mentioned—the numerous writings on him indicate that Meads always changes the subject when his place in the history of the game is discussed).[11]

I have involuntary memories of Meads as a player, which is hardly surprising, since one could not help watching everything he did on the field, even if the "action" was taking place somewhere else. He was *that* compelling. I have to acknowledge that some of this may be due to the fact that I played in the same position, and narcissism being what it is, even today, twenty-five years after I stopped playing rugby, I tend to focus a little bit more on the play of the second-row forwards when I watch a game, whether on television, or on the actual field of play if I attend a game. But there had to be a revision of my sense of the art of the game (a movement from the sensuous sign to the sign of art, in Deleuze's taxonomy of Proustian signs) before I could say that I had indeed become a genuine fan of Meads. But this of course creates a kind of cognitive dissonance—I had seen him play for all those years, and yet at that time was far more excited by the aforementioned Gerald Davies and Jean-Pierre Rives, and also two players who played in the same position as Meads before he retired, namely, the South African Frik du Preez and the Frenchman Benoit Dauga, who once had a memorable confrontation with Meads in a test match. Here is Donald McRae's account of that encounter between Meads and Dauga:

In a 1967 Test in Paris, Meads had been kicked savagely in the head. "We had a Scottish doctor," remembers Fred Allen, then the Kiwis' coach, "and all he seemed to have in his bag was a bottle of gin. In the dressing room he looked at the gash in Piney's [Pine Tree's] head. You could see he was concerned. "I haven't any anaesthetic. I think we'd better take you to the hospital." Piney would have none of that. "Do it here. Now!" he said. I could see some of the players looking away and wincing as the stitches went in. It was a huge and messy gash. Piney didn't say a word.

"I had 17 or 18 stitches," Meads stresses. "Fred Allen reckoned my backside twitched every time the needle went in . . . that night we all went to the after-match dinner. I had a towel around my neck because the wound was weeping, so that made me look a sight. Benoit Dauga came over. I'd cut my hand on his teeth and broken his nose. My hand had turned septic. Hygiene in those days was . . . well, it didn't really exist. Dauga was stammering, trying to find the words to ask me a question. He wanted to know why I'd belted him. I was astonished and pointed to my head. The dirty so-and-so . . ."[12]

Two uncompromising players indeed. To be a fan of Meads (and of Benoit Dauga), and to be a reader of the signs associated with these two players, is certainly to be a fan of the epoch in which they played and of the rugby "imaginary" which subtended that epoch. But there is too much room for another kind of narcissism here, a narcissism that favors one's own time or one's own little patch of the rugby world. This is the ever-present hazard of being a fan; it does not trouble many of us, but for those reflecting on the nature of "fandom," it is a source of serious frustration.

It would certainly be absurd to suggest that rugby has had no truly great players after the time of Meads and that we are left with nothing but nostalgia for a bygone era. One has just to think of the recently retired Englishman Martin Johnson, who captained England to its World Cup victory in 2003, or the great Frenchman Philippe Sella and the sublime Australian David Campese, to know that this is simply not the case. And yet Meads remains the point of comparison for players like Johnson, who played in the same position. It is undeniable that the contemporary professional game is highly demanding: Playing schedules are more crowded because money has to be made by everyone with a finger in the pie, players faced with jammed-up schedules have less time to recover from injuries, and professional players today don't just play the game but also have to lift weights, do endurance training, speed workouts, and so on, this of course being the kind of "systematization" that amateurs like Meads would, and do, frequently regard with disdain. But there is the lingering thought, and some evidence suggests that this may be so, that players now live increasingly in fear of career-affecting, and thus livelihood-terminating, injuries—one "big hit" too many could mean the end of a lucrative career for someone playing top-class rugby today. It was perhaps easier for Meads to play with his trademark unbridled ferocity, since he always had his sheep farm to fall back on if an injury ended his playing career. Training is year-round for the professional rugby player of today, and no contemporary international player could give the time to running a farm in the way that Meads did and still does, while having a fourteen-year international career like his. So perhaps it was in part because he did not have to regard the game as his livelihood that Meads played every game with such fierce abandon.

Becoming a fan is like composing a work of art, which of course can be mediocre or unsurpassingly excellent or anything in between. The composition of a work of art involves a triangulation between an object (in this case a sportsman or -woman), a medium or material (in this case words or discourse), and the artist him- or herself (in this case the fan). It would be futile, however, to judge the merits of being this or that kind of fan—the one who simply goes to a game to yell his head off and have a few drinks before, during, and after the game, or the one who keeps reams of statistics and encyclopedic records and has managed to construct a complex discourse about the object of his fanhood. After all, we count as art everything that extends from a simple etching to a Goya painting. Sporting fanhood is no exception. Where "Pine Tree" Meads is concerned, though—and here I speak as an unabashed fan—neither the etching nor Goya may suffice!

Notes

1   Marcel Proust, *Remembrance of Things Past*, vol. 1: *Swann's Way: Within a Budding Grove*, trans. C. K. Scott Moncrieff and Terence Kilmartin (New York: Vintage, 1981), 50–51. For significant commentary, to which I am much indebted, see Gilles Deleuze, *Proust and Signs*, trans. Richard Howard (New York: George Braziller, 1972). Hereinafter all page references to this work will be given in the main body of the text.

2   On voluntary memory, see Deleuze, *Proust and Signs*, 56.

3   See Ronald Bogue, "Difference and Repetition in Deleuze's Proustian Sign and Time Machine," *Concentric: Studies in English Literature and Linguistics* 27.1 (January 2001): 1–

28. Available on the Web at www.eng.ntnu.edu.tw/concentric-literature/documents/27.1
.PDF/01Bogue.pdf (accessed June 14, 2005). I am much indebted to this fine study of
Deleuze's delineation of the Proustian sign for my own understanding of Deleuze.

4 To quote Deleuze: "The worldly sign appears as the replacement of an action or thought.
It stands for action and thought. It is therefore a sign that does not refer to something
else, to a transcendental signification or to an ideal content, but has usurped the supposed
value of its meaning" (6).

5 Proust, *Swann's Way*, 51.

6 He is even described as such on the Web site of the New Zealand Rugby Museum, at
www.rugbymuseum.co.nz/ABProfilee.asp?level1=All_Blacks&Level2=ABC&IDID=601
(accessed June 16, 2005).

7 See Tom Marcellus, "Happy Birthday to You (Colin Meads's 65th Birthday)," *Rugby Forum*,
vol. 1, week 16, on the Web at www.rugbyforum.co.za/Week16.htm (accessed June 17,
2005).

8 On Meads and Telser, see David Walsh, "The Ultimate All Black," *The Times* (London), on
the Web at www.timesonline.co.uk/printFriendly/0,,1-17909-1651709-17909,00.html
(accessed June 17, 2005).

9 Eddie Butler, "An Audience with Pine Tree Leads to a Right Royal Knees-up in King Country," *The Observer* (London), June 12, 2005, on the Web at http://sport.guardian.co.uk/
lions2005/story/0,15994,1504607,00.html (accessed June 16, 2005). The £10 million
sum is mentioned in "Lions Face Pay Cut on £10m Tour," on the British Lions Web site,
at www.britishlions.com/newsarticle.asp?News_ID=18 (accessed June 17, 2005).

10 Donald McRae, "Today's All Blacks Pale in Comparison to the 'Tree,'" *The Guardian* (London), November 4, 2003, available on the unofficial Colin Meads Fan Site, on the Web at
http://physed.otago.ac.nz/csullivan/meads_files/meads_todays_allblacks.html (accessed
June 16, 2005).

11 Though for us who love repartee and irony, the dietician's reply is just perfect—there
was another level to which the great man could have taken his game if only he had been
vegetarian for a couple of days? Wow!

12 See note 9 above for McRae's article.

Orin Starn

Caddying for the Dalai Lama:
Golf, Heritage Tourism, and the
Pinehurst Resort

"It's always a beautiful day at Pinehurst," an operator will answer in a cheery customer service voice if you call for a reservation at the resort. What golfer has not dreamed of an expedition to Pinehurst's legendary courses? The elegant old Carolina Inn with its shining copper cupola. The perfectly manicured croquet green by the golf clubhouse with players clad in spotless whites. The whispering of the loblolly pines along the fabled Pinehurst No. 2 course, where Jack Nicklaus, Ben Hogan, Tiger Woods, and just about every other golfing great has tested his game. Nowadays you'll find wealthy executives from as far away as Japan and Korea teeing off on one of Pinehurst's eight courses, designed by some of the world's most renowned golf course architects.

I want in this essay to examine the story of Pinehurst and, more generally, of golf itself in twenty-first-century America. Many people, of course, dismiss golf as a tacky, tedious, snotty game for rich white country clubbers in plaid pants. It's a pastime, or so *New York Times* columnist Maureen Dowd classifies it, for "men with guts pretending they are exercising." Even so, a staggering amount of land, money, time,

The *South Atlantic Quarterly* 105:2, Spring 2006.
Copyright © 2006 by Duke University Press.

and passion are tied up in golf today. This country's 16,944 golf courses cover an area more than twice as large as the state of Rhode Island. Golfers spent about $3 billion on putters, drivers, balls, and other equipment in 2004 alone. More than 26 million Americans played at least one round that year. Some 30 million tuned in to watch at least part of the Master's, the U.S. Open, or some other PGA tournament. Like it or not, golf occupies a major place in American culture and society. It's worth trying to make some sense of the history, pleasures, and contradictions of the game.

Those who dislike golf will find plenty to criticize at Pinehurst. None of the glossy resort brochures discloses that black laborers built the resort at pittance wages in this region of North Carolina where the Ku Klux Klan continued to operate into the 1980s—or that poor neighborhoods without sidewalks or sewers lie just behind the pine trees from million-dollar homes along Pinehurst's fairways.[1] The story of Pinehurst is the story of America today in its juxtaposition of wealth and poverty, racial divides, and the brass ring of leisure and luxury only for those who can afford to pay for it. Here, too, one finds the reworking of history for modern commercial purposes. The resort has branded itself as a must-visit, "historic" shrine of "golf tradition" without acknowledging the centrality of racial hierarchy, union-busting, and legalized apartheid in its very origins and development over the last century. Sanitized heritage substitutes for engagement with history's messy, sometimes uncomfortable realities in the portrait of its past that Pinehurst offers to the world.

I must confess that I am a golfer myself. I am not so much the obsessed aficionado as to want to excuse the heavy freight of snobbism and exclusion that has been part of the game's history. Yet I do believe that any black-and-white view of golf's political incorrectness misses the multiple, sometimes unexpected layers of history, experience, and involvement that make the sport something more than just another form of conspicuous consumption for rich white men. It would be a mistake to imagine that Pinehurst, with its moneyed, Lexus-driving corporate clientele, typifies everything about what it means to play golf today. Parallel, less privileged worlds of golf exist as well, especially those many municipal, or "muni," courses where you'll find plumbers and electricians, women and men, blacks, whites, and Latinos, and people of every background out for a round. These more democratically priced public courses may be truest to golf's hardscrabble Scottish origins, and even to Pinehurst's own first years as a resort for retirees of modest means.

Some extravagant claims have been made for golf. In his *Golf for Enlightenment*, for example, the best-selling New Age author Deepak Chopra tells us that "the ball presents a readout of your karma." "Golf is a way to transcend," he explains, because by playing well we "defeat the voice of self-criticism and end the frustration that holds in check deeper, darker, fears."[2] Serious devotees can pay several thousand dollars for a few days at the Chopra Center for Well-Being, combining golf and spiritual instruction at the tony La Costa Resort and Spa in Carlsbad, California.

Is golf a ticket to transcendence and enlightenment? The advancement of such laughably overblown claims for the game's benefits are standard fare in corporate, New Age–flavored, golf instruction–cum–personal growth books these days. At most, I believe golf offers the far more modest pleasures of exercise, being outside, and an absorbing pastime to an overworked, overweight society that spends too much time in front of computer screens and the television. The danger has always been that the game would be hijacked altogether by America's elites, and, more recently, so linked to the voracious sucking up of land for new courses, obscenely large professional purses, and other negative social effects as to make it difficult to mount much of an argument in the game's defense.

That enduring cult classic *Caddyshack* (1980) embraces the more open-ended, even carnivalesque possibilities for the sport. As the whacked-out, golf-addicted, decidedly working-class greenskeeper at a snotty country club, Carl Spackler, played by Bill Murray (an avid golfer in real life), boasts about a special turf-grass mixture of his own invention: "This is a cross, ah, Bluegrass, Kentucky Bluegrass, Featherbed Bent, and Northern California Sensemilla. The amazing stuff about this is, that you can play thirty-six holes on it in the afternoon, take it home and just get stoned to the bejeezus-belt that night." Although celebrating golf in its own way, *Caddyshack* mocks country club pretensions and golfing solemnity at every turn. Enlightenment through golf? That possibility arises only in one of Spackler's hilariously delusional pothead shaggy dog stories, this one about caddying for the Dalai Lama:

> So I jump ship in Hong Kong and make my way over to Tibet, and I get on as a looper at a course over in the Himalayas. A looper, you know, a caddy, a looper, a jock. So, I tell them I'm a pro jock, and who do you think they give me? The Dalai Lama, himself. Twelfth son of the Lama. The flowing robes, the grace, bald . . . striking. So, I'm on the

first tee with him. I give him the driver. He hauls off and whacks one—big hitter, the Lama—long, into a ten-thousand-foot crevice, right at the base of this glacier. And do you know what the Lama says? Gunga galunga . . . gunga—gunga galunga. So we finish the eighteenth and he's gonna stiff me. And I say, "Hey, Lama, hey, how about a little something, you know, for the effort, you know." And he says, "Oh, uh, there won't be any money, but when you die, on your deathbed, you will receive total consciousness." So I got that goin' for me, which is nice.

Soda Fountains, Super-Mex, and the Origins of the Pinehurst Resort

The Boston industrialist James W. Tufts made a fortune manufacturing those classic chrome soda fountains in the old days when you could buy a banana split or a root beer float at the drugstore counter. In 1895, Tufts paid $1.24 an acre for 5,980 acres in the North Carolina sandhills. Most people thought he was crazy.[3] The land was poor, and treeless in the bargain: Its pines had long before been chopped down by Scottish and English settlers to make turpentine. Yet Tufts envisioned an escape from big-city smoke and bustle. The late nineteenth century, after all, witnessed the growth of what historian Jackson Lears calls "antimodernist" yearnings in response to quickening industrialization—and the more enlightened philanthropists of the time wanted to make the bucolic pleasures of nature and the outdoors more available to the masses.[4] Gilded Age industrialists spearheaded the creation of New York's Central Park to provide a leafy retreat for those unable to afford a country vacation. Viewing Pinehurst as a semiphilanthropic endeavor, James Tufts wanted it to be for people of modest means. The resort, he specified, should serve those "who require the beneficial effects of a winter in the South, but cannot afford the usual high price for accommodations."[5]

Golf was an afterthought at Pinehurst, which initially offered riding, croquet, and shooting. In the shadow of the Civil War, Pinehurst was a strange new kind of Yankee outpost. Legend has it that curious southerners would ask northeasterners to repeat such exotically accented phrases as "pahk the cah in Hah-vahd Yahd." Pinehurst's village was laid out by Frederick Law Olmsted, the masterful landscape architect who earlier had joined forces with Calvert Vaux to design New York's Central Park. The evolution of Pinehurst into a resort more centrally focused on golf came in 1900, when a young Scot, Donald Ross, was commissioned to design a first course. Ross, the immigrant son of a stonemason and a nurse, made Pinehurst into his base of operations for the rest of his long career. He became the most sought-after golf course architect of his generation, designing almost four hundred courses. His work included such storied layouts as Florida's Seminole Country Club and Michigan's Oakland Hills Country Club, as well as several courses at Pinehurst itself.

What accounts for golf's growing popularity in the early twentieth century? One writer, Bob Cullen, offers an explanation drawn from evolutionary psychology. Since early hominids supposedly left the forest for the better hunting of the savannah, Cullen suggests that natural selection has left us with a gene pool disposed to attraction to wide-open grasslands. In stepping onto a golf course, he claims, we may be "reenacting the steps taken by some hominid a hundred thousand generations in the past, steps that helped him or her become our ancestors."[6] And what is more: "It could even be that the clubs we carry remind us, on some instinctive level, of the tools they carried in search of food." Cullen offers up one further theory, this one drawn from developmental psychology. Blind babies, he reports, illustrate the "exploratory-motivational assertive system" when they smile on being able to kick a bell to make a sound. The satisfaction of golf lies in gratifying the instinctive pleasure we get from being able to make the world behave as we wish—in this case, by hitting a ball in the right direction.

One can, I suppose, make what one wishes of such explanations for golf's attractions. Some critics, however, have turned instead to the Gilded Age sociologist Thorsten Veblen's trademark concept of "conspicuous consumption." By this way of thinking, embracing a game with pricey equipment, elaborate etiquette, and exclusive clubs allowed America's elites both to mark a special identity and to isolate themselves from their social inferiors.[7] Others have highlighted the xenophobic dimensions of golf's appeal.[8] The sport's early-twentieth-century expansion at Pinehurst and around the United States coincided with spiking anti-immigrant sentiment toward impoverished new arrivals from the Balkans and southern Italy. Golf, a sport perceived as linked to the lifestyle of the Scottish and British aristocracy, possessed an aura of Anglo-Saxon-ness, in contrast to the pastimes of what one observer called the "swarthy, unwashed masses."

Other, less creepy factors also contributed to golf's growth. Unlike, say, basketball or football, this game could be played by people of all ages. It did not demand special physical strength, and women could play as well as men. The rise of golf, too, was more than a country club phenomenon. To the contrary, the success and charisma of American golfers from humble backgrounds helped golf earn a wider public. Twenty-year-old Frances Ouimet, son of a working-class French-Canadian immigrant, upset the fabled British stars Harry Vardon and Ted Ray to win the 1913 U.S. Open; Gene Sarazen, Gino Saraceni by birth, went from a poor family of Sicilian immigrants to champion at the Masters, among the world's most prestigious tournaments. Both men were first exposed to golf as caddies, the servant's job of toting a rich man's clubs. That they crossed over from the caddyshack signaled that golf was not just the province of the privileged.

Contrary to the stereotype of lordly British origins, golf did not originate as the exclusive province of the aristocracy, or as a privilege of club membership. The game grew in Scotland in the sixteenth and seventeenth centuries out of other stick-and-ball games and gained adepts across social lines. "Scots instruct their children in it," one chronicler noted in 1774, "as soon as they can run alone."[9] According to historian David Hamilton, a "long" or "noble" version of the game was played by aristocrats on more developed seaside courses, while ordinary people played a "short game" in village churchyards. The first course in the United States, St. Andrews in Yonkers, New York, was a country club, and more than a thousand private courses were built in the period of golf's massive take-off between the 1890s and the late 1920s. Already by 1895, however, the interest of the less affluent led to the building of the first municipal course. There were several hundred public courses as of 1929, when the Great Depression shut down construction until after World War II.

At least a few of golf's more modern icons come from the world of municipal golf. Lee Trevino, the son of a single mother who cleaned houses in Dallas, grew up in a shack without water, plumbing, or electricity and picked cotton as a child to help put food on the table. "I was twenty-one years old," he joked later, "before I knew Manual Labor wasn't a Mexican." Trevino dropped out of school in the eighth grade to work at a local municipal course in Dallas. There he taught himself the game, eventually becoming so skilled he hustled the unsuspecting by betting that he could beat them playing only with a Dr. Pepper bottle wrapped in masking tape. Trevino went on to win thirty-two tournaments and more than $10 million in prize money. As a rare Latino in the white world of professional golf, Trevino dubbed himself "Super-Mex" and became immensely popular for both his brilliant play and sense of humor and banter with the galleries. Trevino's humor sometimes had a critical edge toward the United States and its treatment of Mexicans. He told reporters after his 1971 U.S. Open triumph that he might use his prize money to "buy the Alamo . . . and give it back to Mexico." But Trevino also loved fast living, making money, and a good laugh, and his politics were never easy to pin down. Later, touring the Alamo, he declared, "Well, I'm not gonna buy this place. It doesn't have indoor plumbing." Although happy to mingle with CEOs in search of endorsement deals, Trevino has never forgotten his own humble origins. "I represent the public courses, the working man, the blue-collar worker," he said in his autobiography, *They Call Me Super-Mex.*[10]

Also worth noting has been golf's openness to women, at least relative to many other American sports. In the late 1800s, it became one of the first sports allowing female participation, including organized tournaments. The new Pinehurst resort was very much part of the growth of women's golf. From the start, the resort established connections with some of the most famous outdoorsy women of the day. Annie Oakley, the legendary Wild West Show deadeye, gave shooting lessons, and Amelia Earhart once landed her plane on the resort's airstrip. Pinehurst hosted the first women's North/South Amateur championship in 1903 and has held the tournament annually ever since. Peggy Kirk Bell, a former professional who became a matriarch of women's golf, ran the Pine Needles resort down the road from Pinehurst. Pine Needles hosted the U.S. Women's Open in 2001 and is well known for its "Golfari" programs for women golfers.

To be sure, the early entry of women into golf measured the power of gender ideologies about female frailty and lack of aptitude for sport. That golf was viewed as a more "refined," less "physical" game meshed with expectations of proper femininity. Early women golfers wore hats and long dresses, as if to wear anything less would be to venture too far into the physicality of the male domain. The greatest early female golfer, Glena Collett, won widespread popularity by playing top-notch golf while remaining (in the judgment of contemporary journalists) "beautiful" and "ladylike." Then, too, the origins of women's golf in the United States were very much tied to the privileges of class and race. At the start it was a sport not for all women, only for rich white ones. Golf, historian Donald Mrozek writes, allowed "women of upper-class instincts and means . . . to isolate themselves" from "working women" and, for that matter, any other American of lesser status.

As the twentieth century advanced, however, the role of women in golf grew more interesting and varied. The most charismatic figure was Mildred "Babe" Didrikson, who some believe was the greatest female athlete of the twentieth century.[11] This tough-talking Texan won two gold medals in track-and-field at the 1932 Olympics, could punt a football eighty yards, bowled 180 on her first try, and swam world-record times. When Didrikson spear-headed the formation of a women's professional golf tour in the 1930s, she transformed the sport with her fierce competitiveness and unabashed reveling in her own power and athleticism. "Watch close, boys," she'd boast to a crowd of reporters before blasting one of her rocketlike long drives, "'coz you're watching the best." Didrikson once yanked her girdle off mid-round, loudly complaining to the gallery that it restricted her swing. Her unashamed refusal to conform to older standards of female modesty and propriety generated a predictable backlash. In 1935, when she entered the Women's Texas Amateur at the posh River Oaks club in Houston, one local club member was quoted in the Houston press as saying, "We don't need any truck driver's daughters in our tournament." A showwoman and self-promoter, Didrikson eventually made concessions like putting on makeup and perming her hair to make herself more marketable. But she helped push women's golf, and sports in general, toward accepting power, force of personality, and the idea of a woman making a living as a professional ath-lete. "I was the first woman to play the game men play," she said not long before her early death from cancer, "to hit—I mean hit the ball instead of swinging at it."[12]

Of course, the constraints facing Didrikson have by no means disap-peared. Female athletes, as cultural theorist Abigail Feder-Kane notes, sometimes feel they must fulfill "popular notions of beauty" in order to avoid being stigmatized as overly "manly" in a society often hostile to gay and lesbian identity.[13] Critics have sometimes grumbled that professional women golfers do not pay enough attention to their appearance—that they too often "fail" to wear lipstick or makeup. One former star, Jan Stephen-son, has called for the tour to do more to "market its sex appeal." But for all its contradictions, golf remains one of the few sports where women can make a good living as professional athletes—sometimes, in the case of top stars, a very good living indeed. Nor are the professional ranks dominated by daughters of the American country club set. More than a third of pro-fessional women golfers come from Korea or Japan, and other prominent professionals in this heavily globalized sport hail from Sweden, Mexico, and Thailand. Golf, too, is one of the only sports where athletes have been willing to come out of the closet. Rosie Jones, a well-known star, announced in 2004 that she was lesbian, and there was minimal backlash. Jones plays in tournaments sporting a cap emblazoned with the logo of Olivia, a lesbian-oriented travel agency with whom she inked an endorsement deal.

Pinehurst, Illusions of Authenticity, and Big-Money Golf

The success of Pinehurst is wrapped up in the marketing of itself as a kind of museum and temple of American golf. Here "history," "tradition," and "heritage" become keywords central to what Pinehurst promises its visitors. Old black-and-white photographs of the early years and famous past champions cover the walls of the Carolina Inn, which has been designated a national historic landmark. The golf clubhouse features still more pictures and memorabilia. Outside, one finds bronze statues of Donald Ross and Richard Tufts, the grandson of the founder and a key twentieth-century figure at Pinehurst, and Payne Stewart, who won the 1999 U.S. Open and died in a plane crash soon after. Like a tour of colonial Williamsburg or the Tall Ships in Boston's Harbor, the allure of Pinehurst is a feeling of connection to the world of the past, a world we like to imagine as having been more interesting and meaningful than our own. A round of golf is a round of golf, or so one might think. At Pinehurst it becomes, or is meant to become, much more than that—a chance to "follow in the footsteps of some of the world's greatest golf legends," according to the official Pinehurst Web site.

But what version of the past is being used to entice visitors? A powerful part of the attraction centers around Donald Ross and the opportunity to play courses designed by America's most legendary golf course architect. Golf course design always reflects the times. Ross was a contemporary of the renowned Greene brothers and other Arts and Crafts architects, who were rejecting Victorian stuffiness for a new, more natural style full of exposed wood and stone. His lovely, intelligent designs place a premium on flow, accessibility, and following and working within the lay of the land. There was little of the desire to subdue, dominate, and pasteurize the land so evident in later Cold War golf course architecture and its massive earth-moving, which paralleled the paving of America for suburbs and strip malls. Nor did Ross add any of the fake waterfalls, man-made island greens, and contrived high-corporate glitz of more contemporary designs. A linchpin of Pinehurst's marketing is the offer of allowing golfers to play Ross's No. 2 course, the jewel of Pinehurst and the "greatest expression of his genius."

Actually, the No. 2 course does not much resemble the course that Ross designed in the early 1900s. The celebrated trademarks of No. 2 are its steeply pitched, wickedly fast, turtleback putting greens—and it's these greens that television golf commentators will discourse upon as an expression of Ross's "genius," the ability of No. 2 to stand the "test of time." But these famous greens bear little resemblance to anything in Ross's design.[14] Like all putting greens in the early twentieth century, the ones at No. 2 were not made of grass at all but of sand hard-packed with tar. They were also relatively flat; it was only decades of top-dressing, once the greens were converted to grass in 1935, that little by little elevated them to create the turtleback effect. What many visitors imagine to be the signature and guarantee of the master designer is, in other words, actually the unintended result of the mundane process of fertilization and maintenance across the years. The amazing speed of the Pinehurst greens is an even more modern invention. Only gradually over the last several decades have turf management companies, a massive high-tech industry of researchers and corporations, figured out how to engineer strains of grass that can now be grown to an astonishing density of about 1,540 plants per square inch—and mowed to the miniscule length of one-eighth of an inch so as to give the golfer a sensation akin to putting on ice.[15] The No. 2 course is lovely and challenging in spite of or perhaps because of the changes across the decades. It nonetheless bears only a partial resemblance to Ross's original plan, no matter how much Pinehurst seeks to portray it as an "authentic," unsullied expression of the great man's creative vision.

To package the past as a matter of picturesque, desirable "heritage" and "tradition," Pinehurst must also ignore some of the most basic, unsavory realities of its actual history. The resort was, after all, very much an artifact of the age of Jim Crow. The hotel and first courses were built in the late nineteenth century in a period of lynching, disenfranchisement of black voters, and backlash against the supposed "coddling" of African Americans in the aftermath of the Yankee triumph in the Civil War. Black men, paid next to nothing and denied the right to vote, did the backbreaking job of transforming the scruffy pine wastelands into golf courses; they were the gardeners and maintenance workers at the resort, and the caddies who carried the bags for white golfers. Their wives and mothers did the brunt of the cooking and laundry at the hotel. Occasional efforts to organize for improved pay were crushed, sometimes by the quick-tempered Donald Ross himself. "One time," recalled a Pinehurst old-timer, "the caddies talked of a strike unless wages were raised. Ross heard of this, walked to the caddie pen, asked the leader what was going on. Hearing the grievance, he whacked the caddie on the head with his ever-present five iron and informed him the strike was over."[16] So strong was early-twentieth-century prejudice that blacks were not allowed the "privilege" of cleaning the rooms until 1960, as if this would violate taboos of pollution and contamination between the races. A statute forbade selling Pinehurst property to "any person of Jewish or Negro descent and lineage."

How does Pinehurst deal with its Jim Crow origins? One way has been by avoiding the history of racism and racial stereotyping altogether. Consider the so-called Putter Boy mascot, based on a 1912 sculpture that stands outside the clubhouse. A carefree, *Little Rascals*–style white child with oversized clubs and a droopy hat, the Putter Boy has long been a Pinehurst advertising trademark. Framed originals of various Putter Boy posters hang around Pinehurst, with replicas available for purchase. But there's one in this series you will not find anywhere in the resort's plentiful public display of historical memorabilia; instead it's filed away in the Pinehurst archives. It's a midcentury scene depicting the boy receiving a trophy while the stereotypical, Little Sambo–style figure of a smiling black caddie deferentially stands nearby. To modern eyes, the poster looks very "incorrect," and in this sense it is what Walter Benjamin would call a "dialectical image" confronting us with the uncomfortable history of racism and discrimination at Pinehurst. One suspects that it is exactly because it does not fit the selective "happy heritage" Pinehurst theme that this Putter Boy poster has been banished from public view by the resort's image-makers. In other cases, Pinehurst has tried to recode the role of African Americans from a matter of servility to a point of pride. In 2001, for example, the resort created the "Pinehurst Caddie Hall of Fame" and held a ceremony honoring the first ten inductees, all of them black. Caddying certainly demands skill. This is especially true at Pinehurst, where the job of "reading" the break to advise the player on the proper line of his putt is doubly demanding due to the fiendishly sloped greens. At the same time, celebrating retired caddies serves Pinehurst both to acknowledge and disarm the explosive topic of race. These men's contribution becomes one more part of the resort's "heritage," yet without any mention of the structures of race, money, and exclusion that limited blacks to the servile job of toting white men's clubs. A chapter called "The Caddies" in *The Spirit of Pinehurst*, a coffee-table history published by Pinehurst, relates "colorful" anecdotes about Fletcher Gaines, Jimmy

Steed, and other old-time caddies. Omitted is any mention that caddying was considered a menial, blacks-only job in the caste system of Jim Crow; that African American were forbidden from living in Pinehurst Village; and that blacks were banned from the PGA tour until 1961, making golf the last major professional sport to integrate. The central role of black women in doing the cleaning and cooking that kept the resort running receives no acknowledgment of any kind in official Pinehurst history.

One recent promotional poster shows two handsome, smiling, well-dressed couples—one black and one white—dining together by sparkling candlelight in the Carolina Inn. The poster's imagery establishes an implicit distance between the old, segregated south of Jim Crow and a new, feel-good Pinehurst of multicultural harmony and inclusion where blacks are now welcome. But the truth is that the resort still has something of a plantation feel to it. One rarely, in fact, sees black diners at the Carolina Inn; an overwhelming majority of the resort's guests are white. By contrast, blacks still do much of the dirty work at Pinehurst—the majority of the maids, shoeshine men, valets, and busboys are African American. Excluded from Pinehurst itself, black workers in the early twentieth century made their homes in poor neighborhoods out of sight of the resort. Today some of these areas—Jackson Hamlet and Monroetown—do not have sewage lines, garbage collection, sidewalks, or other basic amenities. These small black neighborhoods contrast sharply with the plush, million-dollar homes for wealthy vacationers and retirees that have mushroomed around Pinehurst in recent years. At least some black locals worry that Pinehurst wants to see their neighborhoods gone altogether. "All Pinehurst wants to do is put in a darn golf course [here]," says Karen Stanford, a Monroetown activist.[17] The rapid expansion of pricey golf course resorts in South Carolina's Hilton Head Island area has meant the end for a number of old, rural African American communities where residents have sold out to developers, or been forced to move by rising tax rates.

These days, however, money counts as much as or more than race at Pinehurst, or so many area African Americans believe. "It's the color of your money, not your skin," says one older woman from nearby Fayetteville, a sometime golfer herself. A sprinkling of wealthy African Americans, among them several retired sports stars, have bought upscale homes near the resort and play there often. If James Tufts intended Pinehurst to serve those of "modest means," that part of his vision has been lost today. On a summer day, the fee to play the No. 2 course is almost $300; it will set you back another $60 for a caddie, and rooms at the Carolina Inn begin at $130 for a single. In the lead-up to the U.S. Open in 2005, Pinehurst advertised a so-called Championship Package:

> A caddie wearing your name, your tee time announced as you step up to the first tee as Hogan, Snead, Nicklaus and Woods have all done before. Your name and scores posted on our virtual scoreboard. Your moment in time captured with a photo beside Payne Stewart's triumphant statue. And bragging rights in stepping in the footsteps of golf's giants.

It costs $2,005 per person to live out this fantasy, a price tag representing more than a month's salary for a maid or maintenance man at the resort. Unlike most other top U.S. courses, Pinehurst is not a private country club. The resort proudly advertises itself as one of just three recent U.S. Open hosts where the public can also play, the others being New York's Bethpage Black and California's Pebble Beach. The reality is that Pinehurst is public in name only, since the astronomical greens fees mean that only rich golfers can afford a round there.

It would be wrong to single Pinehurst out for criticism. Far from an exception, the recent history of the resort measures much larger trends in golf and society. The number of exclusive, members-only country clubs has stayed more or less the same in the last decades. What has occurred instead has been the rapid expansion of the phenomenon of the upscale, so-called daily fee golf courses and resorts in the manner of Pinehurst. These destinations do not follow in the model of the blue-blooded, Brahminic old money of the traditional country club. They answer to the logic of cash, the free market, and global corporate capitalism. Here money—not social connections—is what matters. If you can pay several thousand dollars, you can spend a weekend at a resort like The Sanctuary in South Carolina, Sea Island in Georgia, or Amelia Island Plantation in Florida. These resorts market themselves in predictably gendered ways—golf for the men; shopping and spa for women. The Web site for The Sanctuary advertises its "spa experience" as a "relaxing ritual of water, steam, and rest . . . in our serene and luxurious surroundings."

In other words, the same dynamics of money and exclusion operate in golf resorts far beyond Pinehurst. The white-collar masters of postmodern corporate capitalism are welcomed onto a fantasy island of "comfort," "amenities," and "luxury"—and the real world of poverty, inconvenience, and social division is fenced out into invisibility. A working class made up disproportionately of people of color, an increasing number of them migrants from Latin America, waits upon these resort "guests" and do the lawn mowing, room cleaning, and ditch digging; they are typically non-unionized, sometimes working two jobs to get by. Geographer Stephen Daniels speaks of the "duplicity of landscape" to describe how particular places may appeal to "subjective experience and pleasure" while betraying no trace of the relations of power and authority that make their very existence possible.[18] A golf course presents an outward appearance of a pristine, parklike beauty belying the hard labor that goes into its making, not to mention the vast amounts of herbicides, pesticides, and other chemicals necessary to create that "natural" green look.

Consider, too, the names of some new golf course resorts in the Carolinas and Georgia—Brunswick Plantation and Golf Links, The Plantation Inn and Golf Resort, the Ritz-Carlton Lodge at Reynolds Plantation, for example. You'd think there'd be reluctance about naming a golf resort after the plantation, an institution so dependent on slavery, the horrors of the Middle Passage, the death and exploitation of millions of people. Think again. For modern marketeers, the word means to conjure a gauzy, azaleas-and-magnolias "heritage" of southern ease, elegance, and privilege—and at the same time, one suspects, an aura of privilege, hierarchy, and racial entitlement of the antebellum South so attractive to white vacationers. The Sanctuary at Kiawah Island bills itself as "captur[ing] the spirit, history, and charm of southern hospitality."

The rise of the upscale, Brunswick Plantation–style golf economy mirrors the dynamics of a winner-take-all society. As many observers have noted, the gap between the rich and the poor has widened shockingly in this country over the last few decades. A CEO at Wal-Mart or McDonald's earns millions more than the poverty-line minimum wages their companies pay to workers or the barely higher salaries paid to day-care workers and school-teachers, who are arguably doing society's most important jobs.[19] The resort offers a pasteurized green wonderland for global capitalism's winners to enjoy the privilege of their status. One morning not long ago, golfers at the Wakefield Plantation course in North Carolina raced their gleaming white golf carts along the sixth fairway. Just off to one side, a crew of Mexican men was digging up a drainage ditch, the type of work that keeps the course in its manicured condition. None of the players raised their hand to acknowledge the men; it was as if the workers were not even there.

Golf, Democracy, and the Muni Course

Fidel Castro shut down Cuba's golf courses after seizing revolutionary power in 1959. Like many critics of the sport, he must have assumed that golf was by its very nature linked to American global capitalism and its excesses of money and injustice. The story of Pinehurst and courses like it do, in fact, bear out some of that harsh view. As I see it, however, the blame lies not with the sport itself, a game anyone from young to old can play and enjoy in principle. The problem lies instead with the uses to which golf has been put and particularly with its continuing linkages to snobbism, domination, and inequality in the United States.

Even today, there are other, more democratic faces of golf in this country. A few blocks from my house in Durham, North Carolina, for example, you can play the Hillandale Golf Course for $20, or $10 at the reduced twilight rate. It's $3.50 for the lunch special of a barbecue sandwich, chips, and soft drink at "Bogey's Grill" by the pro shop. On a midsummer morning, the cars in the parking lot index the great mix of people you'll find there — the van of a housepainter getting in nine holes between jobs; the BMW of a doctor playing hooky from the nearby medical center; the banged-up old Oldsmobile of a retired highway engineer. At least a third of Hillandale's regulars are African American; it's a favorite for women golfers as well, and for beginners who'd be too embarrassed to show up at a high-end resort course. Although the number of low-priced, public courses has declined some, you'll find them in many places nationwide. Here, as novelist and golf nut John Updike notes, "golf is a game of people" where anyone can lose themselves in "the bliss and aggravation" of the sport.[20]

I sometimes see one foursome out early at Hillandale, all in their later years. Three are white, one black. One is a woman, Berta.[21] She's a retiree who, in exchange for free golf, sometimes works as a so-called Course Ranger, driving around in a golf cart to prod slow players along. Berta is weathered and tiny, perhaps four feet tall. But she attacks the ball with an authority that reminds me of my grandmother, a retired secretary, who'd blast it out farther than my grandfather, much to his wounded pride. Berta and her foursome don't smile or joke around much; they take a more serious, concentrated pleasure in a game that gets them outside with others in a shared passion. A few days ago, I stopped to watch Berta teeing off on the par-3 seventeenth hole in a light rain. The ball headed on a low line straight at the flag, bounding up near the hole. "Nice shot, Berta," one of her partners called before they all jumped in their golf carts and sped away in the Carolina mist toward the green.

Notes

I would like to thank Anne Allison, Carolyn Christman, Grant Farred, and Charles Piot for their comments on an earlier draft of this essay. All responsibility for any errors is mine.

1   For the Klan's activities in Moore County, to which Pinehurst belongs, see Morris Dees, *A Season for Justice: The Life and Times of a Civil Rights Lawyer* (New York: Scribner's, 1991). Dees defended prison guard and civil rights activist Bobby Person, who had a cross burned in his front yard and was otherwise threatened by the Klan for challenging the racial discrimination in the Moore County prison system. For more on poverty and social inequality in the area, see the reports of the Cedar Grove Institute and the University of North Carolina's Center for Civil Rights.

2   Deepak Chopra, *Golf for Enlightenment* (New York: Harmony Books, 2003), 159, 186.

3   Bradley Klein, *Discovering Donald Ross: The Architect and His Golf Courses* (Ann Arbor: Clock Tower Press, 2001), 62–105. For more on Pinehurst, see also Pete Moss, *The Village of Pinehurst: A History from 1894 to Today* (Ann Arbor: Clock Tower Press, 2005).

4   T. J. Jackson Lears, *No Place of Grace: Antimodernism and the Transformation of American Culture* (New York: Pantheon, 1981).

5   Klein, *Discovering Donald Ross*, 68.

6   Bob Cullen, *Why Golf?* (New York: Simon and Schuster, 2000), 42.

7   For an elaboration of this argument, see Donald Mrozek, *Sport and American Mentality, 1880–1910* (Knoxville: University of Tennessee Press, 1983), especially chap. 4.

8   For an introduction to the Anglomania and xenophobia of that time, see Karen Brodkin, *How Jews Became White Folks and What That Says about Race in America* (New Brunswick, NJ: Rutgers University Press, 1999). Richard Moss's *Golf and the American Country Club* (Urbana: University of Illinois Press, 2001) explores the perceived links of golf to "Anglo-Saxon tradition" in early-twentieth-century America.

9   Quoted in David Hamilton, *Golf: Scotland's Game* (Kilmacolm, Scotland: Partick Press, 1998), 65.

10 Lee Trevino, *They Call Me Super-Mex* (New York: Random House, 1982), 124.

11 See Susan Cayleff, *Babe: The Life and Legend of Babe Didrickson Zacharias* (Urbana: University of Illinois Press, 1995).

12 Ibid., 159.

13 Abigail Feder-Kane, "'A Radiant Smile from the Lovely Lady': Overdetermined Femininity in 'Ladies' Figure Skating," in Susan Birrell and Mary G. McDonald, eds., *Reading Sport: Critical Essays on Power and Representation*, 206–32 (Boston: Northeastern University Press, 2000), 211.

14 Ron Whitten, "Donald Ross Wouldn't Recognize These Greens," *Golf Digest*, June 2005, 273–78.

15 Thanks to Richard Cooper and John Stier for help with these figures. The plant density figure is for the latest A-4 bent-grass putting green variety.

16 Dick Taylor, "Donald Ross," in Lee Pace, ed., *The Spirit of Pinehurst*, 98–105 (Pinehurst, NC: Sports Media Group, 2004), 104.

17 Quoted in Julia Oliver, "Rift Separates Pinehurst and Monroe Town," *Fayetteville Observer*, May 5, 2005, 3.

18 Quoted in Denis Cosgrove, *Social Formation and Symbolic Landscape* (Madison: University of Wisconsin Press, 1984), xx.

19 An already classic book about the contradictions of wealth and poverty in modern America is Barbara Ehrenreich's *Nickel and Dimed: On (Not) Getting By in America* (New York: Owl Books, 2002).

20 John Updike, *Golf Dreams: Writings on Golf* (New York: Knopf, 1996), 110, 147.

21 "Berta" is a pseudonym.

Jeffrey T. Nealon

Take Me Out to the Slot Machines: Reflections on Gambling and Contemporary American Culture

While for a century it was hailed as "the American pastime," baseball has been eclipsed in recent years by a new American spectacle and cultural metaphor: gambling (or, as its proponents like to call it, "gaming"). According to the American Gaming Association, in 2003 U.S. casinos saw three times more attendees than all Major League Baseball franchises combined. What about participation sports like skiing? Forgetaboutit: There are five times more Americans in the casinos than there are on the slopes. The numbers are truly staggering: 53.4 million American gamblers—defined by the industry as folks who've gone gambling more than five times in a given year. That's 26 percent of this country's adult population. And those numbers cover only *casino* gambling—nearly half of all Americans (46 percent) played some form of Lotto in 2003.[1] And if the endless cable-TV versions of "Celebrity Texas Hold 'Em" are any indication of future trends, the gaming industry seems poised to make even bigger gains. In the national sporting imaginary, Harry Carey's beer-soaked rendition of "Take Me Out to the Ballgame" has been eclipsed by a smarmy, cosmo-sipping lounge singer crooning "Luck Be a Lady."

The *South Atlantic Quarterly* 105:2, Spring 2006.
Copyright © 2006 by Duke University Press.

There is of course much to loathe, and maybe even a few things to like, about the rise of "gaming" as the new American pastime, though I come before you today neither to denounce gambling nor to celebrate it, but rather to try and think about its imbrications within larger cultural formations and economic mutations. Because whether one likes it or not, gambling is here to stay on the American horizon—with casinos and racetracks having generated more than $6.5 billion in tax revenues in 2003 alone.[2] In a rabidly antitax climate, revenue numbers like those are hard for state and municipal governments to ignore. Of course, such an antitax fever constitutes the most obvious, and maybe most compelling, sociological answer to the question "Why gambling now?": because it's a very effective form of regressive taxation. In any case, the bets are down, as they say at the roulette table, and they're likely to stay that way for the foreseeable future.[3]

Sports, from Discipline to Control

In his famous essay on the rise of contemporary "control" societies out of the ashes of eighteenth- through twentieth-century "disciplinary" societies, Gilles Deleuze has odd recourse to sports at a crucial explanatory juncture: "Disciplinary man," Deleuze writes, "produced energy in discrete amounts, while control man undulates, moving among a continuous range of different orbits. *Surfing* has taken over from all the old *sports*."[4] Well, on the face of it, that's a bit puzzling: while I hear surfer-speak like "dude" all over the place, I don't think all that many people actually surf these days. So what could Deleuze possibly be after here? Deleuze expands elsewhere: "All the new sports . . . take the form of entering into an existing wave. There's no longer an origin as a starting point, but a sort of putting-into-orbit. The key thing now is how to get taken up into the motion of a big wave, a column of rising air, to 'get into something' instead of being the origin of an effort."[5]

For Deleuze, the "new sports" of the control society are no longer primarily based on the disciplinary models of discrete individuality, teamwork, and heroic subjective "effort." Baseball, one might say in Deleuzean parlance, was the perfect American metonym for its disciplinary, Fordist period of Empire—tacitly figuring the nation-state as a bunch of position players, each diligently working in his individual place on the great assembly line of team America. Baseball is organized according to what Deleuze calls a disciplinary (which is to say, serial or analog) technology: with each new hitter, as with each new Ford on the assembly line, you start the originary drama all over again. A teleological endgame is then built on these discreet, modular units: three strikes is an out, three outs is an inning, nine innings is a game.

In contrast, the "new" sports of control are what Deleuze calls "digital" in their arrangement, based on the modulating, singular intensities circulating around the undulation of an already-given theme; they are not, in short, role-driven, teleological "team" sports. Rather, one might say that they're "collective assemblage" sports, wherein it's all about joining or tuning into an impersonal or transpersonal flow. These Deleuzean "new" sports are not so much organized by a central disciplinary confrontation beginning ever anew, while simultaneously building to a conclusion (as in pitcher vs. hitter); rather, control-society sports are based on something like an ongoing dance oriented around a subject of practice, who's "taken up into the motion of a big wave," reperforming a set of moves or riffing on a refrain: "extreme" sports like sky surfing, hang gliding, skateboarding, BMX bike competitions. And, I hasten to add (though Deleuze doesn't), gambling.[6]

Indeed, Deleuze's discussion of the contemporary reign of money is one of the linchpins of his notion of the "control society," that postdisciplinary concept that Deleuze sees emerging in the wake of Foucault's disciplinary society: "Money," Deleuze writes, "perhaps best expresses the difference between the two kinds of society, since discipline was always related to molded currencies containing gold as a numerical standard, whereas control is based on floating exchange rates, modulations depending on a code setting sample percentages for various currencies."[7] Money, unmoored from any reference or gold standard, has arrived as the transversal conceptual machinery for constantly modulating "value" throughout the global socius. From the stock market to the corner market and at every playground in between, it's all about floating rates of exchange: an ongoing question of producing, measuring, and evaluating intensity. It's all about gambling.

Gamblers Unanimous

Gambling breeds confession, so here's mine: I learned to read culture by reading the racing form. In the late 1960s, when I was being taught reading, writing, and arithmetic in first and second grade in northern New Jersey, our family spent each summer at the shore, in what amounted to a Quonset hut in Monmouth Beach, New Jersey. Why Monmouth, you ask? The best summer horse racing outside Saratoga, my father might say; and, as "resort" towns go, Saratoga was certainly no place for us—the family of second-generation immigrants, my father working in the soon-to-be-deregulated trucking industry. Trucking went downhill fast—with no jake brakes to stop it—after deregulation by Nixon, but the late 1960s were the days of livin' large for our family, and for my father that meant gambling. Working during the week in Orange, he'd spend long weekends "down the shore" with the family, taking me (his only son) to the track with him three or four days a week.

So began the arduous process of learning to read, my first contact with things that are now as natural to me as breath: a length is one-fifth of a second; in horse racing as in life, class counts; speed ratings; track conditions; quinellas and perfectas; closers versus front-runners. All the winners are right there in the *Daily Racing Form*. You just have to learn to read it.

But of course it means something different to read a novel and to read the racing form. First of all, the racing form is not really about hermeneutics; it has no depth or hidden meanings. It doesn't take you to exotic places. It's not a series of Chinese boxes, each increasingly more esoteric, baffling, and wondrous. Rather, the racing form is a map, some raw material, and a measuring tape. The hermeneutic question "What does it mean?" is completely foreign to a racing form, and to gambling in general. Nobody cares what a five-length victory in a stakes race means; the question is "What can you do with that information?"

And I increasingly learned to measure the world by this kind of yardstick: the "information" of gambling is rarely more than hearsay ("tips" from people in the know) or some cobbled-together excuse for a "system": people who bet nothing but speed ratings, who bet long shots in the rain, or bet exclusively gray horses; some people always place their wager according to the jockey, while others bet by relying on meaningful number combinations (birthdays, anniversaries, shoe sizes) or horse's names ("Look, a horse named Bill's Ghost, and Bill just died"); still others fixate on post positions, bet primarily closers or front-runners, and so on.

As far as my own gambling theory training goes, in what I now recognize as a kind of racy joke, my father has always bet 6-9, 9-6 in the daily double. I now do it too, and when he dies, I'm sure I will continue to do so. Friends of mine have won hundreds of dollars on this "system," and it's ready made for late arrival at the track, before you have a chance to size up the competition: You have a recipe or an algorithm right when you walk through the gate. You only have to know that one race has at least nine horses, and the other has at least six, and you're plugged into a system, a tradition, an inside dope.

So goes the "logic" or "systems theory" that one learns from gambling—a set of numbers can easily mutate from a vaguely pornographic joke to an ironclad necessity. And it is precisely in working these "systems" that I can recognize my earliest interests in what I later came to call academic cultural "theory": Contingency is necessity; every gambler knows this. The question is how one hacks that necessity, whether the response to that necessary contingency can somehow work it otherwise. In the end, gambling is theoretically interesting, to me at least, because it's so thoroughly antihermeneutic: all flows and effects.

Gambling Axiomatics

At first blush gambling may not seem like a topic very fruitful for cultural studies or sociology; or, if it seems productive at all to examine gambling through the lens of social theory, it may seem that gaming provides subject matter for another kind of "subcultural group" analysis familiar from, say, Dick Hebdige's groundbreaking work on the English punk scene.[8] On this vector, examining gamblers and gambling cultures would seem to offer (yet) another set of possibilities for considering what seems to have stubbornly remained a central conundrum of recent cultural studies, what one might call—after Elvis Costello—the "I used to be disgusted, now I try to be amused" quandary: Are everyday contemporary consumption practices to be condemned as the inauthentic canalizing of consumer desire by capitalist marketing masters? Or are such practices to be celebrated as forms of subversive agency performed by market-savvy consumers? Are we, following a certain Frankfurt school trajectory, to be "disgusted" by government-sponsored gambling operations, which disproportionately fleece our poorest citizens? Or are we, following a strain of cultural studies inflected by Michel de Certeau's analysis of everyday subversion, to be "amused" by the multifaceted subjectivities that are born in and around contemporary gambling practices?[9]

Hoping to sidestep that argument, I'd argue that gambling is far from a marginal or subcultural site of coercion or subversion in contemporary culture; instead, gambling is a linchpin of the economic and cultural flows of contemporary capitalist society. And, as such, the question of gambling proves to be somewhat resistant to the "disgusted or amused?" versions of subject formation. There are some games that you don't get to choose.

Of course, I'm not trying to deny that most forms of gambling practice entail a subjective "choice"—no one simply forces you to go to Atlantic City or to buy a Lotto ticket; but there is another way in which gambling behavior is not really about "subjects" or "choices" at all. Rather, gambling is part and parcel of the structural logic of "our" economic moment, and thereby not available to be *simply* celebrated or condemned, chosen or rejected. For example, recent work in economics and cultural theory posits the work of stock-market speculation—venture capital or so-called finance capital— as the defining characteristic and productive engine of "our" moment— variously called "the control society," "Empire," and/or "late" (later? just-in-time?) capitalism. Whatever we may choose to call this moment, today the savvy capitalist no longer wishes to be tied to the difficulties of disciplinary factory production and Fordist markets, nor increasingly is she happy to find herself beholden to the whims of the hegemonic "service" economy. On the contrary, since the collapse of the real estate market in the late 1980s, the real money's been in the stock market, which is by definition an economic sector that's only tangentially tied to what might be called "real" commodities and services. Oddly enough, the "real" money in capitalism's future seems to lie in wagering on "abstract" market speculation devices—futures contracts, stocks, currency trading, derivatives. In other words, the future of capitalism increasingly seems to lie in games of chance.

One might object that the stock market has a kind of (sinister) "rationality" that separates it from other, more traditional forms of gambling: sooner or later, market rationality—a company's profits, losses, and market share—is translated into rising and falling stock prices. Certainly, this is true to a large extent; but there seem to be more striking and high-profile ways in which it's *not* the case—in which the "rationality" of the market defies any kind of traditional notions of economic reasoning concerning production, goods and services, and profits. For example, recently banking giant Wells Fargo posted an enormous second-quarter profit of 48 percent, well above Wall Street estimates and projections for its target earnings. The stock, however, fell $10^3/_8$ for the day, trumped by Federal Reserve Chairman Alan Greenspan's mild worry over inflation (and hence the vague possibility of Fed interest rate hikes) during a morning hearing before the Senate Banking Committee. It seems, in other words, that real profits—where the proverbial rubber hits the supposed road—are less important in today's stock market than misty future projections or vaguely emerging trends, whether or not these projections have any basis in conventional economic "reason."

On the floor of the stock market or on the rail at the racetrack, hunches, rumors, and inside information often count for more than the hard numbers and statistics to be found in the *Wall Street Journal* or the *Daily Racing Form*. Both the *WSJ* and the *DRF* emphasize past performances; but as any horseplayer or stockbroker knows, yesterday's victories are only one part of the equation when it comes to handicapping today's contests.

In the end, it seems clear that the stock market does not function according to any kind of traditional rational or teleological model (in the mid-1980s people insisted the Dow could never run at 2,000, while today it routinely runs above 10,000); as Fredric Jameson writes, the market obeys less a sober, developmental rationality than a kind of spiraling, rumor-laden model of panic: "The system is better seen as a kind of virus . . . and its development is something like an epidemic."[10] The stock market's booms, like its crashes, seem about as predictable as natural disasters like earthquakes or tidal waves. Or as Georg Simmel wrote nearly a century ago, stock market "speculations" amount to "wagers on the future."[11] The stock market, in no uncertain terms, is a gamble, even as it increasingly becomes the template for understanding the logic of contemporary life.

The upshot and effect of all this, as Jameson contends, is a mutation in the workings of capital itself: It seems the future of capital rests no longer in the innovation of products (an industrial model of capital), or in the colonization of new markets (the service economy model), but literally in a kind of futures market on capital itself, in gambling on the future worth of stocks and other investment devices *as* commodities. Following a spate of recent economists, Jameson argues that the future of capitalism lies in speculative investment gambled on a future of supposed or projected worth, rather than in the production of "new" commodities or services. The future of capitalism, as Jameson writes in "Culture and Finance Capital," "is no longer in the factories and the spaces of extraction and production, but on the floor of the stock market, jostling for more intense profitability. But it won't be as one industry competing with another branch, nor even one productive technology against another more advanced one in the same line of manufacturing, but rather in the form of speculation itself."[12] Capitalism's future, in other words, resides not in the extraction of capital from commodities or services, but in the extraction of capital from capital—making money through a very literal process of gambling, wagering on an anticipated outcome. And the future, it seems, is now.

The Futures Market on Gaming and Culture

Given this state of contemporary affairs, it seems that the point in doing an analysis of contemporary capitalism and/as gambling is not primarily to fuel nostalgia for earlier forms of disciplinary capitalism: when sport was authentic and working class, and we "really" knew who the enemy was; when a "successful" worker (who was by definition a man) could look forward to forty years of high-paying but soul-stealing labor performed in a dangerous factory, rather than forty years of low-paying (though equally soul-stealing, it would seem) labor dealing blackjack or filling vending machines. The point of the story, in other words, is not that capital (and with it, our preferred modes of leisure, like sport) has become lamentably "unreal" because money is no longer tied in the same way to the production and exchange of goods and services. As Richard Dienst contends, "The crucial point of this story . . . is not that money suddenly became false and ungrounded—because nobody ever knows if there is a solid ground for the values they are using and pursuing—but that mechanisms and systems that create and 'validate' money changed in a fundamental way."[13] It is in this fundamental change that the control-based logics of gambling—speculation and future profits—begin to take over from the disciplinary logics of commodity production. You got to know when to hold 'em and know when to fold 'em, and how the gambler looks and behaves is often as important as the specific bets she makes.

Contemporary sports or leisure practices, then, are no longer merely the superstructural dross that's "left over" after the real work of capitalism is done from Monday through Friday, nine to five. Increasingly, the mechanisms and practices that validate national currencies and economies are akin to the mechanisms that validate and value sports celebrities and franchises: something like fan support or confidence. Economically speaking, Team America is much more than merely a metaphor. Consider the constant CNN crawl of financial news, or the ubiquitous nightly report of the Dow Jones numbers: Why does the average Joe or Jane care one way or another about a twenty-point drop in the Dow, insofar as very few people own stock in numbers significant enough for the daily ins and outs of the stock market to make any difference? For example, my local news in Pennsylvania, coming out of the lucrative Altoona/Johnstown market, won't even cover Philadelphia Phillies baseball in its nightly sports segment, as they parochially think of themselves as inhabiting the Pirates (Pittsburgh) part of the state. But each and every night, they dutifully report the arcane ups and downs of the Dow Jones numbers. Why, I often wonder? It's almost as if the Dow is America's meta-team — Michael Jordan's Bulls and Roger Staubach's Cowboys, with a healthy dose of Dale Earnhardt, all rolled into one. And at the end of the economic day, it really is something like fan culture (renamed "consumer confidence") that keeps Team America in the economic big leagues.

In terms of the world economy, America is consumption, plain and simple; and without the continuing boosterish economic confidence that fuels our mega-consumption (a confidence buoyed by the nightly touting of otherwise nonsensical Dow Jones averages), Team America would sink to middle of the economic pack, a perennial fourth-place finisher. In the contemporary socioeconomic situation, value tends to free-float, backed as much by a poker player's phantasmatic practices of enthusiasm and confidence as by tangible assets or the hard economic coin of the realm. As Dienst puts it, "Contemporary capitalism can be defined by the way it develops images of value to project relationships between different domains of global existence: not only between worker and boss or between one commodity and another, but between competing currencies, competing environments, and competing hopes for the future."[14] In terms of the very real stakes and consequences tied to phantasmatic hopes and dreams for the future, Americans' obsession with gambling is not merely a marginal formation, passing whimsy, or subcultural practice; rather, gambling is becoming sutured into the very heart of contemporary social and economic problems and policies. We work and play in a world whose economic realities are increasingly coming to look like those of a casino.

Notes

1   American Gaming Association 2004 survey, www.americangaming.org/assets/files/2004_Survey_for_Web.pdf (accessed August 7, 2005).

2   Ibid.

3   Recall that when it was reborn only a few decades ago, widespread casino gaming was sold to voters and taxpayers as a "development" strategy — i.e., by the notion that casinos would help spur related business at restaurants, nightclubs, bars, coffee shops, etc. The

numbers, not surprisingly, have shown quite the opposite: in Atlantic City, for example, there are now fewer restaurants than there were before the advent of casino gambling (Robert Goodman, *The Luck Business* [New York: Free Press, 1995], 20–22), and anyone who's been to a Rust Belt casino (like those in downstate Illinois—Joliet or the Quad Cities) can see the obvious: casinos are completely closed environments. Cheap buffets and free watery cocktails abound inside casinos (where they can be written off as legitimate business expenses), but when the dealing's done, no one mistakes Aurora for Las Vegas: few hang around looking for other diversions. It's axiomatic that casinos make money only for the people who own them and the taxing authorities that allow them to operate. As economist John Warren Kindt puts it: "In reality, the regional and strategic impacts of legalized gambling almost invariably result in a net loss of jobs, increased taxes, and negative economic spiral which is inherently recessionary" (quoted in Jennifer Vogel, ed., *Crapped Out: How Gambling Ruins the Economy and Destroys Lives* [Monroe, ME: Common Courage Press, 1997], 4). Or as casino entrepreneur Steve Wynn put it to a group of businessmen considering a casino in Connecticut, "There is no reason on earth for any of you to expect that just because there are people here, they're going to run into your store, or restaurant, or bar" (quoted in Goodman, *The Luck Business*, 33).

4 Gilles Deleuze, *Negotiations, 1972–1990*, trans. Martin Joughin (New York: Columbia University Press, 1995), 180, emphasis in original.

5 Ibid., 121.

6 Deleuze is hardly a theorist of sports, but see also his extensive comments on tennis in *L'Abécédaire de Gilles Deleuze, avec Claire Parnet*, dir. P. Boutang (Buena Vista DVD, 2004).

7 Deleuze, *Negotiations*, 180.

8 Dick Hebdige, *Subculture: The Meaning of Style* (London: Methuen, 1979).

9 Michel de Certeau, *The Practice of Everyday Life*, trans. Steven F. Rendall (Berkeley: University of California Press, 2002).

10 Fredric Jameson, "Culture and Finance Capital," *Critical Inquiry* 24 (1997): 246–65; quote, 249.

11 Georg Simmel, *Philosophy of Money*, trans. Tom Bottomore and David Frisby (London: Routledge, 1990), 325–26.

12 Jameson, "Culture and Finance Capital," 251.

13 Richard Dienst, "The Futures Market: Global Economics and Cultural Studies," in *Reading the Shape of the World: Toward an International Cultural Studies*, ed. Harry Schwartz and Richard Dienst (Boulder: Westview Press, 1996), 77.

14 Ibid., 83.

Notes on Contributors

DAVID L. ANDREWS is associate professor in the Sport Commerce and Culture Program of the Department of Kinesiology at the University of Maryland in College Park. He is author of *Sport-Commerce-Culture: Essays on Sport in Late Capitalist America* (2006), and coeditor (with Steven J. Jackson) of *Sport, Culture, and Advertising: Identities, Commodities, and the Politics of Representation* (2005).

AMY BASS is director of the Honors Program and assistant professor of history at The College of New Rochelle. She is the author of *Not the Triumph but the Struggle: The 1968 Olympic Games and the Making of the Black Athlete* (2002) and editor of *In the Game: Race, Identity, and Sports in the Twentieth Century* (2005), and has served as research consultant for NBC Sports for the Atlanta, Salt Lake, Sydney, Athens, and Turin Olympic Games. She lives in New York City.

NORMAN K. DENZIN is professor of sociology, cinema studies, and criticism and interpretive theory at the University of Illinois and also Research Professor of Communications within that university's Institute of Communications Research. Denzin's books *The Alcoholic Self* and *The Recovering Alcoholic* won the Charles H. Cooley Award of the Society for the Study of Symbolic Interaction and were nominated for the C. Wright Mills Award. His recent publications include *Screening Race: Hollywood and a Cinema of Racial Violence, Interpretive Ethnography, The Cinematic Society, Images of Postmodern Society, The Research Act, Interpretive Interactionism,* and *Hollywood Shot by Shot.*

GRANT FARRED is associate professor in the Literature Program at Duke University. He is the author of *Midfielder's Moment: Coloured Literature and Culture in Contemporary South Africa* (2000) and *What's My Name: Black Vernacular Intellectuals* (2003) and is editor of the collection *Rethinking C. L. R. James* (1996).

KEYA GANGULY is associate professor in the Department of Cultural Studies and Comparative Literature at the University of Minnesota. Her publications include *States of Exception: Everyday Life and Postcolonial Identity* (2001), and she coedits (with Jochen Schulte-Sasse and John Mowitt) the journal *Cultural Critique.* Her essays have appeared in *camera obscura, Cultural Studies, New Formations,* and *Race and Class;* she is currently completing a book on postcolonial cinema entitled *Cinema, Crisis, and Emergence in the Films of Satyajit Ray.*

JOHN HARTLEY is Australian Research Council Federation Fellow in the ARC Centre of Excellence for Creative Industries and Innovation, and Distinguished Professor at Queensland University of Technology, Australia. He was foundation dean of the Creative Industries Faculty at QUT, and head of the School of Journalism, Media and Cultural Studies at Cardiff University, Wales. Recent books include *Creative Industries* (Blackwell 2005), *A Short History of Cultural Studies* (Sage 2003), *The Indigenous Public Sphere* (with Alan McKee, Oxford 2000), *Uses of Television* (Routledge 1999), and *Popular Reality: Journalism, Modernity, Popular Culture* (Arnold 1996). He is editor of the *International Journal of Cultural Studies* (Sage).

JANE JUFFER is associate professor of English and women's studies and director of the Latina/o Studies Initiative at Pennsylvania State University. She is the author of *Single Mother: The Emergence of the Domestic Intellectual* (New York University Press, forthcoming) and *At Home with Pornography: Women, Sex, and Everyday Life* (New York University Press). She also has published on lingerie, Sammy Sosa, Latina/o studies at the corporate university, and various aspects of the U.S.-Mexican border.

LIZ MOOR teaches in the Department of Media and Cultural Studies at Middlesex University. She is currently writing a book about brands.

JEFFREY T. NEALON is professor of English at Penn State University. He is author of *Alterity Politics: Ethics and Performative Subjectivity* (1998) and *Double Reading: Postmodernism after Deconstruction* (1993), as well as co-author (with Susan Searls Giroux) of *The Theory Toolbox* (2003) and coeditor (with Caren Irr) of *Rethinking the Frankfurt School* (2002). Despite what the blackjack dealer tells you, he strongly advises against hitting 14.

ANNIE PAUL is a writer and critic based at the Sir Arthur Lewis Institute of Social and Economic Studies, University of the West Indies, Jamaica, where she is head of publications. Recipient of a grant from the Prince Claus Fund and a founding editor of the journal *Small Axe*, she is currently working on a book titled *Suitable Subjects: Visual Art and Popular Culture in Postcolonial Jamaica.*

GEORGE RITZER is Distinguished University Professor of Sociology at the University of Maryland. Among his current projects are writing a book on a sociological approach to outsourcing, and editing the 11-volume *Black-*

well Encyclopedia of Sociology. The best-known of his many books is *The McDonaldization of Society.*

JIM SHEPARD is the author of six novels, including most recently *Project X* (Knopf, 2004), and two story collections, including most recently *Love and Hydrogen* (Vintage, 2004). His short fiction has appeared in, among other magazines, *Harper's, McSweeney's,* the *Paris Review,* the *Atlantic Monthly, Esquire, DoubleTake,* the *New Yorker,* and *Playboy,* and he is a columnist on film for the magazine *The Believer.* He teaches at Williams College and in the Warren Wilson MFA program.

ORIN STARN is Sally Dalton Robinson Professor of Cultural Anthropology at Duke University. He is the author of *Nightwatch: The Politics of Protest in the Andes* (1999) and *Ishi's Brain: In Search of America's Last "Wild" Indian* (2004).

KENNETH SURIN is based in the Literature Program at Duke University, where he is also director of the Center for European Studies.

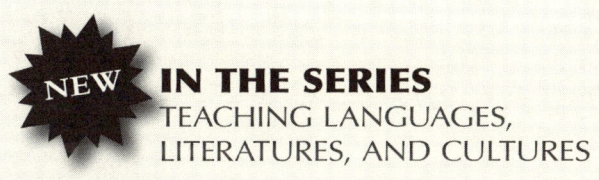

RADICAL *Review*
HISTORY

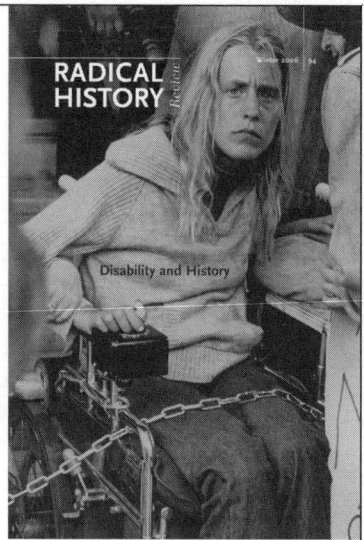

RADICAL
HISTORY *Review*

Disability and History

Disability studies has emerged
as one of the most innovative
transdisciplinary areas of scholarship
in recent years. This *Radical History
Review* special issue, "Disability and
History," discloses how the definition
of "disability" may expose biases
and limitations of a given historical
moment rather than a universal truth.

Essays examine
- How Western definitions of disability, imposed on Botswana
  during colonial rule, have shaped local perceptions
- Labor activism among blind workers in Northern Ireland
  in the 1930s
- Previously untranslated Weimar-era political texts by disabled
  writers and activists that combat their supposed "complacency"
  with the Nazi rise to power
- U.S. radical Randolph Bourne as a philosopher of disability politics
- Disabled feminist theater practice in the 1970s and 1980s

Upcoming special issues

New Imperialisms (95)
Iona Man-Cheong and
Mansour Bonakdarian,
special issue editors

Punishment and Death (96)
Ethan Blue and
Patrick Timmons,
special issue editors